GARDEN VARIETY

ARTS AND TRADITIONS OF THE TABLE:
PERSPECTIVES ON CULINARY HISTORY

Columbia University Press
Publishers Since 1893
New York   Chichester, West Sussex
cup.columbia.edu

Copyright © 2018 Columbia University Press

Library of Congress Cataloging-in-Publication Data
Names: Hoenig, John, author.
Title: Garden variety : the American tomato from corporate to heirloom /
John Hoenig.
Description: New York : Columbia University Press, 2017. | Series: Arts and
traditions of the table | Includes bibliographical references and index.
Identifiers: LCCN 2017015904 | ISBN 978-0-231-17908-9 (cloth : alk. paper) |
ISBN 978-0-231-54638-6 (e-book)
Subjects: LCSH: Tomatoes—United States—History. | Tomato industry—
United States—History.
Classification: LCC SB349 .H64 2017 | DDC 635/.6420973—dc23
LC record available at https://lccn.loc.gov/2017015904

Columbia University Press books are printed on permanent
and durable acid-free paper.
Printed in the United States of America

Cover design and photograph by Catherine Casalino

FOR MY GRANDPARENTS,
MICHAEL AND PATSY SLOAN
AND ANTON AND AILEEN HOENIG

CONTENTS

ACKNOWLEDGMENTS

This project would not have come to fruition without the help, guidance, and support of many people. At the top of that list must be Gary Cross, who worked tirelessly, offering his insight, direction, and attention, from beginning to end. Dr. Cross's tremendous knowledge of history has left its mark on every page of this project, and his continued support helped keep me motivated to finish it. At Pennsylvania State University, Deryck Holdsworth, Tobias Brinkmann, and Bryan McDonald offered invaluable comments, suggestions, and ideas. I am also indebted to Adam Rome, who pushed me to think carefully about my interests in material culture and environmental history. My time working with the Pennsylvania Agricultural History Project, led by Sally McMurry, helped solidify my interest in food history and showed me how agricultural history was relevant to my interests. My graduate colleagues Jeff Rop, Phil Hnatkovich, Spencer Delbridge, Kevin Lowe, Amanda Iacobelli, and Rachel Moran all influenced this project by providing expertise, advice, and support.

I also want to thank Jennifer Crewe, my editor at Columbia University Press, and her assistant, Jonathan Fiedler, who helped guide me through the process of publishing a book. Jennifer, along with the several anonymous reviewers, also offered meaningful and substantive comments on the manuscript and advice on how to revise it.

I am deeply indebted to many librarians and archivists from across the country, beginning first and foremost with Eric Novotny at Penn State. He is among the most knowledgeable librarians I have ever encountered. I am indebted to him for helping me find numerous sources that otherwise would not have been available. I also received great assistance from staff at the University of Delaware; Cornell University; University of California, Davis; Hagley Library; Smithsonian American History Museum; National Agricultural Library; and Library of Congress.

I also want to thank the Penn State history department, which has continued to offer me support long after completing my PhD, even when personal responsibilities have necessitated I live across the country. Specifically, I am deeply indebted to Michael Kulikowski, David Atwill, and Greg Smits.

This book would not be here without the support and strength offered by my friends and family. My parents, David and Sandra Hoenig, have always given me their unwavering support. They have housed and fed me whenever necessary. They have listened to my complaints and frustrations, and, all too often, loaned me money. My sister, Leigh Ann Hoenig, and friends Angela Hodgson, Lucas Holl, Abigail Mattson, Justin Todd, as well as many others, offered emotional support and helped give me confidence to see this project through. Thanks also to the numerous individuals whom I met throughout my travels, especially Maryjo Oster, who provided me with a couch and an instant group of friends while I was doing research in Washington, DC.

Finally, I am most indebted to Grace Heid and Brennyn Leath, who patiently put up with my frequent absence, my constant stress, and my abnormal working hours. Our family movie nights, T-ball practices, and, more recently, weekend trips simply to see each other, offered short respites from work, allowing me to take my mind off this project for brief moments. I am grateful to have such wonderful, intelligent, and caring women in my life.

GARDEN VARIETY

INTRODUCTION

Today, the tomato stands among the most popular vegetables in the United States. In ketchup packets, sliced on burgers and in salads, in sauces slathered on pizza dough and on enchiladas, the tomato can be found in one form or another in almost any restaurant. Upon entering a grocery store, shoppers are met with a wide assortment of fresh tomatoes—Roma, on the vine, cherry, beefsteak, and, increasingly, heirloom varieties. At many grocers, the space given over to canned and jarred tomato products rivals that of all varieties of soup. In short, the tomato dominates American cuisine, telling us much about our food culture. Yet the widespread adoption of the tomato into American culinary culture was anything but inevitable. Over the course of the last two centuries, the tomato went from relative obscurity to its current dominant place in the modern American supermarket. And the process of that transformation helps illuminate many of the changes that have occurred in the larger American culinary culture from 1800 to the present.

Native to the Andes in South America, the tomato was first cultivated in southern Mexico before being introduced to the Caribbean and Europe during the sixteenth century by Spanish explorers. By the end of the sixteenth century, the tomato had made its way to Italy, France, England, and other European countries. The tomato finally "returned" to North America in the eighteenth century, and by the early nineteenth century it had become an important part of the American diet. By 1850, the tomato was established as one of America's most popular vegetables.[1] Served both fresh and processed, in "American" and ethnic dishes, and through organic and heavily industrialized methods, the tomato today represents the expansion and diversity of the American diet while also symbolizing both the promise and anxieties of the industrialization of American food.

The integration of the tomato into the diets of Europe and North America is an unlikely chapter in the story of modern food culture. A member of the *Solanum* genus and related to the deadly nightshades, the tomato was often dismissed as poisonous by European botanists and cooks. The stems and leaves of the tomato plant are, in fact, poisonous. In this way, the tomato shares a similar path to popularity with many other New World crops, like the potato (also a member of the nightshade family), that did not have Old World analogues and which European explorers initially perceived as foreign and potentially dangerous. Many Europeans feared the potato; some even associated its shape with leprosy. Yet even after Europeans accepted the potato (first and foremost because it promised to feed millions of the continent's poor), they continued to regard the tomato with suspicion. More important to the development of tomato consumption in nineteenth-century America, however, since few people beyond botanists knew anything about the *solanum* genus, was the fruit's unusual characteristics. Often brightly colored and soft, the tomato could also be oddly shaped and rough, with a dense core; many early cultivators remained suspicious of its unique appearance and aromatic foliage.[2]

The biggest obstacle preventing the widespread adoption of the tomato, however, was not its distinct appearance or its undervalued nutritional potential, but its fragility and perishability. Because the tomato ripens quickly during the peak of the harvest and thus has a much shorter shelf life than hardy foods such as potatoes and grains, existing technologies of preservation had to be adapted to the tomato. In many ways, the story of the tomato in the United States (and across the globe) is the story of how farmers and cooks overcame the limits of perishable plants to dramatically expand the diet beyond simple staple foods that had dominated civilization since the ancient world's agricultural revolution. Up until the nineteenth century, diets across the world consisted primarily of complex carbohydrates (e.g., wheat, corn, rice, potatoes), storable seeds, or tubers that could be easily preserved and transported. Meat, dairy, hard legumes, and occasionally leaf vegetables (like cabbages) added flavor, protein, and variety to the staple carbohydrate. Soft fruits like grapes and apples entered the staple stream primarily as wine and cider. In this world, the tomato could only be a minor player—a product of kitchen gardens unable to join the grains and tubers in the broader national or international market.

Over the course of the last two centuries, however, the tomato evolved from a rare, seasonal good available only on the farm to being available in a variety of forms in widely dispersed markets and kitchens. This transformation was the work of farmers, corporations, consumers, reformers, and government researchers who have made numerous attempts to refashion the tomato and its place in American culture. What began as an alien food had emerged by the middle of the nineteenth century as one of America's most popular vegetables. It isn't too far fetched to say that the tomato was in the vanguard of a soft-food revolution. The tomato's history reveals the American desire to expand variety in the diet and to transcend the seasonality of the harvest. At the same time, similar to other foods such as wheat, corn, and beef, the tomato was transformed by a wide range of corporate and noncorporate actors who reengineered it, standardizing varieties, extending the growing season, centralizing production, and developing technologies to preserve tomatoes throughout the year.

The tomato, however, is also an example of the limits of commodification. Commercial ideas of tomato consumption (embodied by grocery store tomatoes in cellophane tubes) stand in contrast to the lasting image of the homegrown tomato—in gardens and restaurants, in the kitchen and at farmers' markets. The appeal of the tomato, after all, has always been about expanding the palate of American cuisine. Consumers, farmers, corporations, and others all cooperated and competed to create a distinct and diverse culture of the tomato, one which has produced both three-thousand-pound drums of bland tomato paste and hundreds of varieties of heirloom tomatoes available in an array of different shapes, sizes, and colors.

For many historians and journalists, the tomato industry has recently become a symbol of the cultural, political, economic, and agricultural control that modern corporations have over the food that Americans consume. These researchers and writers see the tomato industry as an example of the troubling state of modern agriculture and food industries—highly centralized, relying on technological control and on the exploitation of labor and the environment. These findings largely mirror those of contemporary scholars studying other aspects of American food production and consumption during the late nineteenth century. For these writers, the can and the food corporation symbolize the annihilation of time, space, and taste in modern American society.[3]

The tomato, however, offers a much more complex and interesting story. The history of the tomato from its popularization in the early nineteenth century through today is a history of culinary curiosity, experimentation, and the expansion of the American diet. The history of the tomato in the United States illuminates continuities and discontinuities not visible in narrow, period-focused analyses. This volume begins by examining food culture in early America and the popularization of the tomato during the nineteenth century, looking specifically at how the tomato was added to the American dinner table by overcoming the primary obstacles to its widespread adoption—seasonality and perishability. In nineteenth-century America, cooks and farmers alike sought and found ways to extend the seasonality of the tomato and to preserve it for off-season consumption. Tomato culture and production changed through two distinct processes of industrialization, the first from roughly 1880 through 1945, which saw the rise of canning and national distribution, the second from 1945 through the 1970s, marked by the centralization of production and the homogenization of food culture. By taking a long view of a single commodity, then, this book follows in a growing tradition of commodity studies revealing what Sidney Mintz refers to as the "interdigitated," or interconnected, relationship between production and consumption.[4]

The tomato's seasonality and perishability and its lack of place in traditional food culture make it unique compared to the long-established traditional staple food crops. At the same time, the tomato is also quite similar to, and thus representative of, many other foods that have also gone unrecognized by historians. Like the tomato, watermelons, peas, broccoli, and cabbage, in contrast to traditional grains and tubers, continued to be grown in many regions of the country through the 1930s. During the first half of the century, these fruits and vegetables were not mechanically harvested and were far less likely than grains and tubers to be produced in small centralized areas. Ultimately, the tomato represents a new class of crops that resisted centralized production and posed special problems regarding their preservation and transportation.[5]

THE TOMATO IN EIGHTEENTH- AND NINETEENTH-CENTURY AMERICAN FOOD CULTURE

The history of the tomato offers a fresh way of thinking about the development of American food culture. For one group of scholars, early Americans treated food primarily as a fuel and insisted on preserving old world tradition. This scholarship focuses on early Americans' heavy reliance on staples such as pork, corn, beef, and wheat. Historian Richard Osborn Cummings observed that "a monotonous round of badly cooked food . . . was the lot of most Americans." In this view, American colonists strictly adhered to English and other European culinary traditions. Waverley Root, in *Eating in America* (1976), argues that despite the New World offering an opportunity for an entirely new food culture, American colonists opted to grow familiar foods that enabled them to replicate English and European culinary styles in the New World. With a bit of "obstinacy," even when facing starvation conditions, Root argues, early Americans "turned their backs on most of the new foods [available in America], often refusing to eat them until after Europe had accepted them and reimported them to the land of their origin."[6]

The view of scholars such as Cummings and Root has in recent years been countered by a celebration of the creativity and novelty of early American cuisine. This newer scholarship, which tends to have a negative assessment on the effects of the later industrialization of food, glorifies the supposed diversity and authenticity of American food culture during the eighteenth and nineteenth centuries, often finding early American food traditions more "pure" or "natural" than the industrial alternative that emerged by the beginning of the twentieth century. In *Kitchen Literacy*, Ann Vileisis celebrates the localness of early American foodways and argues that this required consumers and cooks to have a much greater knowledge of food than consumers of industrial food, where national networks of food production and distribution distance consumers from the food that they consume. So was early American food culture an example of the bad or good old days, of American culinary conservatism or innovation? The history of the tomato in that food culture suggests a more complex picture than a simple contrast between industrial and local allows.[7]

Early America's rejection of the tomato and other less-favored crops was often not simply the result of their being different from traditional European foods but also because they were highly perishable and ripened during a short season. Early Americans' need for a stable food supply, available year-round, made such crops less advantageous to cultivate.

Reliance on corn, beef, wheat, and hard vegetables like squash and pumpkins was often due to the ease with which these foods could be preserved. The early American diet may have been limited, monotonous, and bland, but people accepted it because the foods were easily available on a year-round basis. After all, most Americans in the eighteenth century had little time or energy to devote to cultivating highly perishable foods or to making radical changes to their diets. In a simple cost-benefit analysis, the soft tomato was not worth the effort.

At the same time, the argument that early American farmers and cooks were innovative needs to be investigated from the perspective of the tomato. The tomato's acceptance as part of the American diet coincided

at the state and federal level undertook much of this work. This research helped fuel the expansion of tomato cultivation outside of traditional areas of dominance, such as New Jersey, Indiana, and New York, and into southern and western states like California, Florida, Mississippi, and Arkansas. During the early twentieth century, this helped fuel a decentralized system of production in part designed to fulfill the market need for a year-round supply of tomatoes.

The growing relationship between agriculture and the government is best demonstrated by the development of the mechanical tomato harvester in the early 1960s. The mechanization of many aspects of agriculture—including Cyrus McCormick's reaper (1837) and John Froelich's gasoline tractor (1892)—have generally been viewed as a response to shortages of labor.[13] Developed by one or a few people, these innovations were often supported by the industries that stood to benefit. Agricultural historians have long viewed the early twentieth century as a pivotal period in the mechanization and industrialization of American agriculture. Mechanization of tomato harvesting, by contrast, happened much later and was primarily the result of significant investment and research by the land-grant college system. This was largely due to the complexities and difficulties in mechanizing the production of a soft fruit that did not ripen uniformly. The complexity of harvesting tomatoes by machine required the cooperation of a variety of actors within the university—agronomists, botanists, mechanical engineers, and others. Unlike many other innovations, the tomato harvester was not the direct result of industrial pressure to find a technological solution to labor problems; indeed, until the early 1960s, California tomato producers showed little support for the project, opting instead to lobby the government for increased access to migrant labor. Only after producers repeatedly failed to obtain this cheap labor did they finally accept the need for a mechanical harvester. Perhaps uniquely, the harvester itself was the result of independent academic inquiry as much as a response to market conditions.[14]

The tomato harvester, however, won quick acceptance, making California dominant in the production of canned tomatoes, ending the era of nationwide and decentralized production of canned tomatoes. At the same time, fresh tomato production became divided between California and Florida, as new technologies, improved long-distance distribution, and agricultural practices helped tomato growers achieve a geographically centralized twelve-month tomato (despite some consumer dissatisfaction). All this was part of a larger transition toward a food culture based on convenience and homogenization.

Yet unlike other industrialized food crops, the tomato retained its place in the local truck and home garden, giving it an opportunity to lead a popular resistance to corporate food culture, be it in the form of the often tasteless "fresh" or the processed tomato. Despite a temporary lull in home gardening during the postwar period, it became a very popular hobby beginning in the 1970s as inflation and high food prices coupled with environmental and health concerns led many Americans to consider growing some of their own food. Likewise, by the 1970s farmers' markets, long in decline, again surged in popularity. While historians have also seen the counterculture as the primary challenger to the dominance of industrialized food in the decades following World War II, Americans from all walks of life practiced home gardening and shopped at farmers' markets. Contemporary interest in food trucks, ethnic food, and community-supported agriculture (CSA) programs all contribute to alternative visions of what food should be.[15]

TOWARD A NEW UNDERSTANDING
OF AMERICAN FOOD CULTURE

While the rise of brand-name goods and advertising in the early twentieth century (so often studied by historians) has greatly shaped American food culture, I have sought out new sources that lead to a more balanced understanding of how American food culture changed over the past two centuries. These research materials include seed catalogs, restaurant menus, agricultural journals, cookbooks, and agricultural and mainstream periodicals. Many collections, including the Henry G. Gilbert Seed Trade Catalog Collection at the National Agricultural

Library and Cornell's Restaurant Menu Collection, were extensive and required me to sample available materials rather than complete an exhaustive survey. Likewise, I used many periodicals, most of which are available through online databases such as ProQuest. In cases where exhaustive browsing was not possible, I used broad keyword searches and date sampling.

Of course, advertisements can be deceptive in representing actual eating and purchasing practices, and many of these other sources have similar limitations. Cookbooks offer a glimpse into some culinary options, but they do not necessarily reflect actual eating decisions. Where possible, in dealing with recipes and cookbooks, I have tried to find ways to determine how influential they were (by looking at how many copies of a cookbook were sold, for example). In any case, the appearance of new recipes can point to the beginnings of changes in how Americans understood food.

This story of the tomato offers a new approach to the history of American food culture. While this is a story of the coming of the pink, plastic-looking tomato, so representative of the worst of American agriculture and industrial food, the tomato's history also has led to the organic farmers' market and home garden, often depicted as natural, wholesome, and tasty. These seemingly contradictory images suggest to us that the history of American food culture may not be as simple a story as is often told.

This diverse culture is the result of more than two centuries of agricultural, culinary, and technological experimentation. Rural farmers and cooks, government reformers, and immigrant groups as well as corporations all participated in these innovations. From commercially produced ketchup and frozen pizzas to fresh caprese salads and tomatoes stuffed with meats, cheeses, and vegetables, American tomato culture has thrived on diversity, part of a great broadening of the American diet. In fact, the tomato has been at the vanguard of a food revolution. While the American diet has consistently been criticized as mostly "meat and potatoes," the eighteenth and nineteenth century saw the dramatic increase in possible ingredients and the infusion of new culinary ideas. The rise of the tomato, as well as the emergence of a diverse tomato culture in the United States, reflects this trend. There is little question that this culture suffered between the end of World War II and today, yet the persistence of alternatives to the dominant culture of heat-and-serve spaghetti and tomato sauce—farmers' markets, home gardening, foodie culture, and the like—all indicate that this diverse culture remains alive. In fact, the tomato today is at the center of a debate about the future of what and how Americans eat.

1

THE EARLY AMERICAN TOMATO

T he early history of the tomato in the United States has, until recently, been cloaked in mythology. In 1976, American food historian Waverley Root explained quite succinctly why both the potato and tomato were not cultivated in early America: "They were not there." This explanation is only half true. The tomato is not native to the present-day United States and only made its way here following a circuitous journey: first, in the sixteenth century, from southern Mexico to the Caribbean and Europe and then, during the eighteenth century, from the Caribbean into the American colonies. Although a late arrival to the American colonies, as Andrew Smith has more recently pointed out, the tomato was very much present before 1800. Yet, as discussed in the next chapter, the introduction of the tomato in America occurred over several decades, and it took until the mid-nineteenth century for it to be fully integrated into many Americans' diets. In order to understand this delay we need briefly to consider the early history of the tomato and how it spread from Mexico to the Caribbean, Europe, and America.[1]

As a soft-fruited plant, unlike many other fruits and vegetables popular in Europe, the tomato did not share the advantages of grains, hardrooted, tough-leafed vegetables (like turnips and cabbage) and hard fruits (many of which, like apples, could be transformed into alcoholic beverages). Unlike these traditional foods, which could be relatively easily stored, transported, and transformed into a variety of edible products, the tomato quickly rotted and had no history of use in American diets. As a highly seasonal and perishable plant, it ripened at a time of the year when food supplies were at their peak. Without a tradition of preserving the tomato for out-of-season consumption, and with a pressing need to secure adequate food throughout the year, most colonists had good reason to cultivate other, more durable, crops like potatoes, cabbage, and beans.

THE ORIGINS OF THE TOMATO

The origins of the tomato have long been subject to scholarly debate—from the sixteenth century onward, botanists, archaeologists, and others theorized on the origins of the tomato plant. Though most serious scholars placed the origins of the *Lycopersicon esculentum*, the tomato species cultivated today in the United States, somewhere in South or Central America, scientists and other scholars for centuries found it difficult to narrow down its exact origins. The most popular view—that the modern cultivated tomato originated in a narrow strip that began in Ecuador and went south into northern Chile—was generally accepted until the mid-1940s, when University of California geneticist J. A. Jenkins complicated this story. Now accepted among scholars, Jenkins's argument held that the original location for the emergence of the *Lycopersicon esculentum* species was likely around Peru and that well before Columbus, the tomato, probably through accidental human interaction (e.g., people carrying seeds on clothing, etc.), had expanded northward into southern Mexico. In Mexico, Jenkins suggested, humans began experimenting with the species and cultivating it well before the arrival of Europeans. Thus, in all likelihood, Europe's first encounter with the tomato came in Mexico, in the twenty years after its conquest in 1521, where it had already been altered significantly from its wild origins in Peru.[2]

The earliest known European reference to the tomato occurs in the first edition of Italian doctor and botanist Petrus Andreas Mattioli's *Discourses* (1544). While Europeans often went to the New World for silver and gold, they also collected plants. The tomato's inclusion in Mattioli's *Discourses* indicates that much like other New World plants including the cocao tree and potatoes, the tomato initially was studied for its potential medicinal, rather than culinary, value. European botanists and herbalists shared ideas and specimens in their quest for new medicines, helping to spread knowledge about plants that eventually would be used as food.[3]

Growers in several countries in continental Europe, including Spain, Italy, and France, began cultivating tomatoes as early as the 1540s, but they did not make an appearance in England until the 1590s, when they were first planted at the College of Physicians gardens in Holborn. This location confirms that the tomato was still seen as a medicinal plant. It is likely that the tomato was only rarely served at European tables until the seventeenth century. The most influential cookbooks and food guides of the sixteenth century make no mention of the tomato. As late as 1592, Spanish priest and gardener Gregorio de los Rios observed, "It is said that [tomatoes] are good for sauces," suggesting that while the tomato was beginning to be seen as a useful addition to cuisine, de los Rios himself had never tried them. Another early reference mentions the tomato being used in salads in Seville in 1608. Yet many major cookbooks of the period make little or no mention of the vegetable at all, indicating that it was not in widespread use in European kitchens. It was not until the end of the seventeenth century, beginning with Antonio Latini's *Lo scalco alla moderna* (The Modern Steward, 1692), that tomatoes became regularly featured in European cookbooks. By the early eighteenth century, however, despite concerns among many botanists and other herbalists about the safety of consuming tomatoes, use of the tomato for culinary purposes was expanding dramatically, as cookbooks across Europe began to include recipes for tomato-based dishes.[4]

Before being brought to Europe, the tomato was already cultivated in a modern sense in Mexico. Most notably, while wild tomatoes were very small, sometimes smaller than one centimeter in diameter, in Mexico a variety of sizes of tomatoes could be found, including some that were five or more centimeters in diameter, indicating a long period of seed selection and other breeding practices to increase their size. The tomato's existence in Europe required unintended advancements in tomato stock. Wild tomatoes in South America required *Halictus* bees for pollination. These bees were not present in Europe, meaning that before the tomato was imported into Europe it already had been remade (through either evolution or human interaction) into a self-pollinating plant.[5]

In Europe, further improvements were made to the tomato, and it eventually helped revolutionize several European culinary cultures, including Spanish, French, and Italian cuisine. But this took time. During the seventeenth century, as much of Europe shed its suspicion of vegetables, tomato consumption increased. Italy and Spain, both in Mediterranean climates, were the first places where people integrated the tomato into their diets. French cuisine, highly influential during the seventeenth and eighteenth centuries, did not adopt the tomato until much later, perhaps as late as the 1770s, when for the first time a seed catalog listed the tomato as a vegetable rather than an ornamental. In Britain, too, the tomato was not generally eaten until the mid-eighteenth century, but by 1820 the *Times* could confess that "Love-apples," the common name for the tomato, "are now to be seen in great abundance at all our vegetable markets." In soups and sauces, boiled, roasted, and fried, the tomato had become a significant part of high British cuisine, used as a flavoring agent to diversify the diet.[6]

THE TOMATO COMES TO AMERICA

This story was repeated in North America. The origins of the tomato in the American colonies and the United States were long shrouded in myth, with numerous "introduction" stories, most dating back to the early nineteenth century. These stories typically revolved around Great Men—wealthy, white, and leaders in their community—introducing tomatoes to their local areas in a public fashion. Thomas Jefferson reportedly shocked the citizens of Lynchburg, Virginia, by eating a tomato out of someone's garden. Another story involved Robert Gibbons Johnson, who supposedly ate a tomato on the courthouse steps in Salem, New Jersey, in 1820, while onlookers looked on in disbelief. Though no accounts of this event can be found before the twentieth century, it nevertheless has become an oft-told legend and was featured in a segment of the CBS radio program *You Are There* in 1949. These stories obscured the longer history of the tomato in America and reaffirmed the myth that the tomato was long seen as poisonous or unhealthy.[7]

Actually, the tomato was being grown in parts of America by the early eighteenth century and could be found nearly everywhere within a few years of independence. The first known mention of tomato cultivation in the United States comes from William Salmon's *Botanologia* (1710), where he observes that he has "seen them grown in Carolina." It remains difficult to place the source of these early tomatoes: French Huguenots, British settlers, and the Spanish all had settlements in the area. Trade between the southern colonies and the Caribbean, including the slave trade, could also have brought the tomato to the Carolinas. Nonetheless, by the early eighteenth century the tomato had at least made its way back across the Atlantic and onto American soil.[8]

Numerous other mentions of tomatoes in the southern colonies during the eighteenth century indicate that the tomato was expanding in popularity, even if only within the southern colonies, reaching as far north as Virginia by the 1780s. Thomas Jefferson mentions growing them in his *Notes on the State of Virginia*. They were served at the White House in 1806, and Jefferson noted numerous times that they were available for purchase at markets in Washington during his presidency. The tomato had also made its way as far south as Florida. Archaeological evidence from the excavation of Fort Matanzas, an eighteenth-century fort on the east coast of Florida near Saint Augustine, indicates the presence of tomato seeds from as early as the 1740s. In the early nineteenth century, tomatoes were regularly grown in summer gardens in Florida, in some cases being reported as among the most popular vegetables grown.[9]

These areas of tomato cultivation were all coastal areas in the South, places that would have had regular contact with the outside world, and in particular, with French and Spanish colonists and the Caribbean. Many Americans, however, were much more geographically isolated. For them, first contact with the tomato came later. According to historian Andrew Smith, tomatoes spread to Philadelphia by the middle of the eighteenth century and to New York City in the 1790s, spreading across their states thereafter. Likewise, the tomato was introduced around 1800 to New England, Louisiana, and Ohio. As Americans moved west, they often brought tomatoes with them and introduced them to new territories.[10]

Yet it would take a few generations before the tomato was fully integrated into the American diet, in contrast to the white potato. In the early nineteenth century the American diet remained centered on staple foods, including meat, grains, and cabbage and root vegetables.[11]

THE SEASONALITY OF THE AMERICAN DIET

Cultural theorist Massimo Montanari has argued that one pillar of agricultural advancement is the desire to transcend the natural temporal boundaries of the harvest. There, of course, is a long history of food preservation and agricultural manipulation in order to secure a stable food supply. For example, grinding wheat into flour for preservation dates back at least thirty thousand years, and the earliest known jars existed in 1800 BCE. The need to develop a year-round stock of food played a crucial role in the emergence of American cuisines during the Colonial and Early Republic periods. Even before colonists set foot in the New World they were confronted with the need to provide food for themselves on the long journey across the Atlantic. Inevitably they relied on grains and proteins that had long been subject to preservation techniques. On the moving frontier of American settlement, too, few settlers chose to grow a seasonal and perishable crop like the tomato when hardier crops like grains and tubers were available and often required much less effort to grow and preserve, at a time when labor was scarce. As Richard Hooker argues, "For most Americans the frontier experience, to be repeated in time across the continent, would discourage all but potatoes, pumpkins, cabbages, and a few root crops." Vegetables like the tomato, harvested at the peak of the harvest and with a short shelf life, were at a distinct disadvantage.[12]

Corn became a staple in the American diet in no small part because it could be preserved for year-round consumption in the form of corn meal, hominy, or grits. Pork, likewise, was not valuable simply because the pig could take care of itself but also because pork could easily be preserved for winter and spring consumption either through keeping the animal alive or, when necessary, through the use of copious amounts of salt.

Americans, like their European counterparts, were anxious to expand the arts of food preservation and extend the growing and harvest season of new crops like corn and potatoes. However, in the eighteenth century, many other crops were better suited to this than the tomato. Bernard M'Mahon, writing in *The American Gardener's Calendar* in 1806, advised Philadelphia-area growers to plant tomatoes in the open field around the end of May in order to avoid damage from frost, taking at least 100 days to a harvest no sooner than early September. Thus the tomato ripened when most other summer vegetables were ripening, giving the tomato no special advantage. Moreover, in comparison to other vegetables, the tomato quickly rotted. Cooks surely experimented with traditional preservation methods, but it took decades to make tomatoes suitable for American tastes. Thus, at a time when growers focused on efficiency in creating a year-round supply of food, the tomato was at a marked disadvantage.[13]

As the colonies increased their food security, they often increased their fruit and vegetable consumption. But again the primary beneficiaries of this trend were hardy vegetables, tubers, root crops, and greens that were not highly perishable or could easily be preserved for consumption during the winter and spring in root cellars or, in the case of apples and corn, transformed into alcohol. Upon visiting Swedish colonists in New Jersey in the 1750s, for example, pastor Israel Acrelius reported that gardens were well stocked with "beets, parsnips, onions, parsley, radishes, Turkish beans, large beans, peppergrass, red peppers, lettuce, head-lettuce, German lettuce, and scurvy grass." Most of these plants could be stored or dried for off-season consumption.[14]

By the beginning of the nineteenth century, however, Americans' access to the tomato was expanding. Well beyond Thomas Jefferson in Virginia and Robert Gibbon Johnson in New Jersey, Americans were experimenting with the tomato, gradually making them available for harvesting both for longer periods and earlier in the summer and for preserving in new ways throughout the year. These innovations in cultivation and preservation came not from heroic elites or powerful corporations but from a wide array of local and practical cultivators and cooks, taking small steps to find ways of feeding themselves and earning profit on the market.[15]

2

THE TOMATO ON THE FARM

Culinary and Agricultural Advancements, 1820–1900

I n 1834, Dr. John Cook Bennett, a professor at the Medical College of Lake Erie, in Chagrin, Ohio, gave a public lecture on the importance of tomato consumption to a healthy diet. In addition to declaring it a good food for everyday consumption, he also argued that the tomato was a unique treatment for a variety of stomach ailments. Bennett urged all Americans, but especially those on the move, to eat tomatoes regularly, "either raw, cooked, or in form of a catsup." Reports of his lecture were quickly disseminated across the nation in agricultural journals and mainstream magazines.[1]

Indeed, between the 1830s and 1900, the tomato achieved tremendous popularity, unrivaled by any other vegetable except corn. The larger effect of Bennett's lecture was not a debate in the press on the healthfulness of tomatoes, as Bennett's report was virtually accepted without discussion, but rather how it encouraged new uses of tomatoes. In fact, recipes using tomatoes in diverse ways were often printed alongside reports of Bennett's work. These included not only sauces, stews, and traditional preservation techniques adapted to the tomato such as pickling, preserves, and ketchup but also new ethnic dishes and new forms of preserving tomatoes for the off-season, including tomato paste. Much like with sugar, cola, and other foodstuffs, the widespread adoption of the tomato as a popular addition to the diet was preceded by its (false) claim to be a medicine.[2]

This suggests something extraordinary: during the middle decades of the nineteenth century, housewives and cooks refashioned American cuisine, adapting old cooking techniques to the tomato but also introducing new forms of tomato cookery. As early as the 1820s and 1830s, traditional techniques were being adapted to preserve the tomato for off-season consumption. In the process, the tomato lost its marginal status as a seasonal delicacy subordinate to the age-old staples and became the centerpiece of a food culture where a soft vegetable could be served year-round. In 1865, Fearing Burr confirmed the remarkable successes of both cooks and farmers in *The Field and Garden Vegetables of America*, stating that the tomato was "now so universally relished, that it is furnished to the table, in one form or another, through every season of the year." Thus while the canning industry was still in its infancy, and corporations still had little control over America's agriculture, farmers and cooks were transforming how the tomato was consumed.[3]

For the most part, the tomato did not radically alter the basic structure of American meals: most Americans, like most people everywhere, continued to eat a diet consisting of meat or other protein and complex carbohydrates such as bread or potatoes. But where hard vegetables like squash, onions, or cabbage often had helped freshen this bland and monotonous diet, during the nineteenth century, soft vegetables like the tomato livened up unsavory dishes. The tomato led the way when cooks introduced it as a substitute for existing preserved foods and condiments like pickles and ketchups. By mid-century, the tomato was also featured in dishes entirely new to American cuisine, as French and other cuisines were slowly introduced onto American tables. It was only at the end of the nineteenth century that the canning and seed industries commercialized what cultivators and housewives had created, propelling the tomato as the vanguard of the new American cuisine.[4]

THE TOMATO IN THE KITCHEN

The best sources for observing the growing popularity of the tomato during the mid-nineteenth century are mainstream and agricultural periodicals. Typical was a writer from a New York farmer's magazine who noted in 1835 that tomatoes "are used in various ways, either raw, with sugar, or stewed for sauce, or in fricasses [sic] and soups; for catsup or gravy, for meat and for pies or preserves, as well as for pickles and sweet-meats." The most heavily disseminated recipes during the early nineteenth century were traditional, adapting the tomato to the expectations of diners, yet innovative recipes, including several ethnically influenced dishes, also appeared. This combination of the old and the new account for the dramatic rise in tomato consumption after 1830. Tomato ketchups were by far the most popular of these foods, but tomato preserves, pickles, and even an early version of tomato paste all helped fuel the surge in tomato consumption.[5]

TOMATO KETCHUPS AND SAUCES

Through the extensive use of sauces and ketchups, the nineteenth-century tomato was, first and foremost, a condiment—a flavoring agent for an otherwise bland menu. The transformation of perishable vegetables into ketchups and sauces was not limited to the tomato, but tomato ketchup and sauce quickly made an impact on the American diet. Englishman Launcelot Sturgeon, a member in the Beef-Steak Club, one of London's dining fraternities, wrote rather satirically in his 1823 essay "On the Physical and Political Consequences of Sauces" that "the duty of a good sauce is, to titillate the capillaceous extremities of the maxillary glands, and thus to flatter and excite the appetite." While physicians warn eaters to avoid sauces because they can lead to overeating, said Sturgeon, this amounts to "the finest eulogium that could be passed on" them. As meat remained dominant on American plates, tomato sauces and ketchups also proved vital to salvaging dishes that were overcooked, utilized poor cuts of meat, or generally lacked flavor.[6]

The tomato was hardly the first food transformed into a sauce or ketchup for flavoring dishes. Condiments of various kinds had long served the need to add flavor or cover other inadequacies in the traditional European diet. In the ancient world, Romans used garum—a liquid base made from fish entrails—along with honey and spices in a wide variety of sauces. In the Middle Ages, dishes were heavily seasoned with saffron, ginger, nutmeg, cardamom, and other strong spices. Beginning in the seventeenth century, a large part of the revolution in cuisine introduced by French chefs and cooks was in sauce making. The traditional sauces of the Middle Ages, typically heavily seasoned, were abandoned in favor of sauces that included fewer spices and more locally available herbs and vegetables. French cuisine was based on a small number of ingredients and sauces that when combined allowed for the preparation of a wide variety of dishes. As French cooking flourished, French chefs invented many new sauces.[7]

French innovations that began in the seventeenth century were passed on to the British, who abandoned their sauces made from what one nineteenth-century critic dubbed "the eternal melted butter." Vinegar was the primary ingredient in many of these new sauces, and this contributed to the rising popularity of pickles. While today we usually think of a pickle as a form of cucumber, eighteenth-century pickles were far more diverse, including mushrooms, nuts, and meats. This trend, which was derived from the custom of immersing a solid food into a vinegar or salt solution in order to preserve it for later use, eventually led to the emergence of ketchup, which was essentially a blended version of tomato pickles.[8]

The increasing popularity of pickles and ketchups in British cookery is displayed in eighteenth-century British cookbooks, many of which were distributed (and later even printed) in the American colonies. In the well-known *The Compleat Housewife* (1739), E. Smith provides numerous recipes for pickles, including ones made from mushrooms, walnuts, cucumbers, beans, and red cabbage. Likewise, the 1769 edition of *The Experienced English Housekeeper* gives several ketchup recipes, including two for walnut ketchup, a popular early ketchup variation, and others for mushroom ketchups. These innovations made their way into the only eighteenth-century American cookbook, Amelia Simmons's *American Cookery*. The printing of British cookbooks in America such as Hannah Glasse's *The Art of Cookery Made Plain and Easy* (published in England in 1747 and reprinted in the United States in 1805) gave numerous recipes for pickled walnuts, cucumbers, asparagus, peaches, French beans, cauliflower as well as two different recipes for mushroom ketchup.[9]

These techniques for making pickles and ketchups eventually were adapted to the tomato. The first-known published mention of tomato ketchup is a recipe printed in James Mease's *Archives of Useful Knowledge* (1812), published in Philadelphia. By the 1820s American and English cookbooks were regularly publishing tomato ketchup recipes, along with numerous other tomato-based dishes and sauces. William Kitchiner's *The Cook's Oracle* (published in 1817 in London and 1825 in the United States) included tomato ketchup, as did Mary Randolph's first edition of *The Virginia Housewife* (1828). This suggests that tomato ketchup had become an important solution to the seasonality of the tomato—a clear way of preserving the highly perishable tomato for off-season consumption.[10]

The growing popularity of tomato ketchup may also point to Americans' increasing expectation that food be more diverse and less bland. As food historian Andrew Smith notes, ketchup served "to add zest, color, and flavor to other foods; and to camouflage the taste of unsatisfactory, unfamiliar, or monotonous foods."[11]

The recipes for tomato ketchup also indicate the diversity in flavors that could be achieved by mixing tomatoes with other ingredients. About the only required ingredients were tomatoes and salt. But recipes called for the addition of chopped onions, mace, and black pepper. One of the more popular recipes of the 1830s, offered by the *Cultivator* and other journals, added "cloves, pepper and nutmegs" to the basic mix of tomatoes and salt. Much like the recipes for tomato sauce, such a recipe would have a complex taste profile, with both salty and sweet ingredients. One of the more complex ketchup recipes comes in an 1835 article describing Bennett's lecture. In addition to tomatoes and salt, this recipe calls for horseradish, mustard seed, ginger, pepper, cloves, and mace. It also suggests that some people liked to add onions or garlic. Another called for the addition of sliced onions, black pepper, cayenne, mustard and cloves. After cooling, a large quantity of strong cider or wine vinegar was to be added as well. Tomato ketchup could be made in a wide variety of flavors—sweet, salty, and spicy—depending on the cook's desires and the types of dishes the ketchup was to flavor. This inventiveness of American cooks and their eagerness to experiment is easily forgotten in the modern age when corporate-produced tomato ketchup has been reduced to a predictable uniformity.[12]

At least by 1850 ketchup was effectively wedded to tomatoes in America. While some continued to make ketchup with other ingredients, perhaps most notably mushrooms, tomato ketchup was more prominent in cookbooks and agricultural periodicals and was advertised for sale far more than any other ketchups. As one journal noted in 1834, "It is much better than mushroom ketchup for all kinds of culinary purposes." Cookbook author Lydia Marie Francis Child echoed this sentiment in 1830 when she proclaimed that "the best sort of catsup is made from tomatoes." During the nineteenth century, ketchup was a way for farmers to deal with excess tomatoes. As Edward James Hooper argued, "There can be no loss on this vegetable, for raise as much as you may, what is not sent to market can be converted into catsup, and will bring a price that will fully compensate the gardener." Processing the surplus of the harvest into ketchup was a surefire solution to the unavoidable problem of perishability.[13]

The most important alternative to ketchup was sauce, which also promised to add new flavors to the American meal. In theory, sauces were more complex versions of ketchups, but in fact many sauce recipes closely resembled those of ketchups. One recipe in 1828, for example, called for a dozen tomatoes to be stewed, with two teaspoons of brown sugar, some pepper, and a tablespoon of flour to thicken the sauce. The recipe also indicates that "some persons prefer pounded cracker instead of flour." In many cases, too, sauces were to be prepared much like gravy. Overall, tomato sauces could be flavored to be sweet, with the addition of brown sugar, or spicy, with the addition of pepper or peppers, or in the above case, a little of both. Much like with ketchups, sauces benefited from being able to be preserved in jars for year-round consumption.[14]

PRESERVED TOMATOES

Still, ketchup and sauce weren't the only ways of preserving the vulnerable tomato. For much of the nineteenth century, tomato pickles were common, especially in the South and Midwest. Again the idea seems to have been borrowed from England, where during the late eighteenth century and early nineteenth century, pickled tomatoes were mentioned regularly in American and British sources. It soon made its way to America, where tomatoes were pickled either ripe or green, the latter perhaps indicating a need to find a culinary use for unripe tomatoes.[15]

Other dishes, including tomato preserves and jelly, were often made with surplus tomatoes. A recipe for tomato figs by a Mrs. Steiger was actually deposited at the U.S. Patent Office in July 1841, and made its rounds through the agricultural press. The recipe promised that tomatoes "keep well from year to year, and retain surprisingly their flavor, which is nearly that of the best quality of fresh figs." Other cooks became even more creative, suggesting that the tomato could also be preserved for year-round consumption by turning it into a wine or syrup. It is impossible to know how popular many of these dishes were, but their publication reflects a willingness to experiment and to integrate the tomato into American traditions of preserving and preparing food.[16]

American cooks also dried tomatoes for later rehydration in sauce or stews. A woman from Brooklyn wrote to the *Cultivator* in 1844 offering a recipe for dried tomatoes using a preservation method common for fish and other foods. After peeling the tomatoes and cutting them in half, her recipe directed the cook to "lay them on plates and put them into the oven" to dry. After that, she said, "put them into paper bags and keep in a dry place." They could then be rehydrated for "a mince or stew" simply by dipping them in cool water. As an added benefit, she said, they "are very good to eat out of hand in the dry state," making them serve a similar function to sun-dried tomatoes today.[17]

The appeal of dried tomatoes may have been limited. In fact, one of the motivations for early canning was finding alternatives to drying meats, fruits, and vegetables. So it is not surprising that others provided recipes for preserving tomatoes "fresh." In a recipe lifted from a French journal, the *Workingman's Advocate* reported that tomatoes could be preserved simply by placing them in an earthen pot, whole, uncooked, including the skin, and covering them with salt water. They were said to be able to keep for more than a year in such a state, and when they were desired in the kitchen, they simply needed to be soaked in fresh water for several hours to remove the remnants of the brine. The result would hardly be called fresh by modern standards, but contemporaries saw this as a way to emulate fresh tomatoes as much as possible.[18]

The nineteenth century also saw the first version of what might be described as tomato paste, a concentrated version of tomatoes, preserved in such a way as to allow for thinner tomato sauce to be created months, if not years, after the tomato was processed by adding water. One such method, dubbed the "Turkish Preparation," called for taking the juice of the tomato together with salt, and evaporating it until it created a paste. The paste, the recipe said, would "preserve the true flavor of the fruit for several years." A similar recipe, published in the *Southern Planter*, stated that "a bit [of the paste] not larger than a Lima bean will be sufficient to flavor the soup of a family of twenty persons; and a much smaller quantity for sauces." Yet another recipe, from a woman in Georgia, named "Portable Catsup, or Tomato-Jelly," likely resembled a bouillon cube. It called for straining the juice of tomatoes, adding cloves, pepper, horseradish, mace, and shallots, then baking the tomatoes, and finally drying the mixture in the sun. Once it formed into a hard cake, the cook was to cut it into two-inch squares. These squares, "deposited in a small quantity of warm water, will give a flavor to gravies or soups, equal to fresh Tomatoes." In many ways, these recipes are a logical extension of the development of ketchup. As tomato ketchup was often viewed as a sort of tomato concentrate, where a small amount could season an entire dish, the tomato paste created using the "Turkish Method" could do so while taking up less space and without needing to be sealed in a jar. Some of these grassroots preparations would be adopted by corporate food engineers in the twentieth century.[19]

In still another way, farmers and cooks anticipated industrialization with early versions of canned tomatoes. In the 1850s, when the commercial canning industry was still in its infancy, agricultural journals encouraged families to can their own tomatoes using a process almost identical to that used by early industrial metal canners (in contrast to the glass "mason jars" later commonly used in home canning). After filling a three-quart can with tomatoes, the cook was instructed to solder on the top, leaving only a small hole in the lid. After heating the can over a fire, the cook would finally seal the small hole, leaving a finished product similar to manufactured canned tomatoes that would soon be available in urban and rural stores. Another recipe, published in 1853, asserted that canning in glass rather than in tin-coated iron (a rather expensive material) would "bring it within the means of all." After filling a glass bottle with cooked tomatoes, the bottles were to be corked and then to be covered in wax, thus protecting the jar's contents from the air. The sheer volume of recipes that called for preserving tomatoes—with vinegar, salt, drying, and canning, brought the tomato to the kitchen table year-round and encouraged farmers to grow this seasonal crop.[20]

THE INTRODUCTION OF NEW CUISINE

Through most of the nineteenth century, the tomato was adapted to American foodways rather than really breaking new ground. In fact, often it was a substitute for other foods. For example, housewives directed readers to substitute tomatoes for peach preserves in years that the peach crop failed. "The flavor is almost the precisely the same," one writer noted, "and is altogether an excellent article for the tea table." Tomatoes could also replace peaches in pies, preserves, and tarts, especially when peaches were not available. This practice of substitution and experimentation has a long history and was common in the United States, as may be seen in the extraordinarily wide variety of vegetables and fruits that went into homemade beer and other alcoholic beverages.[21]

The tomato, however, also empowered American cooks to create new dishes, often with ethnic influences. Dishes like fresh tomato salads, "tomatoes fricandeau," and tomatoes cooked according to the "Spanish Method," reflected the growing influence of French and Spanish cuisine during the 1840s and 1850s. Likewise, with the growing popularity of okra, especially in the South and Midwest, several recipes for gumbo, of which tomatoes formed a vital component, were distributed during the period. A dish thought to have its roots in the West Indies, gumbo became popular in areas of French influence, such as New Orleans, but recipes for gumbo were distributed at least as far as Cincinnati. The amazing versatility of the tomato encouraged experimentation and cooking ethnically and culturally diverse foods. "It is among edible vegetables," reported the *Saturday Evening Post* in 1849, "something like India-Rubber or Gum-Elastic and Gutta-Percha are for the purposes for which they are so extensively and variously used." Put simply, the tomato could be molded and shaped by the cook.[22]

By the middle of the nineteenth century, that versatility extended to the idea of serving fresh tomatoes, abandoning the common bias in favor of cooked (even overcooked) vegetables. Edward Hooper remarked in 1840 that "the tomato has become a great favorite sliced and seasoned as we do the cucumber, and has the advantage of being quite wholesome." Elizabeth Putnam provided a recipe for eating raw tomatoes dressed with salt, pepper, and vinegar. Sarah Hale provided a similar recipe, labeling it "Tomatoes en Salade," which suggests a French influence (though it would properly be called *salade de tomates*). However, access to fresh tomatoes was limited to their short harvest season. The desirability of the fresh tomato, however, influenced farmers to make efforts to expand its seasonality.[23]

THE TOMATO IN THE FIELDS

By the mid-nineteenth century, Americans were beginning to consider an alternative to the traditional preserved foods of the past, including tomato ketchups and sauces. This required not the innovations of cooks but the creativity of farmers in extending the growing season of tomato crops. They responded to this demand for the fresh (ultimately throughout the year) by cultivating improved tomato varieties and utilizing existing agricultural technologies to grow better, and earlier, tomatoes. So strong was the demand for out-of-season tomatoes that the *Genesee Farmer and Gardener's Journal* found it newsworthy to report the presence of tomatoes at Philadelphia markets as early as July 10 in 1833, a remarkable feat. In a rare early mention of greenhouse tomatoes, the *New*

England Farmer reported that a few of these still unusual and still costly tomatoes had appeared in Boston in July 1837.[24]

Horticultural and agricultural journals regularly listed prices for produce available at urban markets, presumably to give farmers information on how much profit to expect for their own market crops. These numbers tell us a lot about the seasonal nature of many vegetables, including tomatoes. For example, at Boston's Faneuil Market in 1833, tomatoes dropped from 20 cents per dozen on August 7 to 12.5 cents per dozen on August 14 and 21. In 1835, the figures were even more telling: on July 29, tomatoes cost 50 cents per dozen. By August 19, the price had dropped in half, to 25 cents. On August 26, the price had dropped yet again, to 12.5 cents per dozen. Finally, by September 9, the price bottomed out at 6.5 cents per dozen. In the decades after 1820, when a viable market for tomatoes emerged in urban areas, these price changes provided a strong incentive to bring tomatoes as early as possible in the season, when the prices were high.[25]

During this period, Edmund Morris, a former Philadelphia businessman purchased a ten-acre farm in New Jersey. Devoting one of his ten acres to tomato production, Morris quickly understood the seasonal nature of the Philadelphia and New York vegetable markets and the dramatic advantage of an early (and late) harvest: "For the first few baskets of early tomatoes I sent to market, I obtained two dollars per basket of three pecks each. Other growers coming in competition with me, the price rapidly diminished as the supply increased, until it fell to twenty-five cents a bushel. At less than this the growers refused to pick the [tomatoes]. . . . As the season advanced the supply diminished, and the price again rose to a dollar a basket, the demand continuing as long as any could be procured." These farmers, ever competitive capitalists, sought new ways of marketing tomatoes when the prices were high. Such was the profit potential of early tomatoes, stated Morris, that many New Jersey vegetable farmers "emigrated to Virginia for the purpose of taking advantage of the earlier climate of that genial region." Despite increasing their distance from larger urban markets, Virginia's climate allowed them to produce more tomatoes when prices were high, and thus increased their profit potential. From the 1840s until the Civil War, these farmers utilized improved transportation routes to the cities and were "rewarded by fabulous prices, from the receipt of which large fortunes resulted" simply by providing Philadelphia, Washington, DC, and other northern cities with tomatoes and other vegetables a mere two weeks earlier than their local farmers could provide.[26]

This marketing strategy was widely adopted in the nineteenth century. In 1889, Thomas Baird, a Kentucky farmer, reported to the *National Stockman and Farmer* that the tomato was "the most profitable garden crop [he had] ever offered to the market," in part because he was successful at getting an early crop to market. Not all of these farmers were from the South; some were near urban areas. N. Hallock, a market farmer on Long Island, reported that despite a smaller crop of tomatoes when aiming for the early market, "the first few pickings for market may bring a price that will over-balance the larger crop" that could be obtained later in the season. Thus the early crop remained an ideal, especially for farmers close to fast-growing cities.[27]

EXTENDING THE SEASONS WITH NEW TOMATO VARIETIES

Farmers utilized a variety of techniques to get these early tomatoes, though many resisted change. James Garnett, writing for the *Farmer's Register* in 1841, observed that "strange to say, I have never yet met with any farmer or gardener who had ever taken the trouble, little as that would be, to ascertain how either tomatoes or peas could be rendered most productive; or which among our numerous varieties of the latter ripens the soonest; or which will yield most." Others, though frustrated by the conservatism of farmers, still tried to convince them to improve their own tomato strains: by waiting until their plants are in full bearing, they should "pick from the very best, the most desirable fruit, and save them for seed," argued William Chorlton, writing in the *Horticulturalist* in 1855. Another writer, certainly valuing the earliest crop, advised the readers of the *Southern Cultivator* to "select the earliest and ripest" tomatoes for seed-saving.[28]

Long before the rise of Campbell's, Heinz, and other national manufacturers of tomato soup, sauce, and eventually Spaghetti-Os, American
cooks and farmers introduced American families to the extraordinary
variety of uses of the tomato. Cooks adapted traditional forms of vegetable preservation to the soft tomato, but in the process they also experimented with many new, if sometimes ephemeral, ways of introducing
the tomato to the pot, the skillet, and eventually the plates of American
diners. European culinary influence brought with it pickling and the
use of ketchups, both of which were well-suited uses for the highly perishable tomato in America. Likewise, potential uses of the tomato included preserves, jams, jellies, wines, and syrups.

To these innovations in culinary arts came invention in breeding and
cultivation by farmers who found ways of extending the availability of
fresh tomatoes, a form of the vegetable that became increasingly popular in the nineteenth century. Through carefully selecting desirable tomato plants for saving seeds, farmers produced ripe fruit earlier in the
season. Likewise, hot beds, greenhouses, and other technologies expanded the growing season by shielding plants from the elements in
late winter and early spring, delivering fresh tomatoes to the dinner
tables of millions of increasingly urbanized Americans through retail
markets. In a few cases, farmers had fully transcended the seasons, harvesting tomatoes in every month of the year.

In the decades that followed, the twelve-month tomato would become
an industrial reality. The rise of the canning industry in the late nineteenth and early twentieth century made the twelve-month preserved
tomato a national treasure. Likewise, the continued development of
greenhouse tomatoes, along with expanded production of tomatoes in
nearly every region of the country, assured access to fresh tomatoes at
any time of year. But once again, this development was not the work of
large-scale producers or corporate manufacturers distributing tomatoes and tomato products on a national scale. Rather, it was the effort of
local farmers addressing the cooks' needs for fresh or processed whole
tomatoes that resulted in a year-round supply of what was quickly becoming America's favorite vegetable.

3

A TOMATO FOR ALL SEASONS

The Development of the Twelve-Month Fresh
and Processed Tomato Industries, 1880–1945

A s the nineteenth century drew to a close, the tomato had become a widely popular food. With immigrants and rural Americans flooding American cities, eliminating much urban garden space, the demand for commercially produced tomatoes increased dramatically. At the turn of the century it was not at all clear how the demand for tomatoes in urban areas would be filled. Over the next forty years, both farmers and industry worked to increase the tomato supply; however, their response did not fit with the pattern followed by other major food industries during the period. Instead, it followed a new path: one based on economic and geographic decentralization.

During this period, other food industries, most notably meatpacking, grain, citrus fruit, and lettuce industries, responded to the same situation by consolidating into a few large companies and becoming geographically centralized in particular regions. By the 1880s, for example, over 90 percent of the Chicago meatpacking trade came under the control of just four Chicago-based companies: Swift and Company, Armour and Company, Fairbank Canning Company, and Libby, McNeil, and Libby. By revolutionizing the process of slaughtering and packing meat in factories rather than at butchers, meatpacking served as a model for new production practices in industries across the country. The tomato industry, however, did not follow this model. Tomato production and processing took place in virtually every region of the United States. Most important, a wide cast of characters, from farmers, agricultural researchers, and small-scale canners to large corporations, contributed to the organization of this emerging industry. Into the 1940s, these actors each defined the tomato—its proper growth, marketing and processing—in varied, sometimes even contradictory, ways. This range of approaches helped stave off the dominance of any one particular tomato—no single company, tomato product, tomato variety, or geographic location was able to gain or maintain complete control of the market during the first half of the century.[1]

This chapter traces the roots of the modern tomato industry from the end of the Civil War through the beginning of World War II. This period saw not only the development of the modern tomato canning industry but also the emergence and division of specific industries for the purposes of creating canned, fresh, and greenhouse tomatoes— each made up of different groups of farmers, mechanical and agricultural techniques, researchers, tomato varieties, and industries. While sometimes overlapping, increasingly these became separate industries with distinct varieties and agricultural practices.

This period also saw the rise in heavily processed tomato products, most notably Campbell's Tomato Soup and Heinz Ketchup. The emergence and success of these branded goods fit into the main narrative that scholars have relied on when examining American food culture and industrialization during the early twentieth century. The success of these companies rested on their ability to develop products that could be distinguished through advertising and marketing. Yet despite the growing popularity of heavily processed, brand-name tomato products, these remained much less significant than either fresh tomatoes or minimally processed canned tomato products, which together constituted the vast majority of tomato consumption through the 1940s.

Instead, the most significant aspect of the development of the tomato industry during the first half of the twentieth century was its sustained desire to create a year-round supply of tomatoes. As we have seen, this was not a desire unique to the early twentieth century but instead was rooted in the desires and efforts of traditional farmers and cooks. Yet there is no question that industrialization—of canning, the seed industry, transportation networks, markets, and agriculture—all contributed significantly to the success of the twelve-month tomato.

The quest for the twelve-month tomato meant that the industrialization of the tomato followed a different pattern than that set forth by the meatpackers in Chicago, grain farmers and processors in the Midwest and in Buffalo, New York, or citrus and lettuce growers in California. Indeed, in stark contrast to these other industries, tomato production during the early twentieth century was characterized by a high level of geographic and economic decentralization. That decentralization was not simply a result of the persistence of traditional agricultural and processing practices; rather, it represented the emergence of new ways of understanding the production of tomatoes. Particularly in the case of fresh tomatoes, decentralized production was a direct result of the difficulty in transporting the produce and the desire to extend the seasonality of the harvest. Nearly every region of the country took part in tomato production, and this varied geography helped supply urban markets with tomatoes throughout the year.

The unique decentralized nature of tomato production during the first half of the twentieth century helped increase even further the amount and diversity of actors participating in the making of tomato culture. States across the country, including New Jersey, Maryland, Indiana, West Virginia, Florida, Arkansas, Texas, and Kansas, conducted their own research on the tomato. Seed companies and canners, both national and local, developed and marketed their own seeds and canned local tomato goods for diverse markets. No single group of farmers controlled the production of tomatoes, as well. Ultimately, the emergence of distinct industries focused on different types of tomatoes—canning, truck-farming, long-distance, and greenhouse—meant that throughout the first half of the century no single type or variety of tomato, or even groups of varieties, maintained a dominant position.

In the end, the desire to transcend the seasons and to produce a twelve-month supply of fresh and processed tomatoes resulted in a broadening of the culture of the tomato. Consumers were offered a wide variety of tomatoes and tomato products—each of which was judged according to price, taste, quality, and other factors. The diversity in the production of tomatoes helped further diversify the consumption of tomatoes, ensuring that the tomato's role in American food culture remained many-sided.

THE RISE OF CANNING

At the same time that farmers and cooks were seeking ways to transcend the seasonality of the tomato, enterprising merchants and scientists also pursued industrial methods for extending the seasons for perishable foods. Growing through the second half of the nineteenth century, by the beginning of the twentieth century, the canning industry and the canned tomato emerged as major participants in American food culture. These efforts began with Nicholas Appert's discovery in 1810 that heating and sealing food inside of glass jars using corks could preserve it for an extended period of time, thus providing an alternative to traditional means of food preservation—drying and salting that left food leathery and bitter. Canning left food, including soft foods like whole tomatoes, relatively "fresh," firm, and flavorful. Appert's discovery, which was made in response to Napoleon's offer of a reward for anyone who came up with a new method for preserving foods, established the basic principles by which modern canning continues to operate. It was quickly improved on, however, by the English inventor Peter Durand, who replaced breakable glass bottles with iron "cans" in 1810. Named after the traditional cane "canisters," Durand coated his cans with tin to reduce rusting, thus the "tin can," which he sold to the Royal Navy.[2]

The growth of the canning industry did not immediately follow the inventions of Appert and Durand, however, as canning was expensive and often produced unsafe products. During the first half of the nineteenth century, a few industrious Americans started canning operations. William Underwood, America's first commercial canner, began shipping fruit in jars from Boston overseas. Thomas Kensett first packed fruit in jars in New York in 1825; in 1840, he moved his operations to Baltimore where he began canning oysters from the Chesapeake Bay. Despite these early innovators, however, the canning industry remained a small affair until the American Civil War. Tin cans had to be constructed entirely by hand, with a skilled can-maker able to produce roughly sixty cans in a ten-hour workday. Canned food was often boiled (because processors lacked understanding of how much heating was required for preservation), which turned meats and vegetables into flavorless mush, and (often correctly) consumers questioned the safety of canned food. Thus canning remained an expensive and potentially dangerous process.[3]

The Civil War was the first big test for the canning industry. The Union bought a large volume of canned foods for use in military expeditions. As thousands of soldiers returned home and "told others about canned foods and bought them," demand rose throughout the 1860s and 1870s. By 1870, the total U.S. volume of canned goods was nearly thirty million cans per year, a six-fold increase from prewar figures. The number of canning establishments also ballooned, reaching one hundred by 1870.[4]

Yet the canning industry was limited by two technological and scientific impediments: first, a lack of understanding of bacteriology (which was not fully understood until the 1890s) meant that early canning processes were largely developed by trial and error. Spoiled products remained common. Second, the rudimentary technology implemented in canneries made canning a labor- and resource-intensive process. A can-maker had to manually bend and cut each piece of tin by hand, then solder them together, leaving a large hole in the top to fill the can. This process was laborious, as well as expensive. Constructing ten thousand cans required as much as twenty-five pounds of expensive, lead-based solder (which sometimes tainted and even poisoned the canned food). After the can was filled with food, which had to be skinned, shucked, or otherwise prepared by hand, a cap was soldered onto the hole in the top of the can, and it was cooked for between four and six hours. After this, the hole was soldered shut.[5]

Between the 1850s and 1905, innovators within the industry overcame some of the most significant obstacles to the mass production of canned goods. They did so by improving on and speeding up both the manufacturing of cans and the processing and canning of foods. The late 1840s saw several patents issued for small, hand- or foot-powered machines that stamped or cut out tin for can construction. In 1858, canners began utilizing a method for can construction where the ends were soldered on by being rotated in a solder-bath that increased the average output of a can-maker to about a thousand per day, while also reducing the amount of solder required. During the 1880s, can construction received renewed interest. In 1887, J. D. Cox, a Baltimore canner, created a capper that could cap and solder six cans at a time, further reducing the labor needs in can construction. While Cox's Capper, as one canning expert recalled in 1903, was a "small machine," it helped reduce the labor cost of capping cans by roughly one-third. Other innovations soon followed, and by 1900, the can-making industry was largely mechanized, mass-producing cans at a very high rate.[6]

The technology of canning, however, had significant limitations. The use of large amounts of solder to seal the body and lids and a continued high rate of spoilage produced suspicion of the healthiness of canned foods. These problems were overcome by the introduction of the "Ams" can in the opening years of the twentieth century by canners Max Ams and Amos Cobb. The Ams can, later renamed the "sanitary" can, replaced the practice of soldering the exterior seams of the body and lids with a can with a double-seam construction, eliminating the need for all but a small bit of solder in sealing the can. With crimped double seams replacing the lapped side and sealed with a rubber compound, only a thin coat of solder needed to be applied on the outside of the can, safely away from the food contents. Output from a single machine soon exceeded twenty-five thousand cans per day, and within a decade the "sanitary" can was the dominant format in American canneries (figure 3.1).[7]

The overall success of the canning industry also depended on the emergence of new technologies to help automate food processing and make canning safer. The primary achievements of the canning industry in technological advancement through the end of the nineteenth

ARCHITECTURE OF THE ENAMELED SANITARY TIN CAN

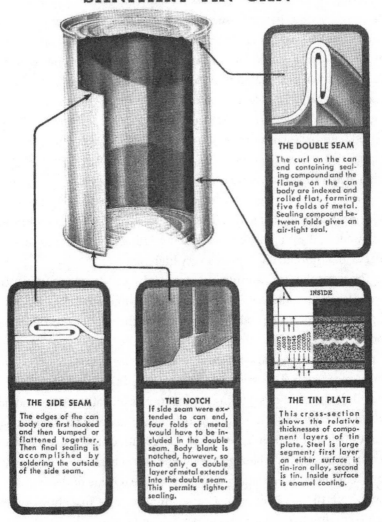

THE DOUBLE SEAM
The curl on the can end containing sealing compound and the flange on the can body are indexed and rolled flat, forming five folds of metal. Sealing compound between folds gives an air-tight seal.

THE SIDE SEAM
The edges of the can body are first hooked and then bumped or flattened together. Then final sealing is accomplished by soldering the outside of the side seam.

THE NOTCH
If side seam were extended to can end, four folds of metal would have to be included in the double seam. Body blank is notched, however, so that only a double layer of metal extends into the double seam. This permits tighter sealing.

THE TIN PLATE
This cross-section shows the relative thicknesses of component layers of tin plate. Steel is large segment; first layer on either surface is tin-iron alloy, second is tin. Inside surface is enamel coating.

INSIDE

FIGURE 3.1 Fabrication of the sanitary can. *The Canning Industry: Its History, Importance, Organization, Methods, and the Public Service of Its Products* (Washington, DC: National Canners Association, 1971), 17.

century were not in creating highly specialized equipment but in changing general cannery procedures and processing technologies. In 1861, for example, Isaac Solomon discovered that the addition of calcium chloride to the water used to process cans allowed the water to reach 240°F. By this method, processing times were reduced from four to six hours to as little as twenty-five to forty minutes. This small improvement allowed a "first-class cannery" to increase production from 2,500 to 20,000 cans per day, and the higher processing temperatures led to a significant drop in the rate of spoilage. The effort to decrease the processing time of canned food was furthered again in 1874, with the introduction of A. K. Shriver's steam-kettle cooker, which utilized externally produced steam in a pressure-controlled kettle to increase cooking temperatures (and thus reduce processing times). The high pressure used to process cans also reduced waste because it helped offset the high pressures within the can when heated. On occasion cans exploded during cooking, which was why factories processed cans with a hole in the top. Canners' overall motive for all these innovations was to reduce processing times and increase the quality of their pack.[8]

While many of the most significant new measures applied to all (or most) canning products, some companies began to develop machinery designed to make the preparation or processing of certain food items more efficient. As the most popular canned food during the period, and among the most labor-intensive, corn led the way. One of the leaders in corn-processing technology was Welcome Sprague, progenitor of the Sprague Canning Machinery Co., based in Chicago. In 1888, Sprague created a corn-cutter capable of processing upward of fifteen thousand cans per day. Others, including Volney Barker and John Winslow Jones, had already developed relatively effective corn cutters, but by using rubber teething rings as springs, Sprague was able to devise a chain-fed corn cutter that was flexible enough to account for differences in the size and shape of individual cobs of corn. The mechanical corn cutter helped overcome the labor-intensive task of individually removing corn from the cob by hand. The most lasting innovation, however, was the development of the "automatic line." Eliminating the need for manually transporting products from station to station, the company Merrell and Soule utilized conveyor belts and an organized factory layout to automate transportation of corn to produce a continuous line of production. While their setup was for canned corn, the idea of a continuous line, developed in the years before Henry Ford's assembly line, was easily adapted to the tomato and other cannery crops.[9]

The tomato industry, already popular by the late-nineteenth century, was not as dependent on specialized technological innovations for its success and benefited greatly from general technological innovations like Shriver's steam kettle and Merrell and Soule's continuous line. The only real requirements of a nineteenth-century tomato cannery were cans, boilers—one for scalding tomatoes and another for processing cans—and a means to remove the tomato skin and close the lids. This made canned tomato production relatively easy and inexpensive, though there were high labor costs in peeling the tomatoes. The addition of new equipment, including conveyor belts, offered increased efficiency but did not require factory specialization. Indeed, as John D. Cox remarked in 1914, the "ease of production and small capital requirement" fueled canned tomato production. Canning machines were mostly generic, and canneries could process a variety of local vegetable and fruit crops in succession as they were harvested. Canners had good reason to produce canned tomatoes, for it required little additional investment. Likewise, opening a tomato cannery, even if on a very small scale, was within the means of many.[10]

By the end of the century other improvements had taken place in tomato processing, including most notably the invention of tomato scalders and fillers. An 1890s catalog for the Canners' Supply Company of Bridgeton, New Jersey, for example, offers numerous models of steam powered tomato-fillers, which could be used to automatically fill cans with tomatoes. One model, Moore and Bristol's Tomato Can Filler, which was "improved for 1894," lists an operating speed of forty to sixty cans per minute, or thirty thousand cans per day. The Haines Perfect Can Filler (figure 3.2), patented in 1890 and advertised by the Canners' Supply Company as "the best machine for packing tomatoes," was offered for only $110 (slightly less than $3,000 in 2014 dollars). While not a requirement for a tomato-canning factory, a tomato filler could be

FIGURE 3.2 Haines Perfect Can Filler. Canners' Supply Company catalog (Bridgeton, NJ; Philadelphia: [1890s]), 68.

used for foods other than tomatoes, making an inexpensive and dynamic addition to any cannery that had upgraded to belt-driven power. Likewise, tomato scalders, to aid in the process of skinning tomatoes, were not required but could be had for as little as $40 (just over $1,000 in 2014).[11]

These innovations helped fuel increased canned food production. In 1891, the total pack of canned tomatoes alone dwarfed the entire canning industry of 1870, producing more than 3 million cases, or 79 million cans. The five-year average for the final five years of the nineteenth century was nearly 4.9 million cases. Baltimore was a canning center in the late nineteenth century. Close proximity to large population centers, access to the sea for both seafood and shipping, and a good climate and fertile soil all benefited the industry. Yet tomato canning in particular existed across the country. As early as 1860, one enterprising farmer, Thomas Duckwell, opened a canning factory near Cincinnati, Ohio. In 1890, tomato packing began in rural Georgia. By 1900, there were at least 1,800 canneries nationwide, up from 100 in 1870. Technological innovations in the canning industry during the late nineteenth century helped drive up (and meet) consumer demand for canned goods, but the proliferation of inexpensive, multifunctional equipment combined with relatively standardized, minimally processed goods, ensured that, during this era, tomato canning would not be highly centralized economically or geographically. The cannery, like the garden, remained dispersed and local.[12]

THE CORPORATE TOMATO

Technological innovations allowed canners to mechanize and increase the speed of production, fulfilling the growing demand for canned whole vegetables and fruits. Yet another trend in food production paralleled these technological innovations and offered the opportunity to revolutionize the canned food industry as well: the development of convenience foods.

The emergence of heavily processed convenience foods has received significant attention from scholars. Susan Strasser, for example, argues in *Satisfaction Guaranteed* that hypercompetition created by new industrial methods led to more heavily processed foods, which could be branded and thus distinguishable within the marketplace. The success of companies such as Campbell's and Heinz depended on their development of brand-name products like Campbell's Tomato Soup and Heinz Tomato Ketchup. Advancements in food-processing technologies like canning were quickly succeeded by the development of convenience foods, which, according to Strasser, played a pivotal role in economic centralization within the food industry, the development of marketing and branding techniques, and the evolution of American food culture.[13]

Heinz and Campbell's both exemplify changes in American food processing during the late nineteenth and early twentieth century. Joseph Campbell grew up on a Bridgeton, New Jersey, farm. As a young man, he became a fruit and vegetable purchasing agent and, in 1869, teamed up with Abraham Anderson and founded Anderson and Campbell, a canning enterprise, in Camden. The company operated until 1877, when the two parted ways over disagreements on whether they should expand. During this time Anderson and Campbell canned several products, including the Celebrated Beefsteak Tomato, so large it was said that a single fruit filled an entire can. They also canned Strictly Fancy Small Peas, Fancy Asparagus, and other products. Also in 1869, in Pittsburgh, Harry Heinz, a young man from Sharpsburg, Pennsylvania, who had been bottling and selling surplus horseradish from his mother's garden since he was eight, teamed up with L. C. Noble and began a small condiment business. The partners, under the Anchor brand, started with Heinz's prized horseradish but soon expanded their line to include pickled cucumbers, sauerkraut, vinegar, and other condiments.[14]

From the outset, both Heinz and Campbell understood the importance of distinguishing their products from competitors. And both offered distinctly labeled and specialty products. Heinz packaged processed goods—sauces and condiments. By 1875, his company had emerged as one of the largest condiment companies in the nation. His original three-quarters of an acre of farmland had expanded to 160 acres. His company's production capacity had increased similarly. The company annually produced three thousand barrels of sauerkraut, fifteen thousand barrels of pickles, and fifty thousand barrels of vinegar. After going bankrupt, Harry Heinz re-formed the company in 1876 with his cousin Frederick, and they specialized in cucumber pickles and tomato ketchup. In 1887, after just two decades in operation, the company's sales exceeded $100,000. By the turn of the century, Heinz was the largest condiment company in the United States.[15]

While Campbell originally packed mostly raw ingredients—minimally processed vegetables—he nonetheless tried to market them as unique products unavailable elsewhere on the market. In 1893, Arthur Dorrance bought the Joseph Campbell Company and quickly sought a new direction. In 1897, Arthur's nephew John, who had received a degree from MIT and had recently earned a PhD from the University of Göttingen, began working for the company and immediately began experimenting with condensed soups. Campbell's first introduced five varieties of condensed soups in late 1897, including tomato, consommé, vegetable, chicken, and oxtail. They were an immediate hit. The year that John Dorrance came to work at Campbell's, the company lost $60,000. Within a year, the business was profitable. Condensed soup dominated sales, as early as 1905 accounting for $750,000 of the company's $900,000 in total sales. Most of the several hundred products sold by Campbell's in the 1890s were soon discontinued to focus on the soup business. In 1907, sales of condensed soup topped $1 million per year. By the late 1910s, sales had increased to twelve million cans per year. Thus, much like Heinz, Campbell's success depended largely on finding niche markets for heavily processed, highly distinguishable goods.[16]

Both Heinz and Campbell's played a pivotal role in expanding agricultural research related to tomatoes. John Dorrance, who had experimented with tomato cultivation at his Cinnaminson, New Jersey, farm before coming to Campbell's, hired Harry Hall, a leading agricultural expert, to conduct agricultural research on the major crops used in the company's soups, especially tomatoes. As the superintendent of Campbell's Soup Farms, Hall's primary job was to advise farmers on proper agricultural techniques and practices. As Campbell's factories were often overloaded during the tomato harvest season, even having to shut down all other production during the peak of the tomato harvest, one member of Hall's staff, R. Vincent Crine, came up with the idea in 1918 of planting tomato seeds in Georgia in January and February and shipping the vines north to be replanted to New Jersey after the last frost, thus extending the harvest season and reducing stress on Campbell's overloaded plants. Likewise, Heinz was interested in advancing the quality of their tomato varieties. As early as 1901, Heinz annually planted eighteen thousand acres of its own land. The company completed its first tomato yield trials in 1916 and hired a full-time agricultural researcher in 1920. Much like Campbell's, Heinz was committed to thoroughly controlling the production of its raw ingredients: in 1924, Heinz oversaw 150,000 acres of cropland. Through 1936, the company annually grew its own tomato plants and distributed them to farmers contracted to grow the crop. In 1949, Heinz provided seed and seedlings for upward of fifty million tomato plants to around forty thousand farmers, mostly on a contract basis.[17]

In addition to controlling the cultivation of the raw ingredients used in their products, both Heinz and Campbell's recognized the importance of marketing and branding their products to find consumers for their increased production. This marketing effort encompassed not only brand differentiation but also the introduction of new foods and dietary habits to the American consumer, including an expanded line of Heinz condiments and Campbell's soups. At the same time, other manufacturers were encouraging Americans to adopt other new foods and ways of serving them (Jell-O flavored gelatin, Kellogg's Corn Flakes, Post Postum, etc.).[18]

Of course, even as Campbell's and Heinz innovated by creating highly processed tomato products—one Heinz biographer labeled them "reciped products" to distinguish them from products like canned whole tomatoes that did not require a complicated recipe—they were not alone in this venture. Franco-American, later bought out by Campbell's, was canning soup well before Campbell's began marketing its condensed soup. Heinz, too, was a major seller of soups through the first half of the twentieth century. But whatever the product, Heinz and Campbell's sought to increase its value, strengthen consumer loyalty, and reduce the effects of competition through careful marketing and advertising. By appealing directly to consumers, as Strasser has noted, businesses like Heinz and Campbell's increased sales and ensured that storekeepers would carry their items. Arthur Dorrance understood the need for this: "When you have the consumer sold you have finished the worst part of the campaign. If the consumer makes the demand, the dealer will stock, and if the dealer stocks, the jobber is bound to get the business, and if he lists it for the dealer, we have to make the soup. It is perfectly simple and eliminates a complexity of selling methods." With the understanding that the way to drive up sales was through connecting directly to consumers, Campbell's was able to keep a small sales office with only a few hundred employees. In its place, Campbell's spent its money on advertisements. The company's advertising budget ballooned from only $10,000 in 1899 to $50,000 in 1901, $400,000 in 1911, and $1 million, or roughly 5 percent of sales, in 1920. Likewise Heinz's advertising budget increased to $4 million in 1933, in the midst of the Great Depression.[19]

Advertisements for Heinz and Campbell's products abounded, especially in mainstream national publications like the *Ladies' Home Journal* and *Good Housekeeping*. Both companies understood the growing power of women as the primary purchasers of food, and sought ways to advertise directly to them. One popular image was of the "Campbell's kids," two pudgy red-apple-cheeked youngsters in overalls created by Grace Drayton, that first appeared in 1905. These advertisements, labeled by advertising historian Roland Marchand as "the paradox of the captivated child," appealed to women as mothers who wanted to delight their offspring with child-pleasing food that also was wholesome and promised to produce vital and healthy youngsters at a time when parents were still fearful of high child and infant mortality rates.[20]

Heinz often appealed to the healthfulness of their tomato ketchup, especially in light of the Pure Food Movement of the early twentieth century and the subsequent banning of benzoate of soda as a preservative in ketchup. In 1908 and 1909, in some of the company's first advertisements placed in national magazines, Heinz repeatedly attacked its competitors who "drugged" their ketchup with benzoate of soda. In a period when advertising in magazines was fairly new and when many magazines had only a few full page ads in each issue, Heinz took out one- and two-page ads in leading magazines citing the results of government investigations into the effects of the chemical and questioning whether the Pure Food and Drugs Act of 1906 had gone far enough. Seeing the use of benzoate of soda as a sure sign of other adulterations, Heinz added a sticker to the neck of its ketchup bottle proclaiming it was free from the substance. And to its competitors it asked, "If there is any good in it when used in Ketchup, why doesn't the manufacturer who uses it blazon it in great letters on the label instead of whispering it in the smallest type he can find?" Or put simply, "The labels tell the story." To ensure the healthfulness of their products, Heinz regularly invited consumers to its factory in Pittsburgh, where they received a first-class tour to see for themselves the sanitary facilities in which their products were produced.[21]

Campbell's and Heinz advertisements took diverse forms. Both advertised in magazines, in newspapers, and on streetcars. Heinz, in particular, advertised on nearly any medium it could find: in 1893, at Chicago's World Columbian Exposition, the company handed out tens of thousands of pickle pins, a symbol which became its trademark for decades. Both companies regularly advertised their agricultural research: by the 1920s, Heinz commonly mentioned that its tomatoes were grown from the company's own seeds, and the name of its variety, the "Aristocrat," was a marketing tool in and of itself. Similarly, Campbell's displayed images of its agricultural experiment station and claimed that "this work of the Campbell experts has established a definitely higher standard of tomato perfection everywhere." In newspapers and magazines, on streetcars and city buildings, even on the boardwalk at Atlantic City, consumers were flooded with images of the corporate tomato. The success that both Heinz and Campbell's had in developing highly processed tomato products and marketing those products to the public is significant, and by the second half of the twentieth century, both companies were among the largest food corporations in the United States.[22]

THE CANNED WHOLE TOMATO

Despite the growing influence of companies like Heinz and Campbell's in branding tomato products, defining tomato consumption, and even in designing and shaping the tomato itself, their importance has been

overstated. These companies, above all, stand as early, and thus important, innovators in the fields of marketing, advertising, and product development, but they did not dominate American culinary culture during
the first half of the twentieth century. Despite the power of their advertising and innovations in processed convenience foods, Americans did
not abandon traditionally prepared meals or the ingredients that went
into them, even if those ingredients came in cans.

Canned whole tomatoes and other minimally processed tomato
products made up the vast majority of processed-tomato consumption
in the United States before 1945. In 1905, for example, Campbell's sold
around 24 million cans of soup, yet that figure represents less than one
can for every four citizens in the country, hardly evidence of Campbell's
soup as an essential part of the daily meal. In 1909, the U.S. Department
of Agriculture (USDA) estimated that consumers purchased a per capita
average of six pounds of canned whole tomatoes but only three-tenths of
a pound of canned soups (of all varieties, not just tomato soup). Ketchup
use was limited enough so that the USDA did not estimate its consumption at all. Dorrance, long dismissive of tomato juice due to it being minimally processed and hard to brand, capitulated to market pressure in
1931, and Campbell's began selling tomato juice as an alternative to condensed soup. It was only in 1948, as the trend toward value-added goods
picked up steam, that Campbell's purchased V8, a more heavily processed
and branded version of tomato juice. Likewise, by 1940 Heinz could boast
$8 million in ketchup sales. The trend was toward more processed canned
foods. Yet as late as 1950 per-capita consumption of all ready-made tomato products remained less than five pounds annually. At the same time,
for an American population of roughly 132 million people, the canning
industry packed around 600 million cans of tomatoes in 1940, in addition to more than 360 million cans of tomato juice and 50 million cans
of tomato pulp. The ready-made products, including both soup and
ketchup, would have contained less water than canned whole tomatoes
and thus given a consumer more pounds of fresh tomatoes per pound of
processed food. Nonetheless, these statistics demonstrate that consumers purchased processed products far less often than whole tomatoes or
minimally processed tomato products.[23]

Canning industry publications illustrate the persistence of these minimally processed items. In the 1918 edition of the *Almanac of the Canning Industry*, canned whole tomatoes, ketchup, and tomato puree are the only canned tomato products mentioned. Likewise, despite the growing popularity of ketchup during the early twentieth century, as well as evidence that suggests that companies were producing tomato paste between the world wars, the National Canners Association, which annually printed statistics on the total pack of tomato products, only kept track of numbers for canned whole tomatoes, juice, and pulp through 1943, when it began printing statistics for ketchup as well. At least through 1948, it did not publish numbers for tomato paste or other tomato products. Apparently, they were simply not important, even at that late date.[24]

These statistics suggest that Americans before World War II primarily consumed minimally processed goods like canned whole and pureed tomatoes. This had several significant effects: first, as discussed in the following chapter, by canning minimally processed goods, canned tomatoes remained versatile and could easily be adjusted to the needs of the cook. Canned tomatoes remained raw ingredients that could be used for most purposes. Second, the popularity of minimally processed tomato products encouraged and enabled a dispersed and localized industry to survive, despite the advantages that Heinz, Campbell's, and other national name-brand food corporations had in manufacturing, advertising, and retail distribution. Minimally processed canned products made processing tomatoes for canning relatively easy, where little expertise or specialization was necessary. Because of the basic uniformity of the canned tomatoes, the advantages of name-brand and product-differentiating advertising (as done by Campbell's soups) was minimized. This allowed tomato canning to be taken up by both large and small producers nearly anywhere in the country. With minimal equipment requirements, tomato canning could be completed in buildings of almost any size. The efforts made by the National Canners Association and others to rationalize production, beginning after its founding in 1907, furthered this cause, as canned tomato production, even for more heavily processed goods like chili sauce and ketchup, became more standardized. To help canners successfully process these goods, Clyde Campbell, a twenty-year veteran of Heinz and a former food chemist for the Pennsylvania Department of Agriculture, first published *Campbell's Book* in 1929, effectively a how-to guide for canning. In addition to describing how to successfully prepare and process tomatoes for canning, he offered standard recipes for chili sauce and spaghetti sauce, explained to canners how to instruct farmers to grow tomatoes, and described how tomatoes should be graded and handled during shipment. He encouraged mechanization, arguing that the most successful plant was one with an "automatic method of handling [tomatoes] from time of the arrival until packed in cans," yet he admitted that "hand-packed" tomatoes were often "used for special or fancy grade," indicating that a nonmechanized setup, where tomatoes were still packed by hand, were often viewed by consumers as a superior canned product. Ultimately, this guide, along with numerous others, served as a textbook for canners. Thus rationalization and standardization, two trends that have often resulted in centralized and concentrated production in many food industries, in the case of the canned tomato industry actually made tomato canning more accessible to a larger group of people.[25]

Equipment for tomato canning, much like in the late nineteenth century, remained minimal. Washers, scalders, fillers, and mechanized conveyer belt systems were needed to run a tomato cannery. Yet much of this equipment remained inexpensive and could be used for multiple purposes. In the early 1910s, for example, the Sprague Canning Machinery Co. sold a tomato scalder capable of scalding 7,500 cans worth of tomatoes per day for $85 and a double capacity model for $125. Likewise, a Remington washer, able to wash enough tomatoes for 70,000 cans per day, sold for $150. Unlike the tomato scalder, the washer could be used with numerous fruits and vegetables, making it a versatile investment. Many tomato canneries continued operating with only kettles, manually heating the tomatoes before processing them. Stanley Macklem, manager of production for the Curtice Brothers cannery during the 1920s, recalled that during this time it was still possible to "jump into the canning business" with little cash or credit. The peeling of tomatoes

FIGURE 3.3 The Triumph Platform Conveyor Peeling Table. Sprague Canning Machinery Co., *Sprague General Catalogue of Canning Machinery and Supplies* (Chicago, ca. 1913), 141. National Museum of American History, Washington, DC.

remained the most labor-intensive aspect of tomato canning, and efforts were made to automate this process as much as possible. Edward Judge wrote in 1903 that "there [was] an opportunity for an exceeding great fortune to anyone who will give us a practical tomato peeling machine." Still, canning machinery companies sold specialized conveyer belt systems to speed up the peeling process, such as the Triumph Platform Conveyor Peeling Table offered by Sprague around 1913 (figure 3.3). Fast turnover of canning equipment, as canneries sought to expand or replace their existing machinery, likely led to an affordable second-hand canning-equipment market as well.[26]

The increasingly standardized but minimally processed canned tomato, along with the relatively low cost of (and need for) canning equipment, led to the emergence of thousands of canneries across the United States. Many of these operated only seasonally and produced a small pack, often specializing in one or a few products. Farmers, too, were often encouraged to start their own canning operations. In 1911, the Georgia Experiment Station tested out a home canning kit that cost as little as fifteen dollars. For many farmers, the *Market Growers' Journal* reported in 1908, canning on the farm offered a profitable way to dispose of the remainder of their crop after the choicest tomatoes had been sold and the market was no longer favorable. Manufacturers of home and farm canning equipment advertised regularly in the journal, and in 1910, in an issue largely dedicated to the topic of "Saving the Surplus," farmer George Demuth asserted that with a minimal investment he was operating a small outfit out of his farm producing, on average, five hundred cans of tomatoes per day. He claimed that local grocers were happy to sell his wares, deeming them superior to the larger canning companies' products. In other cases, such as those of Mrs. Harry Brown of Pennsylvania and C. W. Brown of Massachusetts, women practiced home canning and sold their products on local markets. Unlike Heinz and Campbell's, tomato canners of all sizes often marketed their products under numerous labels or brands, sometimes their own but often also brands of wholesalers and other purchasers. One cannery, the H. S. Mill Canning Company, located in Bucks County, Pennsylvania, canned tomatoes under numerous labels during the first decade of the twentieth century, including "Luxury," "Iron Mountain," and "Spring Mountain." The company was also willing to can under private labels if supplied by resellers. Similarly, as late as the 1940s the canneries operated by the Curtice Burns Corporation in New York canned under both their own label and those of wholesalers.[27]

Thus tomato canning stood between the practices and economics of traditional cottage industry and those of modern mechanized industry. Yet the industry in the early twentieth century was not simply in a transitional phase between small-scale and large-scale manufacturing. Instead, the persistence of small-scale tomato canners created a thriving industry that expanded across most regions and states, especially after 1900, precisely at the time when other industries were being centralized. In addition to the comparatively low cost needed to operate a tomato cannery, the adaptability of the tomato to be grown in nearly every American climate and environment encouraged tomato production and the proliferation of canneries across this wide geography.

Before 1900, tomato canning was centered in New Jersey and Maryland, with each state packing more than 800,000 cases of tomatoes in

1892. By 1900, both fresh and processed-tomato production had spread west along the 39th parallel—from New Jersey, Maryland, Delaware, and Virginia across to Indiana, Ohio, Illinois, and Missouri. The four Atlantic states planted almost 48 percent of the nation's commercial tomato crop. The total acreage of all eight states represented nearly 70 percent of the nation's total. This geographic distribution existed for several reasons, including proximity to eastern and Midwestern urban markets, fertile soil, and temperate climates. Even into the 1920s, many farmers and agriculture experts believed these areas were destined by natural advantage to remain the dominant sites of production for the nation's tomato supply. In a 1922 bulletin for the Maryland Agricultural Experiment Station, Henry James declared, "Maryland is destined by location, soil and climate to be an important tomato producing state. The large consuming markets are close at hand favoring Maryland in the competition with the western states which must ship their goods longer distances." Likewise, Frank App and Allen G. Waller, writing in 1921 for the New Jersey Experiment Station, argued that high shipping costs prohibited the development of tomato canning outside these regions. While New Jersey canners could ship a ton of canned tomatoes to New York for $2.64, shipping would cost Oakland, California, canners more than thirteen dollars, and even Indiana growers upward of seven. Thus, despite higher production costs near population centers, App and Waller argued that New Jersey producers "should be able to grow tomatoes at an advantage over the more remote regions." This geography persisted during the first two decades of the twentieth century, and the government's need for canned tomatoes during World War I maintained the Atlantic states' dominance in processed-tomato production through the war years. Benefiting from proximity to Atlantic ports, acreage of processing tomatoes in New Jersey more than tripled, from 101,000 in 1915 to 317,000 in 1918.[28]

However, this dominance changed in the 1920s, and the predictions of agricultural experts proved to be wrong. The four Atlantic states, which produced nearly 45 percent of all processing tomatoes in 1918, produced less than 35 percent between 1925 and 1929, and less than 30 percent between 1930 and 1934. In 1921, the USDA's James Beattie declared,

"The very fact that the tomato can be so easily produced under a wide variety of conditions has in the past led to the development of the industry in sections where there have been and are few economic reasons for its continuance." But, by the 1920s, as nationwide transportation became quicker and more efficient, Beattie's assessment proved incorrect. Tomatoes continued to be produced widely in the United States, and tomato production outside the Mid-Atlantic and Midwest became increasingly profitable, leading to the expansion of production in nearly every region in America.[29]

The tomato-processing industry became more decentralized between the end of World War I and the end of World War II. While Ohio, Indiana, and California reaped the biggest rewards from this shift, tomato canning extended into a host of states led by small canning factories and companies. In sum, common factors encouraged the expansion of canneries all over the country—the comparatively small amount of capital to open a cannery, the need for canneries close to tomato production because of the vegetable's rapid deterioration, the capacity to grow tomatoes nearly anywhere in the country, and the relatively simple and standardized practice of canning whole tomatoes. By 1925, the National Canners Association reported no fewer than 1,530 businesses operating canneries that processed tomatoes (many with multiple factories). Although half of these were operating in the Atlantic states, tomato canning took place in twenty-nine states, with at least thirty businesses operating in twelve states, and at least ten in nineteen states (figures 3.4–3.6).[30]

The development of the processed-tomato industry also helped lead to specialization in agricultural research. Much like with the geography of production, however, this did not result in a radical narrowing of the varieties available. As research was spread across numerous state agricultural experiment stations, no single institution, corporate or government, had complete control over the direction that tomato research would progress. As such, no single variety gained dominance from the research to find tomatoes that produced high quality canned products suitable for mass production. Indeed, at least until the 1940s, canners all over the country continued to use dozens of varieties. There were often several preferred varieties within a single state or county. Some longstanding

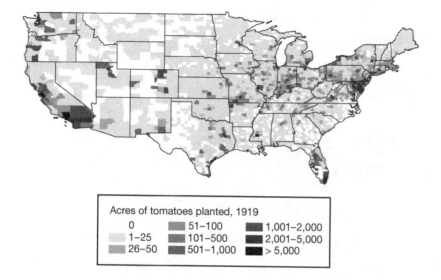

Acres of tomatoes planted, 1919
0	51–100	1,001–2,000
1–25	101–500	2,001–5,000
26–50	501–1,000	> 5,000

FIGURE 3.4 Acres of tomatoes planted, 1919. Data compiled from U.S. Census Bureau, *Fourteenth Census of the United States: 1920; Agriculture* (Washington, DC: Government Printing Office, 1922). Unfortunately, the census does not distinguish between tomatoes produced for fresh and processed production, but it does indicate a general trend away from the traditional areas of tomato production into new states and regions through the early twentieth century.

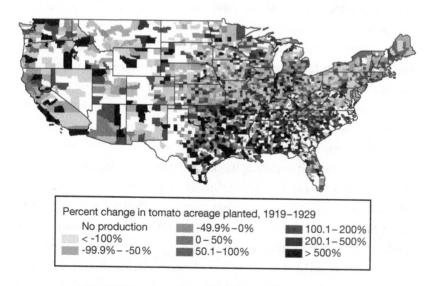

Percent change in tomato acreage planted, 1919–1929
No production	-49.9%–0%	100.1–200%
< -100%	0–50%	200.1–500%
-99.9%– -50%	50.1–100%	> 500%

FIGURE 3.5 Percent change in acres of tomatoes planted, 1919–1929. Data compiled from U.S. Census Bureau, *U.S. Census: 1920; Agriculture*; U.S. Census Bureau, *Fifteenth Census of the United States: 1930; Agriculture* (Washington, DC: Government Printing Office, 1932).

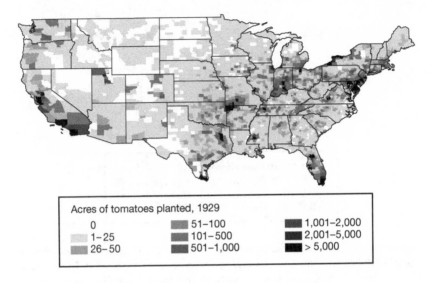

FIGURE 3.6 Acres of tomatoes planted, 1929. Data compiled from U.S. Census Bureau, *U.S. Census: 1930; Agriculture.*

late-season favorites were Stone, Bonny's Best, and Matchless, but other varieties—including Red Rock, Greater Baltimore, Royal Red, Perfection, Paragon, and dozens of others—were also grown to be sent to canneries.

Over time, however, the varieties that were planted for canning were increasingly similar tomatoes. The need for a standardized product and particular cultural ideas of the tomato led both farmers and canneries (as well as consumers) to expect a uniform tomato. The ideal canning tomato became almost universally a red tomato. Despite the existence of other colors, each having unique taste properties, the red tomato came to dominate the canning industry. Advertising, in effect, branded the ideal tomato as red—representing ripeness and juiciness. In a 1912 bulletin issued by the Delaware experiment station, C. A. McCue dismissed as a potential canning tomato any variety that did not produce red fruit. Likewise, among the dozen or more varieties used as canning tomatoes in 1915 all across New Jersey, Charles Arthur did not list a single variety of tomato that was not red. Research on the canning tomato industry did not yet emphasize a single variety as the perfect canning tomato, but it did begin to narrow the options available. Of great importance for many canners, for example, was producing varieties that ripened during a short period so as to save on labor and transportation costs. Increasingly, research followed Livingston's example—focusing on a particular set of attributes, including color, shape, size, and texture—to create a more predictable, standardized tomato based on specific ideas of taste and aesthetics.[31]

Ultimately, unlike the fresh tomato industry, whose geography and research was a vital component of providing consumers with unprocessed fresh tomatoes across the year, the canning industry relied primarily on the technology of the can to create the twelve-month tomato through preservation. Despite this, the decentralized nature of tomato canning produced an industry unlike most other food industries. Canning produced not widespread distribution but yearlong access to locally grown tomatoes. As late as the 1940s, the canning industry remained largely a regional affair. In 1939 and again in 1944 the Purdue University Agricultural Experiment Station conducted a study of canned tomato products available at Indiana retailers. In 1939, a total of 390 different brands of canned tomatoes were purchased during the three-year survey period. Interestingly, however, more than 85 percent of those brands were packed in Indiana. Though tomatoes packed in Maryland, Virginia, California, and Delaware were all available, the Indiana canned tomato dominated, even over those from nearby states like Michigan and Ohio. In the 1944 survey, there were similar results, with around 85 percent of the canned tomatoes consumed in Indiana canned there. Canning of tomatoes, in this period at least, did not necessarily lead to national distribution but instead to anytime access based on localized production and consumption.[32]

Thus the geographic decentralization of the tomato industry, which was fueled by readily available and inexpensive canning equipment, helped ensure that no single tomato producer or group of producers would control the production and processing of canning tomatoes during the first half of the twentieth century. Similarly, the continued popularity of minimally processed tomato goods, like canned whole tomatoes, in addition to ensuring the tomato remained a dynamic ingredient in the kitchen, also helped encourage increased competition in the marketplace, as anyone with canning equipment and a little know-how could successfully can tomatoes. The result was the proliferation of hundreds of canneries and brands of canned tomatoes during the early twentieth century.

THE TWELVE-MONTH FRESH TOMATO

Despite the tremendous growth in canned tomatoes, Americans hardly abandoned the fresh tomato. Consumption of fresh tomatoes (both commercial and homegrown) remained remarkably stable until after World War II (figure 3.7). There are a number of possible explanations

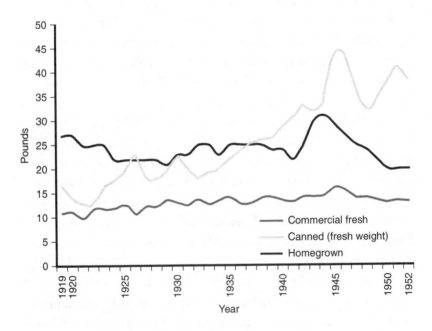

FIGURE 3.7 Per capita consumption of tomatoes in the United States, 1919–1952. U.S. Department of Agriculture (USDA) Bureau of Agricultural Economics (BAE), *Supplement for 1961 to Consumption of Food in the United States, 1909–1952*, supplement to Agricultural Handbook 62 (Washington, DC, 1962), 25; USDA BAE, *Consumption of Food in the United States, 1909–1952*, Agricultural Handbook 62 (Washington, DC, 1953), 117, 119, 121, 142.

for this: some consumers likely continued to perceive a quality difference between canned and fresh tomatoes; others sustained ethnic traditions of cooking and preserving fresh tomatoes themselves; finally, and perhaps most persuasively, there remained distinct uses for both fresh and preserved tomatoes. And, while producing fresh tomatoes raised different problems and required different solutions than canned, both sides of the industry shared the same goal—transcending the seasonality of the vegetable—and produced a similar result—a geographically dispersed and localized industry.

The fresh-tomato industry focused on constructing the right tomato and the right environment for producing fresh tomatoes throughout the year. The look and taste, as well as the harvest time and shelf life, of the fresh tomato were far more important than for the canned. To meet these and other stringent requirements, growers drew heavily on agricultural research. Researchers initially aimed at creating varieties that produced the earliest tomatoes. The names of many varieties, including Earliana and First of All, stressed the primacy of earliness as a desirable characteristic in fresh-market tomatoes. These helped farmers supply local consumers several weeks earlier than with main-crop tomato varieties. In their advertisements, claims of earliness featured prominently. In a 1908 advertisement for May's First of All Tomatoes, for example, the seed house of L. L. May & Co. proclaimed the tomato "The Earliest in the World," promising that First of All tomatoes would ripen "a week to ten days ahead of any other known variety" (figure 3.8). Earliness remained the most important quality.[33]

While big seed houses like Livingston and W. Atlee Burpee, of Philadelphia, created many of the most important varieties during the early twentieth century, varietal development continued to come from a number of sources, including farmers themselves. One of the most important early varieties, the Earliana, dubbed by Burpee to be "the most famous and actually the 'Earliest of All' first-early tomatoes," was developed by George Sparks, of Salem County, New Jersey. Often referred to as Sparks' Earliana, this variety was distributed by virtually every seed house in the country. Likewise, Chalk's Early Jewel, another popular variety, got its name from James Chalk, of Montgomery County,

FIGURE 3.8 "The Earliest in the World" (May's Tomato Seed ad), *Market Growers Journal*, Feb. 5, 1908, 3.

Pennsylvania, who developed it in the late nineteenth century. Thus, both seed houses and farmers developed new varieties. The USDA and numerous state agricultural experiment stations, too, conducted regular tomato variety trials and created vitally important tomato varieties, including the Rutgers tomato, developed at Rutgers University and released in the fall of 1934.[34]

The lack of patent protection for developed varieties, too, meant that even varieties developed by Livingston or Burpee were quickly picked up by others and sold. While Livingston himself believed that some form of patent protection was necessary to encourage variety development, such protection was not achieved for the tomato until the second half of the century, after hybrid varieties made such protection far less important. In the interim, Livingston, Burpee, and others tried to brand their products as higher quality. While concerns over seed quality and the existence of copycat varieties remained prevalent during the early twentieth century, the lack of patent protection of varieties did not seem to limit new varieties being developed. Instead, what resulted was a flood of new varieties, some of which became very popular, especially those that were among the earliest on the market.[35]

The success of seedsmen, farmers, and government researchers in developing earlier strains of tomatoes can be seen in decreasing ripening times. In 1890, N. Hallock reported on some of the most valuable tomato varieties on the market, including analyzing the number of days each variety took to ripen. In general, he found that most varieties took between 125 and 140 days from the time of planting until ripe fruit could be picked from the vine. By 1900, D. Landreth and Sons, a Philadelphia seed house, offered several varieties that reportedly ripened around 100 days. In 1905, the Nebraska Seed Company marketed seed of the Extra Early Advance variety that they claimed would ripen in a mere 95 days. By 1915, Landreth offered several varieties, including the Earliana and Chalk's Early Jewel, that could be harvested within 90 to 100 days of planting. In 1920, the Leonard Seed Co. in Chicago promised that its Red Rock tomato, which it deemed especially useful as a main-crop tomato, would begin ripening within 110 days. Thus by the 1920s, at least some main-crop tomato varieties were producing tomatoes faster and earlier than the early tomatoes of the late nineteenth century.[36]

Consumers' desires for fresh vegetables throughout the year drove the push for the early tomato. In an attempt to diversify their diets, and to transcend the traditional limitations on obtaining fresh produce, increasingly affluent northern urban consumers were willing to pay significantly higher prices for tomatoes and other vegetables outside of the traditional harvest season. At the very least, regardless of whether they actually profited from producing early tomatoes, farmers *believed* that they had an economic incentive to produce out-of-season early tomatoes. As the *Market Growers' Journal* remarked in 1912, "The first two weeks of marketing bring the cream of the prices." The journal reported that farmers received as much as 25 percent less after the first two weeks of the harvest, with a similar drop in prices following a few more weeks. Thus, a few weeks' delay in ripening could determine whether a year's crop was profitable at all. In addition, an early frost (in the North) or stifling heat or drought could also cut short the tomato-harvest season.

By finding tomato plants that would produce early tomatoes, the number of tomatoes on each plant necessarily increased. Farmers, trying to produce a profitable tomato crop, adopted common practices—using early variety seeds, starting plants in hot beds, and even obtaining plants germinated in the South and shipped north. Many of these techniques required minimal cost. For example, a single hot bed frame could germinate several hundred plants, a cheap way of getting the jump on the early harvest market. In pursuit of profitable sale, farmers and agricultural researchers well into the twentieth century tried to alter the tomato and its growing environment to expand its harvest season.[37]

And just as the tomato canning industry shifted out of Atlantic states, production of fresh tomatoes for market also expanded out of this region. Before 1900, because of the limitations in transportation, fresh tomatoes had, in fact, been grown locally for sale in nearby cities and towns, and the population density of the urban northeast made the Atlantic states critical sites of fresh tomato production. During the first half of the twentieth century, however, the production of fresh tomatoes expanded to regions across the country and among tropical areas such as the west coast of Mexico. By 1928, the Atlantic states had lost their position in the fresh-tomato industry. While New Jersey produced 1.75 million bushels, a little more than 10 percent of the national total, Florida, Texas, and California combined to produce more than 40 percent of the nation's supply of fresh tomatoes. Overall, ten states scattered across the country produced at least 500,000 bushels of fresh tomatoes (see figures 3.1–3.3).[38]

At the root of this geographic redistribution of fresh tomato production was the quest for the twelve-month tomato, the sale of which was made possible by reduced costs of transportation. Agricultural research encouraged this trend toward extending the tomato-production season by introducing tomato cultivation to new regions, especially in the South and West, thus providing major urban markets with tomatoes throughout the year. Florida emerged early as a dominant leader producing winter and spring tomatoes. Already by 1918, Florida was shipping thousands of car-lots of tomatoes to urban markets in the Northeast and Midwest, mostly between March and June. In the years that followed, Florida pushed seasonal boundaries, producing greater quantities for shipment in the winter months. By 1924, more than half of shipments from the eastern shore of Florida came in February and March, representing a much earlier crop than five years before.[39]

During the early twentieth century, the production of fresh tomatoes and other vegetables for American consumers extended outside American borders. Guatemala, Cuba, England, Canada, and other nations exported fresh tomatoes to the United States, but this emerging international production centered on the west coast of Mexico. In a single season's time, between 1923 and 1924, Mexico increased its tomato imports into the United States by almost 20 percent, from 47 million pounds to more than 56 million. During the first half of 1925, total imports of fresh tomatoes from all foreign nations increased 25 percent over the previous year. Much as in Florida, the demand for winter and early spring tomatoes drove increased imports of fresh tomatoes from Mexico. High transportation costs limited Mexico's shipping season to times of the year when fresh tomatoes were in short supply. Mexican tomatoes were shipped in large volumes into the United States between December and June, peaking in April and May, when there was significantly less competition.[40]

The early summer months, too, became periods of intense competition between many states, particularly in the South. During these months, numerous states sought a time when they faced the least competition and earned the highest prices for their tomatoes in urban markets. Gibson County, Tennessee, illustrates this marketing strategy. Commercial-tomato production began in the county during the late nineteenth century, and, by 1910, Gibson County remained the only county in Tennessee with substantial tomato production, thanks in part to three railroad lines running through the county that sent several hundred car-lots of tomatoes to northern cities each year. Yet Gibson County's position in the market was fragile. As S. H. Essary explained in a Tennessee Agricultural Experiment Station bulletin, "Tomatoes ripen in the Gibson section just after the close of the shipping season in states further south and before tomatoes began to ripen north of the Ohio. This gives the section only a few weeks of open market, usually from about the middle of June until the first of August. After this time, it is not profitable to ship them."[41]

Similarly, the state of Mississippi emerged as a dominant site of production for early tomatoes. As early as 1918, Mississippi tomato growers, based almost entirely in Hinds and Copiah counties, were providing several thousand car-lots of tomatoes to urban markets almost exclusively during the month of June, when it had an advantage. In 1924, Mississippi growers shipped tomatoes to 102 cities in 31 states, several dozen car-lots even making their way into Canada. By 1930, rail shipments of fresh tomatoes were providing urban northerners, and increasingly urban dwellers elsewhere, with a relatively constant supply of fresh tomatoes all year long. To do this, regions, states, and even counties carefully carved out a slice of the newly expanded tomato season that they could profitably provide urban markets with long-distance fresh tomatoes. As a result, during the 1920s, the difference between the availability of tomatoes in summer and winter declined. For example, in 1918, New York City received eleven carloads of tomatoes in January, or a mere 2 percent of the 466 carloads unloaded in June. From 1928 to 1930, by contrast, the city received an average of 472 carloads of tomatoes in January, representing more than a third of the 1,409 carloads unloaded in June (figure 3.9). These changes in the geography and timing of tomato production were critical components of achieving a

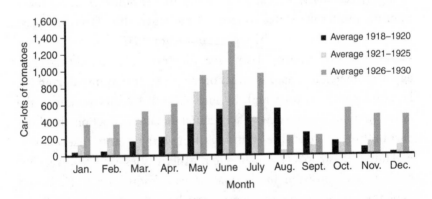

FIGURE 3.9 Car-lot shipments of tomatoes to New York City markets, 1918–1930, by month. USDA BAE, "Shipments and Unloads of Certain Fruits and Vegetables,1918–1923," Statistical Bulletin 7 (Apr. 1925); "Car-Lot Shipments and Unloads of Important Fruits and Vegetables for the Calendar Years 1924–1926," Statistical Bulletin 23 (Apr. 1928); "Car-Lot Shipments and Unloads of Important Fruits and Vegetables for the Calendar Years 1927 and 1928," Statistical Bulletin 30 (May 1930); "Car-Lot Shipments and Unloads of Important Fruits and Vegetables for the Calendar Years 1929 and 1930," Statistical Bulletin 35 (Oct. 1931).

year-round supply of tomatoes. While today the twelve-month tomato comes from centralization and concentration, at least until the end of World War II, the primary method for achieving year-round access to fresh tomatoes remained geographic decentralization and the dividing up of the "natural advantage" in tomato production of different regions and climates corresponding with different times of the year.[42]

THE SOUTHERN TOMATO VERSUS THE GREENHOUSE-TOMATO INDUSTRY

While southern states such as Florida, Tennessee, Texas, and Mississippi successfully delivered out-of-season fresh tomatoes to urban markets, consumers were often disappointed. In a 1920 USDA bulletin, Charles Sando admitted, "In spite of the fact that thousands of cars of Florida tomatoes are shipped to the North each year, the quality of a large percentage that reaches the consumer is admittedly inferior." Likewise, in 1912, horticulture expert W. F. Massey found the entirety of the early crop of Florida tomatoes "pink and hollow" and argued that he had "not seen a solitary red Tomato from Florida." The consistent problems with producing quality tomatoes led many Florida growers to use ripening houses in the late 1910s, to ensure both that their tomatoes ripened prior to getting to market and that diseased and bruised tomatoes would be sorted out prior to being shipped north. But these complaints and efforts to rectify them suggest that as the out-of-season tomato became readily available, consumers expected these winter and spring tomatoes to be of high quality: firm, ripe, red, and juicy.[43]

Yet the advantage of all-season tomatoes often prevailed over quality, assuring a dominance of the southern product in northern urban markets. Any tomato in January for a salad was better than none. In 1924, for example, almost 80 percent of the tomatoes reaching New York City markets via rail came from the South, California, Mexico, and other distant places, compared to less than 1 percent arriving from New Jersey. While these numbers are distorted by the fact that many were brought to New York City from New Jersey via truck, E. V. Wilcox noted in 1925 that a "craze for early stuff" helped undermine New Jersey tomato production in favor of more distant sites of production. "Thus," he argued, the urban New Yorker "is willing to pay 15 to 30 cents a pound for the pale pink, anemic, sweat house ripened tomatoes of the premature birth, simply because they come in January and can't see 50 cents value in a bushel of *real* tomatoes in July."[44]

But mid-Atlantic and Midwestern tomato producers did not give up without a fight. And they responded by attempting to address the aesthetic failings of the out-of-season tomatoes from the South and West, as well as compete with them by extending their own growing season. Northern farmers, recognizing the poor quality of the southern winter tomatoes, as early as 1900, began to force tomatoes under glass (starting plants in greenhouses before their usual growing season). By 1910, while virtually every state produced some vegetables in greenhouses, New England, the Middle Atlantic, East North-Central, and West North-Central regions produced almost $14 million of the nation's $15.5 million market in greenhouse vegetables. Greenhouses of all sizes devoted to tomatoes, among other vegetables, emerged in many of these states, often in close proximity to major cities. Despite the large capital investment required for their construction and maintenance, James Beattie of the USDA argued that with proper planning and placement, greenhouses "are usually able to compete successfully with tomatoes grown at distant points out of doors."[45]

The success of greenhouse tomatoes depended on the superior quality of the early greenhouse tomato over southern early tomatoes. Beattie noted, "When ripened on the vine, greenhouse tomatoes are far superior in quality to those grown outside in warm sections, where it is necessary to pick the fruit green in order to get it into the hands of the distant consumer without undue loss." In fact, the superior quality of greenhouse tomatoes relatively close to market allowed producers to demand and obtain high enough prices for their product to offset the high costs of building and maintaining greenhouses. Here, the expectation of winter tomatoes (made possible by rail transport of southern tomatoes to northern urban markets) created the possibility of selling high-priced hothouse tomatoes during these months. As early as 1908 C. W. Waid of the Ohio State Experiment Station observed that greenhouse tomatoes, produced earlier than other locally and regionally produced tomatoes, could secure significantly higher prices than southern-grown field tomatoes.[46]

More important than whether or not greenhouse tomatoes were in fact of superior quality was whether consumers *perceived* greenhouse tomatoes to be superior to southern-grown tomatoes. In 1908, Waid commented, "It requires considerable argument to persuade some people, who have not had an opportunity to test the quality of hothouse Tomatoes, that Tomatoes grown under glass should bring higher prices than Southern grown Tomatoes on the same markets." In order to foster consumer recognition of the value of hothouse tomatoes, in 1912, Waid urged greenhouse growers to use standardized packaging and labels that would distinguish greenhouse tomatoes from southern-grown field tomatoes with "an attractive trademark or stamp attached to each package [to] help to make identification easy."[47]

Waid was not alone in this marketing strategy. Soon after, E. E. Adams, a grower from the Lake Erie section of Ontario, responded to Waid's article, describing his firm's container and the image of the logo affixed to each box (figure 3.10). Although growers in his area did not use standard packages, Adams suggested that his firm's "smooth pine" boxes, measuring six by nine and a half by nineteen and a half inches with a capacity of twenty pounds, had produced satisfactory results. They lined the boxes "with corrugated paper, sides, top and bottom, and [wrapped] each Tomato in tissue paper, on which is printed in red a picture of a Tomato and the grower's name." Overall, these early efforts by greenhouse growers to use packaging and labels to distinguish their products demonstrates their understanding of the larger changes taking place in the American economy and consumer culture and their willingness to adapt in order to compete in the emerging food industry. The perception of quality through packaging had become more important than the actual characteristics of the hothouse tomato itself.[48]

Although the hothouse tomato never displaced or seriously threatened the market for southern-grown tomatoes, it did emerge as a viable industry in its own right, one that continues to hold significant cultural and

FIGURE 3.10 E. E. Adams, "Packages for Hothouse Tomatoes," *Market Growers Journal*, June 29, 1912, 2.

economic value. During the first half of the twentieth century, a variety of sizes of greenhouses emerged to fulfill the growing demand for greenhouse tomatoes. By the mid-1920s, numerous large greenhouse complexes supplied northern cities with spring and early summer hothouse tomatoes. In 1924, with fifteen greenhouses comprising more than a quarter of a million square feet under glass, Zuck Greenhouses, in Erie, Pennsylvania, produced fifteen thousand ten-pound baskets of tomatoes, along with other vegetables. With more than twenty-nine acres of greenhouses, Davis Gardens in Terre Haute, Indiana, claimed to be the world's largest greenhouse facility in 1925. Producing around 350,000 pounds of tomatoes annually, Davis Gardens shipped their product all over the nation, as far north as Alaska and even to the southern tip of Florida.[49]

Unlike the beef, corn, citrus, and other food industries, the commercialization of the tomato during the late nineteenth and early twentieth century did not result in an economically and geographically concentrated industry, where production and processing took place in one or a few geographic regions and was controlled by a handful of companies. Instead, through the 1930s, tomato production and processing became decentralized, with almost every region of the country growing and processing a significant amount of tomatoes and tomato products. The low capital costs of opening a tomato cannery, and a need to can tomatoes close to where they were produced, coupled with the ability to grow tomatoes in virtually every American environment, ensured that small and large tomato canneries were present in states and regions across the country. The desire to create a twelve-month fresh tomato helped further decentralize fresh-tomato production, as states carved up the harvest season to find times when they could profitably sell fresh tomatoes in urban markets. The greenhouse tomato industry, which emerged during the final decades of the nineteenth century, grew during the early twentieth century in part as a response to the lower quality off-season tomatoes offered by southern states. Thus the longstanding desire for a twelve-month tomato, an idea conceived and largely achieved during the nineteenth century, culminated in the early twentieth century with the creation of a diverse and widely distributed tomato industry that was relatively unique.

All this meant that a diverse tomato culture, with its large cast of characters—local farmers, agriculture extension officials, seed entrepreneurs, and others—continued to thrive, despite the rise of Heinz and Campbell's. Because large-scale growers and processors did not control the production of tomatoes, no single idea of the tomato prevailed. Instead, tomato production expanded to include new farmers, canners, and agricultural researchers. Both fresh and processed tomato production remained strong throughout the period. Despite the growing significance of Heinz, Campbell's, and other large companies producing soups, pastes, and condiments, the primary tomato products during the early twentieth century remained fresh and minimally processed tomato products, like canned whole tomatoes. The tomato industry, decentralized, diverse, driven by a quest for the twelve-month tomato, and coupled with minimally processed tomatoes, helped ensure that corporate interests would not control the tomato and its many uses, at least before the middle of the twentieth century.

In addition to changing methods of tomato production, tomato consumption, the subject of the following chapter, changed dramatically between the late nineteenth century and the onset of World War II. With an increasing urban population, especially among Italian and other ethnic immigrants, tomato culture continued to expand. Moreover, a home gardening movement, featuring the tomato as its most celebrated crop, actually grew during the world wars. In surprising ways, the canning and fresh tomato industries promoted innovation in home use of tomatoes as the vegetable, in both canned and fresh form, became accessible (and more affordable) throughout the year.

4

CONSUMING TOMATOES

Culinary Creativity and Expansion
in the Age of Industrialization

During the nineteenth century, the tomato became a major crop and menu item thanks to small farmers and rural homemakers. By end of that century, however, an emerging urban culture set off a culinary revolution in America, and new uses for the tomato led the way. By the 1830s, American cooks, with roots in rural crafts, had adapted the tomato to traditional ways of preserving and serving food and discovered the joys of fresh tomatoes. Later, American farmers (with help from an assortment of experts) found ways of providing processed and fresh tomatoes to American consumers across the year. After the Civil War, however, new players—corporate promoters, of course, but also immigrants and middle-class homemakers, mostly located in cities—developed new ways of consuming tomatoes. Between the 1870s and the end of World War II these different groups produced an unusually diverse tomato culture that prevented any narrow corporate or nutritional notion of the tomato from predominating.

The story of the tomato, then, stands in stark contrast to the picture painted by many historians on the major trends in food history during the first half of the twentieth century. On the one hand, scholars of consumer culture like Susan Strasser see the rise of corporate advertising and early convenience foods as signs of a changing food culture, one that was largely controlled by corporate interests during the period. On the other hand, Harvey Levenstein argues that in addition to corporate forces, middle-class and elite reformers and government policy makers and bureaucrats formed a near omnipotent triumvirate that was able to "Americanize" and standardize American food culture as early as the 1920s. Both find that elites shaped the use and meanings of the tomato and food culture in general.[1]

Yet, as the previous chapter demonstrated, despite the successes of early food-processing companies like Campbell's and Heinz in creating and marketing brand-name goods, these companies did not dominate tomato production during the first half of the twentieth century. Likewise, despite their influence on the consuming public, national brands did not control the ways that tomatoes were cooked, processed, or consumed either, as small producers and grass-roots culinary innovation played a critical role in tomato culture during the first half of the century.

Similarly, reformers along with government policy makers and bureaucrats had only limited success at "Americanizing" or standardizing the American diet during the early twentieth century. As Levenstein notes, these reformers were often met with staunch resistance from the working class and immigrant groups. They were much more successful in shaping middle-class culinary habits, but the result was less the standardization of American cuisine, as many reformers sought, and more a vast expansion in American food culture, as new foods and new dishes were introduced into the American diet alongside the old.

Likewise, new immigrant groups brought with them their own ideas of tomato culture. Despite the efforts of reformers, many ethnic cuisines flourished in the early twentieth century. The tomato, in part because of its preexisting popularity in the United States, became a staple of Italian American cuisine, as Italian immigrants developed a unique cuisine based on regional Italian food traditions and American conditions. Italian food, in particular, not only flourished during the early twentieth century but also greatly influenced middle-class American cuisine. By the middle of the century Italian American dishes such as spaghetti and pizza had become popular with many Americans.

The tomato was a key component in diversifying the American diet. Long used as a way to add variety and flavor to otherwise monotonous dishes, the tomato also became a featured component of many new dishes, especially as new dietary ideas and the discovery of vitamins led nutritionists and other food experts to reevaluate the value of fruits and vegetables in a healthy diet.

These new ways of consuming tomatoes were built on and adapted to the twelve-month tomato. Having fresh tomatoes throughout the year enabled cooks to prepare more dishes from scratch, including those that utilized raw tomatoes. Similarly, the availability of canned tomatoes allowed cooks great flexibility in the preparation of tomato dishes.

TRANSITIONING FROM RURAL
TO URBAN AMERICA

America's transition from a rural to an urban nation around the turn of the twentieth century set the stage for a culinary revolution. Already by 1870, America had 226 cities with populations of at least eight thousand. By 1900, the trend toward an urban America was even clearer. There were 212 towns, for example, with populations between four and five thousand, almost the same number of towns that exceeded four thousand residents just thirty years before. While in 1870 there was not an American city with a population greater than one million, by 1900 there were three, and three more had populations greater than half a million. In 1900, fully 47 percent of the population lived in incorporated places, and this was especially pronounced in the Northeast and upper Midwest.[2]

Two distinct processes fueled urbanization: first, migration from farm to town and city; second, beginning in the late nineteenth century and continuing through the 1920s, immigrants flooded mostly cities and towns. Immigration shifted from Western European nations to Eastern Europe and the Mediterranean. During the 1890s, more than 650,000 Italian immigrants, for example, entered the United States, compared to around 500,000 Germans, and most settled in cities.[3]

Urbanization and immigration helped tomato culture spread into American cities, and urban cooks took advantage of access to processed and the twelve-month supply of fresh tomatoes. This trend was furthered by the proliferation of cookbooks and magazines geared toward the expanding ideal of American domesticity. Thus while tomato production was still largely a rural phenomenon—farms, canneries, and seed firms were primarily rural enterprises—tomato consumption blossomed in American towns and cities during the early twentieth century.

NUTRITIONAL REFORM AND THE TOMATO

At the same time that Americans and immigrants flooded America's cities, reformers sought to overcome the many problems these cities faced, including poverty, poor health conditions, and a lack of open public space. Increasingly, they also sought to shape urban residents' culinary habits. Of great importance to these efforts, as numerous scholars have pointed out, was the growing influence of the fields of nutrition and home economics. The USDA, through the Department of Chemistry, became deeply involved in the nutrition movement during the late nineteenth century, and Wilbur Atwater, Wesleyan University's first chemistry professor, became the primary voice on nutrition for the USDA. Atwater is perhaps best known for his invention in the 1890s of the calorimeter, a device that could accurately determine the caloric content of food. Obsessed by the emerging "urban crisis" of the late nineteenth century, Atwater's interest in nutrition was primarily in what he called "food economy," or the maximization of nutritional food for the lowest possible cost to feed the urban poor. He believed that taste should have little influence in human diets and that the poor were some of the most wasteful when it came to food. The calorimeter, while undoubtedly a revolutionary device, represents the biases and limitations of early nutrition studies. Atwater likened the proper maintenance of the human body to the operation of a machine, where nutrition amounted to the study of "definite quantities of income and expenditure," or what he aptly termed "chemical book-keeping." Central to this chemical book-keeping was the counting of calories. This new way of evaluating the value of various articles of food suggested that many vegetables, including tomatoes, were of little food value. Atwater distinguished between different types of foods, including proteids (proteins), carbohydrates, and fats, but in his estimation, proteins and fats were of far greater importance than carbohydrates, a readily available source of energy and a traditional staple of the working classes.[4]

This is not to say that Atwater suggested a one-sided diet, one made up primarily of meat. Indeed, he argued consistently for a "mixed diet" that included a variety of foods. Yet his idea of a mixed diet included less fatty cuts of meat, wheat products, and potatoes. Beans also served as an inexpensive source of protein. According to Atwater, other vegetables, including the tomato, were generally of little nutritional value, to be consumed only sparingly due to their high cost compared to their nutritional (caloric) value. These positions were codified as USDA policy in 1894 with the publishing of Atwater's food guide, *Foods: Nutritive Value and Costs*. During the late nineteenth century, reformers attempted to turn Atwater's nutritional guidelines into culinary reality by opening public kitchens that would supply working-class urban residents with inexpensive but nutritious foods. In Boston, for instance, Helen Richards and others provided inexpensive soups and stews to the working poor. Fortunately, both for the fate of the tomato and the nutrition of these poor urbanites, the efforts at reforming the diets of the poor largely failed. As Harvey Levenstein has pointed out, poor Americans, especially immigrants, mostly ignored the public kitchen movement. As the story of the tomato during the late nineteenth century attests, Americans had little interest in reformers dictating their diets, altering their ethnic identities, or dismissing the value of foods, like tomatoes, that they deemed both healthy and useful additions to the kitchen table.[5]

Despite the early failures of the nutrition movement to radically redefine American cuisine, it did have several lasting effects. It continued a precedent of high consumption of meat, wheat, and potatoes that continues to this day, offering scientific legitimacy to a diet that many Americans already practiced. It also created a tradition of the scientific study of food. While such studies initially were confined only to counting calories, in the 1910s they led to the discovery of new compounds in food products.

In the years leading up to World War I, scientists from the United States and Europe discovered the existence of a small substance in foods, which they called the vitamin. Almost immediately, this discovery undermined Atwater's sole reliance on the calorie, and in its place nutritionists came to believe that vitamins and other minerals played a vital part in proper nutrition as well. In 1911, Dr. Casimer Funk of the Lister Institute began research that resulted in the discovery of vitamins. Soon, Funk and Dr. E. V. McCollum of Johns Hopkins University became leaders in the field. The original discovery of vitamins A, B, and C expanded into five with vitamin A being split into A and E, and vitamin B split into B and D. As late as 1921, scientists remained unable to isolate vitamins from other compounds in food, but they could detect their existence by determining whether certain foods prevented the harmful effects associated with a lack of vitamins.[6]

The discovery of vitamins led to a revolution in nutrition studies. It meant not only a shift away from calories and the idea of food as fuel but also a move toward appealing to the middle class rather than challenging working-class or immigrant diets. Nutritionists quickly deemed the vegetable to be a vital component to a healthy diet and, with this claim, won a middle-class audience. Although these vitamins were sometimes found in meat, dairy products, and major staple grains, it became clear that they were often most prevalent in fruits and vegetables. Already by the 1910s the tomato was fully accepted as part of the American diet, but with the discovery of vitamins, and the tomato's high content of vitamin C and other vitamins, the nutritional value of the tomato quickly received scientific backing.[7]

While Atwater's concept of nutrition focused almost exclusively on calorie intake, his daughter, Helen Atwater, was forced to reconcile the existence of vitamins in her own 1918 food guide, which called for the daily consumption of more than a pound of fruits and vegetables. Moreover, Helen's work indicates a clear link between the nutrition and home economics movements by the 1910s. Her father dismissed the value of "taste" in food, but Helen's experience in the home economics movement led her to understand the value of producing appetizing meals, a central focus of many of the recipes and cookbooks of the period. Flavorings, seasonings, and condiments, while often not always adding extensively to the nutritional value of a meal, "may . . . be very useful in making an otherwise unattractive diet taste good." Thus, for Helen Atwater, proper eating was a combination of nutritious and appetizing meals. The tomato increasingly played a critical role in both.[8]

The discovery of the vitamin was not a necessary part of the tomato becoming accepted by mainstream America. Yet home economists and nutritionists challenged Wilbur Atwater by actively promoting this diversity during the early twentieth century. Scholars have focused on reformers' efforts to "Americanize" immigrants and criticize their food budgeting. Still, many published cookbooks (along with popular middle-class magazines like Ladies' Home Journal and American Family Home) encouraged increased diversity and variety in the American diet. While many of their recipes drew on traditional American cookery, the nutrition and home economics movements helped foster a dramatic increase in tomato consumption.[9]

Early twentieth-century reformers had more success remaking the middle-class diet than they had had with the working-class one. They made significant gains in increasing the cleanliness of American kitchens and in teaching homemakers how to budget and plan meals. Most of all, however, these reformers helped oversee a tremendous broadening of foods. Atwater's meat, bread, and potatoes gave way to more variety in fruits, vegetables, and other foods. Middle-class and increasingly urbanized women learned from these experts (and from each other) in and through a wide expansion of cookbooks and the new women's magazines that emerged after 1880. Especially important was the introduction of salads and other tomato-dominated dishes. These culinary ideas did filter down to the broader public but did not dominate the early twentieth-century American kitchen table. The result, in some respects unintentionally, was a more diverse American cuisine.[10]

By the end of the nineteenth century, especially as market gardening became more prevalent, the popularity of tomatoes exploded in urban areas, especially among elites and the middle class. In many ways, the uses of tomatoes followed the traditions set forth by rural nineteenth-century cooks and farmers—including fresh tomatoes, ketchups, sauces, and other side dishes. Yet home economics and other reformers also had an influence, even as magazines and new cookbooks offered new ways of preparing and using the tomato.

INNOVATION IN THE KITCHEN: THE COOKED TOMATO

In the late nineteenth and early twentieth centuries, cooks followed traditional methods of preparing tomatoes, using commercially available canned or fresh tomatoes. Recipes for homemade ketchup, for example, continued to be published in cookbooks and periodicals even as commercially prepared ketchup grew more widely available. Much like in the middle of the nineteenth century, these recipes tended to be complex, with several ingredients and offering a variety of tastes. Most recipes called for a combination of sweet, salty, and spicy flavors. One recipe, for example, called for onions, garlic, salt, brown sugar, cayenne, and vinegar. While recipes tended to call for red, ripe, some, including one called "Southern Catsup," required green tomatoes, giving cooks a way to use tomatoes either early in the season, before they had ripened, or late in the season, as green tomatoes were salvaged before the first frost. For those without access to fresh tomatoes, one 1915 cookbook offered a recipe for making ketchup from canned tomatoes. Making ketchup allowed cooks to use the recipe and ingredients of their choice, and perhaps to avoid the possibility of adulteration (the fight during the 1900s over the use of sodium benzoate as a preservative was waged largely over its use in ketchup). And newer canning methods allowed cooks to store their ketchup more reliably and for longer periods of time.[11]

Similar to ketchup, recipes for tomato pickles continued to be widely available during the early twentieth century. The wide variety of these recipes reflects the ability of the tomato to take on complex flavors. While most favored green tomatoes over ripe tomatoes, both yellow and red tomatoes were considered suitable for pickling as late as 1917. Some recipes favored salty and spicy flavors, perhaps close in taste to today's dill cucumber pickles. Ground pepper, red peppers, green peppers, and onions were all common ingredients in spicy pickle recipes. Another common ingredient was horseradish. Most recipes required small amounts of grated horseradish, but one actually calls for the addition of a pint of horseradish to a pickled mixture of one gallon green tomatoes, four green peppers and a dozen onions. This recipe certainly packed punch.[12]

Other tomato pickle recipes combined salty and sweet flavors. Cinnamon, cloves, and especially sugar were common ingredients. In one recipe, eight pounds of sugar was added to twenty pounds of tomatoes. Another called for two pounds of brown sugar for every gallon of tomato and vinegar mixture. In most cases, however, horseradish, red pepper, or mustard helped balance out the sweetness with a little spice. Despite the introduction of standardized and limited selection of manufactured condiments by the likes of Heinz, published recipes appealed to a wide variety of tastes. By encouraging home cooks to continue making their own ketchup and pickles (even as they became readily available on grocers' shelves), cookbook authors and other professional home economists inspired experimentation and innovation in the American kitchen.[13]

Pickled tomato recipes were often associated with different regions and places. The mid-Atlantic and southern regions were particularly well represented, with recipes for the Pottsville Pickle (of Pennsylvania), Philadelphia Pickle, and Maryland Pickle. Virginia, too, had "Virginia Mixed Pickles." These recipes, while sometimes similar, had distinguishing characteristics. The Pottsville Pickle, for example, contained green and red tomatoes, as well as onions and peppers. The Philadelphia Pickle added raisins, peppers, brown sugar, and celery. The Maryland Pickle called for brown sugar, red and green tomatoes, horseradish, yellow mustard seed, cabbage, and red peppers.[14]

Yet Americans went well beyond traditional pickling recipes during the early twentieth century. Many cooks embraced the innovations promoted by the home economics and nutrition movements. One of these was the introduction of mixed pickles and relishes, which were likely served as a way to make use of leftover produce—a large theme of home economics. One recipe, aptly named "Rummage Pickles," called for green and ripe tomatoes, cucumbers, onions, celery, and red and green peppers. Yet these were relatively informal recipes, allowing cooks to substitute what they had on hand. Some, for example, called for cauliflower and cabbage in addition to tomatoes.[15]

Far more common than mixed pickles, however, was the introduction of various relishes (mixtures of chopped or diced vegetables that were then pickled). The two dominant types of relishes were piccalilli, a Western take on the Indian pickle, and chow chow, developed in the Americas (although the two types were often very similar). Much like with pickles and ketchups, recipes for relishes contained a variety of vegetables and spices. Yet these condiments did provide something new: they offered a way for tomatoes to be served in bright, colorful, and flavorful ways, appealing directly to the aesthetics of the American meal. Served as a garnish or a side to a meat entrée or sandwich these relishes offered new and more complex tastes to the standard American diet, and they helped integrate the tomato more fully into mainstream, middle-class American cuisine. Expanded access to tomatoes (even outside of the traditional growing season) facilitated more complex culinary preparation and creativity.[16]

While many housewives continued to preserve tomatoes at home, they increasingly used store bought tomatoes rather than homegrown. Many continued to can tomatoes from their own gardens, but the low prices offered in urban markets at the peak of the harvest also offered opportunities to can commercially produced fresh tomatoes. In fact, this availability and affordability helped make it possible for the rural tradition of preserving tomatoes to migrate to the city. Home canning was especially popular during World War I, as home economists and government leaders saw the practice as an important part of the war effort. Between the late nineteenth century and through the 1910s, recipes for canning tomatoes were commonly offered in domestic periodicals, cookbooks, and nutrition guides. Most called for canning whole tomatoes, just as commercial canners did, usually only adding water and salt. Much like their commercial counterparts, tomatoes canned at home were minimally processed, maximizing their usability by the cook.[17]

At the same time, some cooks developed more heavily processed canned tomato products, including chili sauce and tomato sauce, pulp, and paste. These enabled cooks to do preparation work during the canning process. Whether prepared in advance or from fresh and canned tomatoes, tomato sauces continued to be seen as an important way to add variety to otherwise monotonous and bland dishes. Yet compared to the nineteenth century, early twentieth-century recipes for tomato sauces found in cookbooks and periodicals were even more diverse and were used in a wider array of dishes. Different recipes could create dramatically different taste profiles: some called for sugar and cinnamon, and others included gravy, beef fat, onions, or green peppers. Perhaps most common were recipes for beefsteaks, chops, lamb, and veal. Numerous other tomato sauce recipes existed for cod, haddock, bass and other types of fish, as well as for polenta, eggs, and cauliflower.[18]

Cooked tomatoes continued to be served as a side dish to meats and other staple foods. Recipes abound for hamburger steak with tomatoes and for beans and tomatoes. Stewed tomatoes were also commonly prepared with other vegetables, including corn, okra, and potatoes. Other dishes, including curried tomatoes and tomatoes with rice, were also common. There were even desserts, including tomato and cheese pudding and tomato custard.[19]

Tomatoes also continued to be used as a complementary ingredient in soups. Much like with sauces, these recipes often combined tomatoes with either carbohydrate staples like rice or potatoes or sources of protein, including chicken, beef, and beans. Tomatoes were an especially important part of the development of gumbo and okra-based soups originating in Creole cuisine from Louisiana. Simpler soups that combined tomatoes and rice likely emerged from a similar culinary impulse, as many of the areas of the United States that grew rice, including South Carolina, had French influences. Recipes for tomato and bean soup were common, but others included other sources of protein, including peanuts (or in one case, peanut butter) and lentils. Tomatoes mostly provided flavor to recipes, but, as in the case of pickles, they also served as a vehicle for culinary sharing and exploration, allowing cultural and ethnic dishes to be popularized for mainstream consumption.[20]

An important factor in the transformation of tomato preparations was the rise of urbanized middle-class homemakers and cooks willing to experiment with a more cosmopolitan diet. We can see this in the increasing popularity of tomato soup, which marked a shift from using tomatoes as a complementary component to employing them as the main ingredient. As home economists and nutritionists increasingly sought to reduce the amount of meat in the American diet by encouraging increased vegetable consumption, dishes featuring the tomato as the dominant ingredient became much more common.[21]

Middle-class Americans also commonly prepared stuffed tomatoes. Tomatoes were often stuffed with other vegetables, including onions, but they were also used as a vehicle for serving meat. One such recipe, offered by Christine Herrick, called for tomatoes to be stuffed with ham and mushrooms. Declaring it to be "a very nice dish for a luncheon, or Sunday evening or informal supper," Herrick admitted that the unique qualities of the tomato made the dish very versatile. If ham was unavailable, "cold chicken or veal, or any nice cold meat may be used." Tomatoes could also be baked, not unlike Irish and sweet potatoes. As American cuisine continued to expand, integrating elite cuisine with those of middle-class reformers and new immigrant cultures, middle-class Americans increasingly used the tomato not simply as a minor ingredient but as a featured ingredient in their diets.[22]

THE FRESH TOMATO

Until the twentieth century, most vegetables were cooked or preserved. Given their perishability and unpalatability raw, this isn't surprising. But soon thereafter the fresh came into vogue, and the raw tomato proved exceptionally tasty when fresh. By 1897, New York City's Waldorf Hotel was already offering not only cooked and processed tomatoes every day but also fresh tomatoes. This restaurant offered fresh farm tomatoes as an hors d'oeuvre every day until mid-November when they were replaced briefly by hothouse tomatoes and in December by tomato pickles (except for a surprise delight of fresh tomatoes for Christmas day).[23]

The fresh tomato was a hit with the rich and this taste trickled down to the middle class. Just as the middle-class borrowed tomato-based soups from the elite, they also showed a desire for luxuries like fresh tomatoes, which were becoming more widely available.

The unique taste qualities of the tomato were showcased in new recipes. One, for example, called for tomatoes to be sliced and eaten raw, either plain, or with the addition of "sugar and cream as a dessert." As the author of this recipe noted, the sweetened tomato became "a close rival to strawberries." If the cook preferred a non-sweetened version of the dish, the author noted that the tomato, due to its high acid content, "needs very little vinegar" and that excessive spicing or vinegar might irritate the mouth and stomach. While the tomato as a desert never caught on, the culinary inventiveness displayed in this and other recipes was extraordinary. It was a trend that declined with the growing acceptance of convenience foods in the latter half of the century.[24]

Encouraged by the increasing popularity of fresh tomatoes, one of the biggest transformations of the American diet was the rise of salads. Heavily influenced by French cookery and the cuisine of American elites, the salad became a mainstay on middle-class tables in the early twentieth century. Already in 1905, home economist Christine Herrick, an author of more than thirty books and a frequent contributor to *Ladies' Home Journal* and other periodicals, declared that "the salad is the prince of the menu, and though the dinner may be perfect in every detail, it is incomplete without a good salad." Early forms of salads typically included only one primary ingredient—lettuce, cucumber, or tomato, for example—typically dressed with oil or mayonnaise. Only rarely would one find a salad with a combination of ingredients like lettuce and tomato. Dinner and banquet menus from the Hotel Bellevue in Philadelphia in 1886 and 1887 and several banquet menus from New York City's famous Delmonico's in the same years list lettuce salad. Published recipes from the late nineteenth century also indicate this trend. One recipe, printed in *Good Housekeeping* in 1886 described a tomato salad that consisted simply of sliced tomatoes topped with a dressing of oil, vinegar, mustard, salt, and pepper. Likewise, in 1887 the magazine printed a recipe for raw tomatoes "as served and eaten in San Francisco." This recipe called for tomatoes to be skinned, chilled, and served topped with a "thick mayonnaise sauce." Similar recipes continued to be printed by *Good Housekeeping* and other periodicals well into the twentieth century.[25]

By the first decade of the century, however, salads were beginning to evolve from a single-ingredient dish to more complex mixtures of different fresh ingredients. In 1895 a *Good Housekeeping* author reported that "one of the prettiest and most palatable dishes for a summer lunch is a fresh tomato salad." While in the past this would have most likely indicated a salad made up almost entirely of fresh sliced or chopped tomatoes, this recipe called for each tomato to be placed on its own bed of lettuce. During the first decade of the twentieth century, this was a common dish at upscale restaurants. In June 1905 the upscale Hotel Astor in New York City offered "Salade de laitues et tomates" on its dinner menu. Likewise, the Pennsylvania Railroad offered riders a similar dish at least as early as 1911.[26]

In the 1910s, as home economists encouraged increased vegetable consumption and home cooks continued to expand their culinary palate, the category of salad expanded dramatically to include dozens of new ingredients, and increasingly, recipes for salads included two or more main ingredients. As Emma Conley, a Wisconsin state domestic science inspector, reported in her *Principles of Cooking* that "salads are made of cold meat or fish, eggs, cheese, raw or cooked vegetables or fruits, combined with a salad dressing." The home economist Ruth Wardall added, "A salad is a wholesome and a favorite way of serving vegetables, both fresh and cooked. Combinations of meat, eggs, fruit, nuts, and cheese with vegetables are frequently made in salads." Whether combined with cucumbers and lettuce, stuffed with crab and served on lettuce, or served in the "Spanish" style, with lettuce, cucumber, onions, pickles, and French dressing, the tomato became one of the most popular ingredients in the increasingly popular salad. For Americans interested in proving their patriotism by preparing an Independence Day–themed salad, the tomato was absolutely vital. Herrick provided not one but two recipes for such a salad, both relying on tomatoes for their bright red color. Herrick, unable to find an appropriate blue-colored ingredient, opted instead for the use of a blue serving plate. For those unable to obtain a supply of fresh tomatoes in time for Independence Day, one of Herrick's recipes provided a solution: instead of using raw tomatoes, one could easily substitute a "red tomato jelly" made from cooked tomatoes combined with gelatin. Numerous other recipes called for similar tomato jellies; one even used a mold pan to shape a tomato aspic.[27]

Whether in fresh or cooked form, the tomato played a central role in the expansion of the diet of the early twentieth century middle-class American. These innovations were made possible by the dramatic surge in tomato production and the success of the fresh and processed twelve-month tomato. Rather than limiting the American diet, the industrialization of the tomato encouraged culinary creativity and the expansion of middle-class food culture. Yet ethnic, especially Italian, immigrants also helped redefine the place of the tomato in American food.

THE ITALIAN TOMATO, 1880–1945

Spanish, Mexican, and even German and Polish immigrants put tomatoes on their dinner tables, but none shaped American food culture like the Italian tomato. The sudden influx of Italian immigrants after 1880 introduced these Mediterranean people and their distinct cuisine to the United States. Despite the efforts of nutritionists and reformers to "Americanize" and standardize the immigrants' diets during the period, Italian immigrants went their own way, creating an Italian American cuisine that mixed traditional Italian food habits with the American environment, which, in turn, had a distinct impact on new American eating habits. Americans of every stripe embraced Italian uses of the tomato.

Between 1870 and 1945, at least five million Italian immigrants arrived in America. Interestingly, the Italians that came to America during the late nineteenth and early twentieth century did not eat "Italian" food. As numerous historians have commented, even after the Italian nation was created in 1861, Italy was more a political construction than a cultural reality, as "Italians" continued to identify with their regional origins. In fact, historian Donna Gabaccia argues that "no sooner did Italy have its own state than Italians began to abandon it in record numbers." The Italian immigrants who flooded America during the late nineteenth and early twentieth century brought with them regional cuisines and culinary ideas. Northern and southern Italy, especially, had fairly distinct cuisines. Ironically, as David Gentilcore contends, modern Italian food as a unified cuisine was in many ways constructed in the United States by Italian immigrants. Gabaccia maintains that this is true of Italian culture more broadly, as "it is quite possible that peasants and workers more often came to think of themselves as Italian while abroad than at home." This was especially true of food, given the primacy of food in Italian American culture. In the words of Hasia Diner, "by engaging with American food realities, immigrants created an Italian American cultural system heavily centered on food."[28]

The first Italian immigrants to arrive en masse to American cities were mostly men, often hoping to save enough money to return to their homeland with money in their pockets. Despite the lack of wives and daughters, who were the traditional food preparers in Italy, these Italian men expected food they were familiar with. Often living together in groups in boarding houses, these men resisted the urge to simply adopt the eating habits of other Americans, trying instead to eat food that mostly resembled their traditional fare as much as possible. In many cases, groups from the same regions, and even towns, gathered together, allowing them to stay true to their own regional and local diets. When this was not possible, they almost always stuck with other Italians, allowing for an exchange and a sharing of different regional and local diets. In many cases, Italian neighborhoods in American cities were virtually self-sufficient, and immigrants had little need or desire to leave them. As women arrived in the country, as one immigrant named Rosa recounted, they typically filled the role of food preparer. Even as Italian families began to settle and find their own homes, they often took in Italian immigrants as boarders, whom they generally accepted as part of the family.[29]

Replicating "Italian" cookery in America was difficult, especially given that Italian (and even regional) cuisines were in flux just as immigration rose in the late nineteenth century. Pasta, a Neapolitan specialty dating back to the sixteenth century, was transitioning from a very soft (even overcooked) dish topped with dry ingredients like nuts, or cheese, or served with milk or cream, toward a more lightly cooked version with liquid sauces, including tomato sauce. While the tomato was already widely consumed in Italy, it was just beginning to be served as a sauce on pasta during the 1850s, a few decades before Italian immigration to the United States. The full integration of both pasta and tomatoes into Italian diets did not take place until the late nineteenth century, when industrialization increased access to these foods. Thus, especially for Italian immigrants arriving before 1900, spaghetti with tomato sauce was a recent addition to their diets. Some of the largest groups of immigrants came from southern Italy, where pasta and tomatoes were most prominent.[30]

Yet it was the Italian American restaurant, which also appeared during the late nineteenth century, that brought together the culinary ideas of Italian immigrants and helped create a relatively consistent food culture that appealed to commonalities in different regional styles. It was a commercial establishment designed as an alternative to boardinghouse cooking, and thus sought to find a common denominator in the food preferences of its customers. Given the importance immigrants placed on food, these restaurants quickly became important cultural institutions in Italian American neighborhoods of American cities. Italian restaurants popped up from New York to San Francisco, and from Chicago to Tampa. At least into the 1920s, these restaurants catered to Italian, rather than American, eaters.[31]

The developing Italian American cuisine was affirmed and reinforced by other cultural institutions, including the Catholic Church, mutual aid societies, and community festivals and gatherings. At Italian American gatherings food, rather than alcohol, was the centerpiece. Food, too, was an integral part of religious life, from baptism to the funeral. Meetings of community organizations commonly featured large amounts of Italian food. Community festivals, often held on religious holidays and other important days, helped present a unified Italian cuisine. In the words of one scholar, "the *feste* showcased the emergence of an Italian consciousness in America through food." In most cases, these institutions remained popular with immigrants' children. Despite their gradual acceptance of the English language, American political and other ideas, and consumer goods, second- and third-generation Italian immigrants held fast to the culinary ideas practiced by their parents and grandparents. Even in later generations, one scholar argues, "most [Italians] prefer pasta over potatoes and wine over beer or hard liquor." Over time, many Italians came to celebrate Thanksgiving with a turkey, but they did so after eating an antipasto salad, and the turkey was served alongside Italian dishes like spaghetti or lasagna, and it was followed with Italian desserts like spumoni or cannoli.[32]

The influx of Italian immigrants to the United States came at the same time that American food industries were beginning a massive expansion. Despite this, "authentic" Italian food was still imported, including Italian-style tomato products. In 1878, more than 132,000 pounds of tomato paste were exported annually from Italy, and most of this was sent to the United States. In 1905 more than 11,000 tons of tomato paste and concentrate were exported from Italy, and this number peaked in 1929, when 150,000 tons were exported; up to half of this total went to Italian immigrants in America. Soon ethnic Italians who had settled in the United States began to replace imports with their own processed Italian foods. By the late 1930s, as Gentilcore points out, a dozen Italian American companies producing tomato products in California exceeded the total volume of tomato products imported from Italy. This Italian American production "was a hybrid that in sometimes paradoxical ways looked back to Italy while taking advantage of what the new continent had to offer."[33]

Italian Americans not only substituted imports with their own products, but they actively developed their own markets, farms, and canneries to grow and distribute foods suitable to their culinary tastes. Very early on Italians practiced truck farming outside of Italian enclaves in American cities, and a significant number distributed that produce via pushcarts. Even in Mormon-dominated Utah, Italian immigrants produced and distributed their own produce and other foods to their country folk. Italian American food stores also became increasingly common during the early twentieth century. These stores helped produce an image of a unified, national Italian cuisine. While Italian food stores continued to cater to regional differences, as early as 1900, according to historian Hasia Diner, "merchants linked the food they sold to the idea of a nation, embellishing the word 'Italian' with such adjectives as 'fine,' 'fresh,' 'genuine,' 'imported,' 'real,' and 'tasty.'" By doing so, and by offering credit to marginal members of the community, much like other cultural institutions, these stores "wound the fabric of the community around food."[34]

In the opening decades of the twentieth century, Italian immigrants quickly established pasta industries in their new host countries. This was especially the case in the United States, where inexpensive and plentiful wheat encouraged the development of a large pasta industry. During the 1920s, American pasta production doubled, and imports dropped by 92 percent. Most of these factories were in states with large Italian populations, including New York, California, Illinois, and Pennsylvania. These companies, often starting as small immigrant ventures, often led the way by modernizing the packaging of pasta. Whereas in Italy most pasta was packed in bulk, often coming in boxes of close to 100 pounds, demand for smaller and more sanitary packages led American producers to produce pasta in one pound containers. After 1920, cellophane packaging was used to draw out the aesthetic quality of pasta while keeping it safe from contamination. Thus these producers followed a growing trend among American food companies toward smaller packages— suitable for a single or a few meals.[35]

Italian Americans succeeded in becoming major producers of canned vegetables, especially tomatoes. For example, Del Monte, a large producer of canned whole tomatoes during the early twentieth century, began as a small immigrant concern. Marco J. Fontana, a former employee of a small cannery, A. Galli and Company, opened his own cannery in his home kitchen in northern California. After years of financial struggle, Fontana played a big role in the formation of the California Fruit Canners' Association, which came to can under the Del Monte name (originally in reference to a northern California hotel, not an Italian family) in 1898. By the late nineteenth century, Del Monte employed several hundred employees during the peak of the season, most of them women.[36]

The development of more heavily processed tomato products, most notably tomato paste, was also the result of Italian immigration. During the early twentieth century, Italy exported somewhere between thirteen and twenty thousand tons of tomato products annually, primarily to countries with high numbers of Italian immigrants. Like their American counterparts, Italian producers packed unskinned whole tomatoes (*pomodoro al naturale*), and peeled whole tomatoes (*pomodoro pelati*), but they also sold canned tomato sauce (*salsa di pomodora*) and, even in larger quantities, tomato paste and tomato puree. These products were especially popular among Italian immigrants. By the 1910s, and especially after the outbreak of war in Europe cut off the Italian supply of these products, Italian American producers became interested in manufacturing these products at home for American consumption.[37]

There were a variety of practical reasons for the production of more concentrated tomato products. One of the more common arguments was that tomato paste greatly reduced waste. Proponents of paste claimed that eliminating legitimate waste, including the skin, core, and seeds, meant that upward of 50 percent of the tomato juices were also lost in packing whole tomatoes.[38]

Producing paste had other advantages as well: it greatly reduced labor costs, as the processes of removing the skins, seeds, and core could finally be mechanized. Without the concern for damaging the tomatoes, they could be cooked, crushed, strained, and boiled down via machines rather than human hands. And "since no hands touch[ed] the product" from the time the tomatoes enter the factory until canning is completed, proponents of tomato paste claimed that it was more sanitary. Further, since it was a concentrated product, paste production also saved space in storage, transportation, and a reduced need for metal in cans. As J. H. Shrader argued, "a 6-oz. paste can contains practically the equivalent of a 32-oz. ordinary tomato can." Finally, despite it being a more heavily processed tomato product, tomato paste still gave cooks great opportunity to shape the product to their needs and desires. Diluted in water, tomato paste could be turned into a sauce, added to stews or soups, and spiced appropriately. While it reduced some of the skill and labor of the cook, as it was no longer necessary to boil down tomatoes to produce a puree or sauce, tomato paste retained much of the creativity that skilled cooks desired. Tomato paste was often favored among Italian immigrants and those of Italian descent, and increasingly, by the 1940s and 1950s, it was favored among other American consumers as well.[39]

Early twentieth-century Italian American cooking is surprisingly hard to catalog. Many of the studies of Italian immigration and immigrant life pay little, if any, attention to Italian cooking, despite its prominent place in Italian culture. And, as Donna Gabaccia notes, there were very few Italian American cookbooks printed during the early twentieth century. One of the few, and more popular, was *The Italian Cookbook*, published in New York in 1919 by Maria Gentile in an effort to popularize Italian food in America. Once again, the tomato figured prominently. It was featured primarily as a sauce, as an addition to pastas of all kinds, including spaghetti and ravioli, as well as with chicken and other meats.[40]

Italian American cookery relied on the tomato as more than just a sauce. Niccolo de Quattrociocchi, one of the many Italian immigrants who went on to open their own restaurants, was a lifelong collector of recipes and published many of his favorites in his memoir. In addition to Neapolitan- and Sicilian-style spaghetti and spaghetti with meat sauce, Quattrociocchi also published recipes for Italian antipasto (salad), lentil soup, and *pasta e fagioli* soup, all with tomatoes as a major ingredient.[41]

Thus, during the first half of the twentieth century, as Italians came to the United States in record numbers, they brought with them ideas about cooking and eating. These ideas developed in the United States as a unique cuisine, one based on the memory, sometimes imagined, of their homeland and adapted to fit their new American environment. Italian Americans were not, as some have suggested, simply an isolated ethnic enclave but instead a vibrant ethnic community that built their own culture based on a blending of old and new. In constructing their cuisine, Italian Americans relied heavily on the tomato, a food many had not had regular access to in Italy, and tomato sauce, a dish popularized in

Italy just prior to Italian immigration. Tomato and pasta dishes were also adapted to the American environment with the addition of meats, especially beef, which were much less plentiful in Italy. Indeed, just as pasta became the prominent source of carbohydrates in many Italian Americans' diets, and meatballs, sausage, veal and others became a major source of protein, the tomato, primarily in the form of tomato sauce, became a vital flavoring agent and source of vegetable-based nutrients.[42]

Despite the efforts of reformers to "Americanize" the immigrant diet, Italian Americans had not only created their own cuisine but also influenced the larger American culinary culture. As early as the 1910s, Italian-influenced dishes received regular attention in American cookbooks and periodicals. By far the most common recipe printed was for "macaroni and tomato sauce." Occasionally recipes were printed for tomato and pasta soups as well as ravioli. During the 1920s, Italian American restaurants became popular among bohemian urbanites, and by the 1940s and 1950s, American families across the country enjoyed at least an occasional Italian American meal. In the 1970s, *American Cooking: The Melting Pot*, a volume containing a wide variety of traditional and ethnically inspired meals popular in America, reflected the broad acceptance of Italian American food by mainstream America. Despite the diversity of the contribution of Italian American cuisine to the United States, the most popular innovation of Italians in America was to combine spaghetti with hamburger meatballs in a tomato sauce, producing the quintessential, signature item on the menu of Italian American restaurants by the 1920s. This was not intended solely to attract an American audience. Quattrociocchi, on first trying the dish, found it "extremely satisfying" and felt that "someone in Italy should invent [it] for the Italians over there [in Italy]." Yet the inclusion of the meatball into spaghetti also helped Italian American cuisine appeal to a wider audience, combining Italian spaghetti with the American love of beef.[43]

The emergence of the tomato as a staple in Italian American cuisine benefited from the preexisting tomato culture in the United States. The prevalence of the tomato as a condiment (ketchup) and a form of soup meant that Americans had already accepted the tomato as a useful article of the daily diet. By the end of World War II, spaghetti and meatballs, along with numerous other Italian American influenced dishes, commonly appeared on the American dinner table. Tomato paste was available on most grocers' shelves by the 1930s, and pasta with tomato sauce was a quick, easy to prepare, and tasty meal (with an appealing mixture of textures and flavors). The tomato, along with pasta, formed the basis for this new cuisine, and American acceptance of Italian American cuisine propelled the tomato to an even higher place in American cuisine.[44]

THE HOMEGROWN TOMATO, 1914-1945

Americans had long grown their own tomatoes in their gardens. While urbanization and the availability of store-bought fresh and canned tomatoes certainly replaced seasonal homegrown foods, the family garden hardly disappeared. One important factor encouraging its survival was the world wars. With shortages of staples like meat, wheat, and sugar during World War I, the U.S. government encouraged Americans to rely on fruits and vegetables to satisfy their nutritional needs. The government also bought a significant portion of the commercial supply of canned vegetables to supply Europe and the soldiers of the Allies. In 1917 and 1918, the government purchased almost a quarter of the pack of canned tomatoes, and in 1919, with a significantly smaller pack, it acquired more than 40 percent. During World War II, in 1943, federal government purchases of canned vegetables totaled nearly 60 percent of total production, and 50 percent of canned tomatoes for use abroad. To fill the shortage of vegetables on the home front, during both world wars, the government conducted a massive campaign to encourage citizens to grow their own produce, especially the highly adaptable tomato.[45]

Despite urbanization and the convenience of store-bought foods, Americans embraced this call to cultivate home vegetable gardens with enthusiasm. Many, of course, had never given it up. Further, this gardening culture provided a deep connection between rural America and the rapidly expanding cities and suburbs. Immigrants groups also continued their gardening traditions as a vital connection to their pasts, often going to great lengths to secure harvests in urban settings. As Americans moved into cities and towns, they brought with them both their gardening experiences and traditions and their specific ideas of tomato cultivation and cooking.[46]

The promotion of fruits and vegetables by government officials and food reformers beginning during World War I was motivated by the desire to improve the American diet, especially after the discovery of the benefits of vitamins in fruits and vegetables. Typical were these words: "an increase in the use of vegetables and fruits is practically sure to mean an increase in health" and thus a more fit nation for the struggles ahead. Moreover, it was often argued that by substituting vegetables for meat and grains, American citizens could do their patriotic duty to increase the amount of staple foods available for soldiers in Europe while also benefiting from a healthier diet. By growing their own food during the war, gardeners reduced their (and their families') reliance on commercially produced food. One writer noted that vegetables "can be produced in quantity in three or four months on unused land by labor that otherwise might not be used." Thus growing and preserving food became an act of patriotic duty and a challenge that many Americans accepted.[47]

Americans responded quickly to the dwindling supply of canned vegetables and called for home production as a form of patriotic action. In 1917–1918, Americans produced almost 530 million pounds of vegetables in more than five million war gardens. Children and other young people in Indiana reportedly tended half a million gardens. Eight thousands acres in and around Los Angeles were planted with vegetables, along with twelve thousand New York City lots. Overall, the total value of war garden vegetable production was estimated at more than $350 million; the production in children's gardens alone was estimated at $100 million. During World War II the government asked even more Americans to augment the supply of commercially produced vegetables with Victory Garden vegetables. In 1942, there were an estimated 15 million Victory Gardens, and in 1944, the government was calling for 22 million Victory Gardens, including 450,000 in the New York City area.[48]

Throughout World War II, approximately two-thirds of the Victory Gardens were built in cities, suburbs, and towns. These gardens sprang up in backyards, on skyscraper balconies, and on empty lots in major cities, including a large field of corn and tomatoes planted on the corner of Sixth Avenue and Fifty-Second Street, in the heart of Manhattan's nightclub district. While it is difficult to assess the total production of tomatoes in Victory Gardens, the relative ease of growing them in a variety of conditions and environments and their popularity as a food combined to make them one of the more popular Victory Garden crops. One observer even labeled them the "Queen" of Victory Gardens, second only to sweet corn. Experts estimated that a family of four would need the produce from only three dozen tomato plants in order to supply the family for the entire year.[49]

Thus, even as the world wars facilitated tremendous growth in the tomato-processing industry, it was still necessary for consumers to produce their own and indeed to find new ways of using the tomatoes they produced. *New York Times* columnist Jane Holt regularly provided recipes that catered to the bounties of the Victory Garden. These recipes varied widely, from stuffed tomatoes and a casserole containing eggs, cheese, and tomatoes to Spanish rice and scalloped onions and tomatoes. Esther Grayson argued that the Victory Garden promoted increased salad consumption, providing virtually every ingredient necessary for fresh salads. Holt even argued that Victory Garden produce should be used not simply to provide basic foods but to diversify and spice up the diet. Offering readers a recipe for a tomato-based chili sauce, Holt argued, "Home-made condiments can hardly be called essential to a wartime diet, and yet they offer a pleasant way to vary it."[50]

At the same time that urban Americans were learning to enjoy the fresh bounty from their Victory Gardens, they were increasingly urged to learn the traditional practice of preserving their autumn harvests for the winter. Canning demonstrations were held in cities across the country, and the production of home canning equipment grew tremendously during the war. When shortages of equipment limited consumer access, community-canning centers emerged to provide women with access to the equipment necessary to preserve their Victory Garden tomatoes and other vegetables. In 1917, for example, there were 142 community canning centers in North Carolina alone. In New York State, more than one hundred opened. Westchester County had eighteen that put up a combined thirty thousand quarts of food.[51]

Americans' experience with gardening during the first half of the twentieth century encouraged Americans to experiment and vary their diets in order to maximize nutrition. They also enjoyed the pleasures of doing it themselves and freedom from dependence on the market. While many Americans were regular gardeners, there is little doubt that during each world war home gardening became more popular, as intermittent or new gardeners sought to help solve the nation's, and their own, food shortages. "Joe Novice," a New Yorker, planted his first garden with his wife during the war. Planting the garden to fulfill their patriotic duty, the couple soon realized that gardening allowed them to be "creative, producing things that never have existed before." It made them think about the quality of the farm produce they could purchase. "Their vegetables," reported the *New York Times*, "fresh from the garden and wet with the morning dew, are more toothsome and pack more vitamins than the finest green produce that can be bought in the stores." While this experience certainly did not radically challenge store-bought foods, it invited, even forced, many Americans to think about the difference between the home-grown and the commercial, a recognition that would be revived later in the century when the tomato, the "Queen of the Garden," would again be the centerpiece of a new appreciation of seasonal and local food.[52]

THE PREPACKAGED TOMATO

Even as commercially produced and homegrown tomatoes were transforming how Americans ate, industrialization also led to prepackaged convenience food, ready-made meals—including soup and canned spaghetti with tomato sauce. By the 1950s, these heavily processed food products had become mainstays on the shelves of the rapidly expanding supermarket industry.

While commercially produced ketchup became popular during the late nineteenth century, and canned tomato soup was widely consumed by the early twentieth century, more substantial ready-made foods did not appear until the 1930s. Products like canned spaghetti with tomato sauce were not intended as condiments or side dishes but instead as complete heat-and-eat meals. These foods represented a new way of thinking about food, one that gained acceptance across much of America during the 1950s and 1960s. Ready-made meals minimized the importance of the cook. Preparing, mixing, spicing, and thoroughly cooking the dish was unnecessary. On the stovetop, it could be heated and consumed in a few minutes.

Historians of the industrialization of food in America have long concerned themselves with the rise of such products, lamenting the loss of unique food cultures and cooking habits in America. Many of these scholars, including Harvey Levenstein, see this trend as part of the larger nutrition and home economics movements of the late nineteenth and early twentieth century. However, the influence of early examples of these types of products, including Campbell's soup, has been overemphasized, as we have seen. Moreover, increasing consumption of ready-made meals, rather than being created or nurtured by reformers, was the result of very real circumstances of poverty originating during the Great Depression that led many consumers to buy convenience foods for the first time, as it was often possible to prepare a meal from processed foods more cheaply than from scratch. Likewise, while Ernest Dichter suggested in 1952 that Chef Boyardee's spaghetti in a can appealed to homemakers' desire to "have tonight or tomorrow night off," more important was the fact that an increased percentage of women worked outside of the home by the 1950s and 1960s.[53]

Thus the commercial growth of canned soup and ketchup was topped during the 1930s with the popularization of ready-made meals like canned spaghetti. Franco-American was probably the first company to introduce canned spaghetti. Heinz followed suit by the 1920s. The product was not widely consumed, however, until the end of the 1920s, when Italian immigrant Ettore "Hector" Boiardi successfully introduced, marketed, and branded Chef Boy-Ar-Dee canned spaghetti.[54]

Boiardi may be the quintessential example of the Italian immigrant processed-food entrepreneur. He emigrated from Italy to New York City in 1917, eventually relocating to Cleveland, where he opened an Italian restaurant, Il Giardino d'Italia, in 1926. After repeated requests from his

customers, he began selling prepared, take-home meals at his restaurant. Boiardi opened a factory for his products in 1928. He packaged
uncooked spaghetti with cheese and his popular tomato sauce in empty
milk bottles. Demand continued to grow, and within a decade he relo-
cated to Milton, Pennsylvania, where he established a canning facility
where he packaged under the name "Chef Boy-Ar-Dee," (later renamed
Chef Boyardee) intentionally Americanizing the spelling of the name to
make it more recognizable (while still "ethnic") to American consumers. By the 1930s, in the midst of the Great Depression, Chef Boy-Ar-Dee
was distributed in A&P stores and had become a national brand. During World War II, Chef Boy-Ar-Dee had become so popular that it was
distributed to American GIs in military rations.[55]

The growing popularity of ready-made meals during the 1930s and beyond represents a much larger shift in American culinary habits than the
flood of industrial changes that preceded it. Ettore Boiardi developed and
marketed an Italian (or perhaps more accurately, Italian American) dish
for mass consumption. In so doing, he popularized a homogenized, relatively bland idea of Italian food to the American public. At the same time,
Boiardi's product undermined the role of the cook, creating a product
that even the most unskilled cooks could prepare. While the emerging
ready-made meal industry commonly touted the convenience and time-
saving qualities of such food products, it also resulted in the homogenization of the diet toward bland food and a deskilling of cooking. With
ready-made meals, opening a can and heating the contents became the
only skills necessary for meal preparation. In the decades following
World War II, ready-made meals became increasingly popular, with far
more serious consequences for American cuisine, consequences that perhaps inevitably led to a backlash, with the revival of the home garden.

There is little question that the period from 1870 to 1945 radically
changed American food culture. But is it correct to hold, as some scholars have done, that this meant the standardization and "Americanization" of the American diet? While food industries and various reformers

certainly played a role, they hardly homogenized American cuisine and made Americans into passive consumers of mass-produced foods. Moreover, even as reformers had some success in defining acceptable culinary ideas, the early twentieth century also saw the introduction of many new ingredients and dishes.

The history of the tomato tells a different story, one in which consumers and cooks also participated in making culinary culture. The initial development of tomato-based food products was radical only insofar as it greatly expanded Americans' access to the tomato, especially during the winter and spring. The legacy of expanded tomato production and the emergence of the twelve-month tomato, both in fresh and canned forms, then, was not the "Americanization" of food culture but instead a highly diverse and aesthetically rich tomato culture. There were certainly downsides to large-scale production of both fresh and canned tomatoes: fresh tomatoes hauled across the country were often of low quality. Similarly, canned tomatoes, especially after the introduction of pulp, puree, and paste, could mask low-quality tomatoes from consumers' eyes. Yet the largest effect of the development of the twelve-month tomato and increased production was to expand consumer access to tomatoes, opening the way for this culinary revolution—in a wide range of salads, soups, mixed vegetable dishes, and pastas, along with more traditional recipes like pickles and ketchup. Even canned tomatoes contributed to culinary innovation because they were usually packed in an adaptable, minimally processed form. The middle-class American homemaker adopted new and surprisingly diverse uses of the tomato, whether canned or fresh.

The tomato also illustrates how Americans adapted to culinary innovation. Some might view this as a bad thing. Many early scholars of American food history lamented what they saw as a break with "traditional" American food habits during the late nineteenth century. Others complained that Americans lacked culinary traditions like many European cultures and thus succumbed to corporate influences by embracing Campbell's soup and Chef Boyardee's canned spaghetti. But that "lack" also facilitated cultural sharing, blending, and innovation. The tomato served as an ambassador between different cultures that were emerging in the United States, especially with the immigration boom of the late nineteenth century. Just as the tomato's acceptance in America benefited Italian immigrants by ensuring their access to cheap fresh and processed tomatoes year-round, the particular uses of the tomato imported from Italy, in pastas especially, introduced other Americans to a unique line of foods. While the concept of America as a "melting pot" has long been dismissed, to the extent that it existed concerning food in the early twentieth century, the tomato was one of its major ingredients.

This period also saw the growth of several important tomato-processing companies, including Campbell's, Heinz, and Chef Boyardee, which produced heavily processed, heat-and-eat foods. The introduction of these products reflects the emergence of a trend that became prevalent during the second half of the century. Until World War II, however, their importance was overshadowed by the dramatic expansion of access to fresh and minimally processed tomato products, which encouraged rather than suppressed diversity in the food culture.

5

"A POOR TOMATO IS BETTER THAN NO TOMATO"

The Harvester and the Commodification of the Tomato

The tomato industry, which had long thrived on economic and geographic decentralization, reversed course after World War II. By the end of the twentieth century, domestic tomato production was centered in two states: California, which focused almost exclusively on processing tomatoes, and Florida, which produced the majority of the nation's winter and off-season fresh tomatoes.[1]

A number of critical factors help explain the dramatic shift toward geographic centralization and economic concentration. The loss of prime farm land due to suburbanization in the Mid-Atlantic and Midwest drove many tomato growers out of business in these regions. Labor shortages across the nation during World War II and in the decades that followed were an impediment to the industry and ultimately helped lead to mechanization and other technological innovations. Many state and federal agricultural research programs related to breeding, processing, and transportation disappeared, leaving just a few states and an increasing number of private companies to undertake the vast majority of tomato related research.

More importantly, however, these changes in breeding, growing, harvesting, and processing tomatoes themselves contributed to a much larger story in American culinary history. Deborah Fitzgerald has argued that the industrialization of agriculture, which had begun in earnest by the 1920s, was the result of complex "technical, social, and ideological relationships that both created and sustained the change." I argue that industrialization was not only confined to the economic and technological structures of production—machinery, chemicals, lending industries, and so on—but instead encompassed new ways of thinking about and encouraging consumption. The importance of the tomato industry during the postwar period is not simply that it succumbed to the pressures placed on other foods earlier in the century but that these changes helped lead to a nearly complete commodification of the tomato and made the tomato a key player in the development of a new food marketplace after 1945. The changing American food culture increasingly focused on heavily processed, often heat-and-eat, convenience foods. With mechanization and new varieties, the tomato became more uniform and significantly cheaper to produce. Tomato paste, a product introduced in the United States as early as World War I, developed into an industrial raw ingredient—an interchangeable, standardized product—for most tomato-based goods, including soups, sauces and juice. Complementing this increasingly West Coast commodity was the mass-produced fresh tomato of Florida in its cellophane-wrapped tube. By the 1990s, the development of the Flavr Savr tomato, the first genetically modified fresh produce to hit grocery stores, represented man's dominance over nature and an ultimately failed effort to market and sell such a product to American consumers.[2]

These industrial and agricultural changes combined with the growing popularity of several tomato-based dishes, including spaghetti, pizza, and even French fries served with ketchup, made the tomato increasingly popular in American kitchens and restaurants. Other factors, including freezing technology, the proliferation of kitchen appliances like the home freezer, and the reduced time available to cook dinners as women pitched aside their aprons and joined the workforce, contributed to an American cuisine increasingly based on convenience, which often meant prepackaged meals. The revolution in tomato production played a pivotal role in the proliferation of TV dinners, frozen pizza, canned spaghetti, and a host of other heat-and-serve meals. The tomato also served a critical role in the fast food industry, which began in earnest in the

1950s, with burger joints serving sliced tomatoes and ketchup, and America's new favorite meal, pizza, becoming a staple with the growing number of both mom and pop and chain pizzerias like Domino's (originally Dominick's) from 1960.[3]

Thus the development of the tomato industry and evolution of tomato consumption during the second half of the twentieth century illuminate several important changes in American culture. While historians have often focused on the convenience foods of the early twentieth century, including condiments like ketchup, as well as tomato soup, Jell-O, and store-baked bread, the introduction of convenience foods after 1945 was far more important. The tomato played a critical role in this process.

TOMATO PRODUCTION DURING
THE POSTWAR PERIOD

While in the previous half century, the tomato industry was defined by localized year-round production, the postwar period saw a dramatic shift toward geographic and economic concentration. By the end of the twentieth century domestic production had moved away from traditional centers of production in the Mid-Atlantic and Midwest and was almost entirely centered in California and Florida.

Tomato production during the first half of the twentieth century had been geographically decentralized, with states across the country playing a significant role in providing the nation's urban areas with tomatoes throughout the year. The Mid-Atlantic and Midwest, continued to produce tomatoes, but California, Texas, and Florida became major sites of tomato production as well, and a host of other states often distant from urban markets, including Mississippi, Tennessee, and Utah, provided significant supplies of tomatoes to cities. In the postwar period, following a trend for the nation as a whole, acreage in many of these states declined, in part as a result of increased yields. Even so, in California, and to a lesser extent in Florida, acreage actually increased sharply (figure 5.1). At

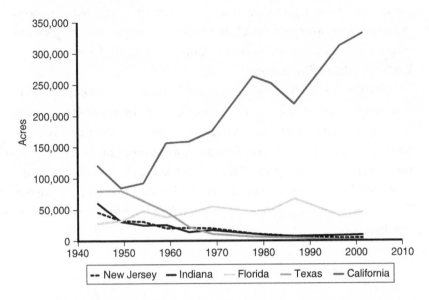

FIGURE 5.1 Tomato acreage by state, 1944–2002. This figure and the following two use data compiled from the following sources: U.S. Census Bureau, *1935 Census of Agriculture*, vol. 3, part 6 (Washington, DC: Government Printing Office, 1937), 390; *1945 Census of Agriculture*, vol. 2, part 8 (Washington, DC: Government Printing Office, 1946), 525; *1954 Census of Agriculture*, vol. 2, part 7 (Washington, DC: Government Printing Office, 1956), 785; *1959 Census of Agriculture*, vol. 2, part 7 (Washington, DC: Government Printing Office, 1962), 875; *1969 Census of Agriculture*, vol. 2, part 6 (Washington, DC: Government Printing Office, 1973), 84; *1978 Census of Agriculture*, vol. 1, part 5 (Washington, DC: Government Printing Office, 1981), 188; *1987 Census of Agriculture*, vol. 1, part 51 (Washington, DC: Government Printing Office, 1989), 373–74; and U.S. Department of Agriculture, *2002 Census of Agriculture*, vol. 1, part 2 (Washington, DC: Government Printing Office, 2004), 477.

the same time, a dramatic decrease in the number of farms growing tomatoes coincided with a sharp increase in average acreage per farm, particularly from 1944 to the late 1960s (figures 5.2–5.3).

Another key part of the new tomato industry was its division in production. While many traditional tomato states continued to grow tomatoes both for market and canneries, Florida and California became highly specialized producers. Florida remained devoted to producing out-of-season fresh tomatoes. California, while continuing to produce a significant amount of tomatoes for fresh consumption, largely wedded

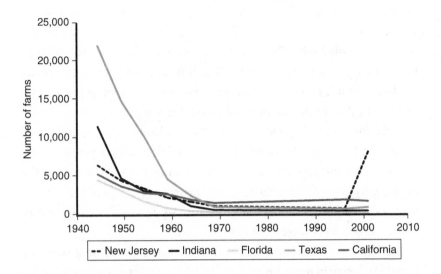

FIGURE 5.2 Number of tomato farms, 1944–2002.

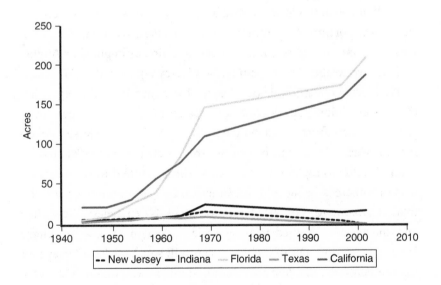

FIGURE 5.3 Acreage of tomatoes per farm, 1944–2002.

itself to the cannery. California had long produced fresh tomatoes for out-of-season consumption, but the long distance the fresh tomatoes had to travel coupled with the fact that it could not consistently produce tomatoes in the dead of winter, made it difficult to compete with Florida producers. While many California growers continued to plant fresh tomatoes for the late spring and summer months, many grew tomatoes almost entirely for processing facilities. By the mid-1960s, California could boast that it produced around 60 percent of the nation's processed tomatoes. This number climbed steadily during the second half of the century. By 2002, California produced nearly 93 percent of the nation's processed tomatoes, cultivating more than 290,000 of the nation's 315,000 acres of processed tomato crop.[4]

Environmental and social factors contributed to the demise of the tomato industry in many areas, including in New Jersey and Long Island. The Mid-Atlantic, in particular, was hit with wave after wave of crop failures during the late 1940s and early 1950s. During the 1946 season, a blight that began in Florida spread across the Mid-Atlantic, affecting a significant portion of the tomato harvest. In Pennsylvania, Maryland, Delaware, and New Jersey, 40,000 acres were already blighted by August 14. Just a week later, Union County, New Jersey reported that 60 percent of its expected one million pound harvest was ruined. By the beginning of October, Union County's total loss was estimated at 75 percent. Just a year later, a late frost wiped out ten million plants in New Jersey, delaying the season by a month. Despite this, increased prices offered by canneries due to the previous season's failure resulted in record numbers of tomatoes being sold to canneries. In 1947, canneries packed a total of 270,000 tons of New Jersey tomatoes. Nevertheless, these gluts and shortages continued to plague the region: in 1948, a late blight wiped out around half of the tomato crop in southern New Jersey and eastern Pennsylvania. Just a few hundred miles away, on Long Island, a heat wave decimated entire fields of tomatoes. Nassau County, New York reported a total loss of $500,000 in tomatoes. These environmental challenges put the Mid-Atlantic, as well as other regions, in a fragile position. Farmers and canneries alike could be destroyed by a single bad season.[5]

Added to the fragile state of the tomato industry in these areas was a second trend: suburbanization. The suburban explosion that took place in the years following 1945 often absorbed prime truck farming land. New Jersey, site of much of the first waves of postwar suburban growth, quickly transitioned from the "Garden State" to a site of sprawl and pavement. In places nearby New York City, like Rockland County and Long Island, farms were quickly swallowed up by suburban growth. As early as 1962, the number of farms in Nassau County, on Long Island, was 10 percent of what it had been at the end of World War II. Remaining fields were mostly devoted to the raising of flowers and shrubs. The effects of higher taxes caused by increasing property values due to suburbanization were also felt in Rockland County, where at least one large tomato grower shut down operations in 1956. Even in Florida, where the tomato industry continued to develop, suburban development often eliminated tomato acreage. In 1967, a 640-acre tomato farm twelve miles south of Miami was bought out and a "$75-million 'town'" was constructed.[6]

Poor harvests and suburbanization offer a partial explanation for the dramatic shift in tomato production from the Mid-Atlantic and Midwest to California and Florida, but they do not fully explain this transformation. After all, the population of California and Florida exploded during and after World War II as well, and other tomato-producing states, including Texas, had far more acreage available for production. But nationwide farm labor shortages that had begun during World War II continued through the 1960s. The tomato, being a very labor-intensive crop, was among the hardest hit industries. Labor shortages existed in nearly every geographic area that grew tomatoes, and were especially acute in California and Florida, even as these states continued to expand tomato production. However, compared to Midwestern and mid-Atlantic growers, California and Florida growers, benefiting from closer proximity to migrant labor, also proved more adept at lobbying the federal government to allow migrants to work the tomato harvest. Unlike in many other sectors, where the private sector overcame labor shortages through technological change and mechanization, California and Florida growers continued to rely on migrant labor even after the federal government signaled the end of favorable immigration policies. Without several decades of friendly labor policies, it seems unlikely that the Florida and California tomato industries would have succeeded.

In contrast to other industries, the major technological change in the tomato industry, the mechanical harvester, was the product of almost twenty years of research by agricultural engineers and breeders at the University of California, Davis, among other universities. Only after the demonstration of a successful mechanical harvester did the private sector, growers, and canners develop significant interest in labor-saving technologies. While labor shortages played a role in the formation of the mechanical harvester project, ironically the impetus for its invention came not from the growers facing these labor shortages but, as was partially the case with the development of the twelve-month tomato, from a public university.

ALWAYS SEARCHING FOR LABOR

The rapid development of the California and Florida tomato industries occurred during a nationwide labor shortage. Labor shortages within the tomato industry could have easily ruined the entire industry: in most cases, the difference between a successful harvest and a complete failure is a matter of weeks. A labor shortage that disrupted the harvest season could have quickly ruined the entire tomato crop. While a dearth of workers in California, where growers continually planted more tomatoes than the domestic labor market could harvest, was particularly troubling, the labor shortage was truly a nationwide problem, and it certainly played a role in undermining the tomato industry in other parts of the country. It also contributed to the politicization of the tomato, as California growers lobbied Congress to help save the tomato industry by allowing migrant farm workers from Mexico and elsewhere into the country. Intentionally or not, these policies, which together form the core of the Bracero Program, helped realign the geography of tomato production.

During World War II, when millions of Americans were sent to Europe and Asia to fight and millions more worked in war-related industries, the scarcity of farm labor became a national crisis. Beginning in 1942, the federal government allowed some Mexican migrant farm workers into the United States to help harvest crops. By the mid-1940s, the practice became codified in Public Law 45. Additional laws extended this program, and in 1951, Congress passed Public Law 78, which became the face of what was known as the Bracero Program and was routinely extended into the early 1960s. The solution offered by these laws was the importation of migrant laborers, most of whom came from Mexico, in order to harvest a multitude of crops. Tomato growers were one of the key beneficiaries of this policy. California's tomato industry in particular, due to the state's close proximity to Mexico, was in a unique position to benefit from the policy.[7]

Despite the efforts of the federal government to secure migrant labor for farmers, labor shortages abounded, particularly in states in the Mid-Atlantic and Midwest. In 1945, Illinois farmer Charles Neubert found it impossible to acquire labor to harvest his large crop of tomatoes. After attempting to go through all of the legal channels to acquire field workers, he had hired a Mexican to travel to Mexico and recruit workers. Neubert's agent picked up fifty-three Mexicans who had waded across the Rio Grande and drove them to Neubert's farm, about 20 miles south of Chicago, to harvest tomatoes. Immigration officers raided Neubert's farm and arrested the farmer and his Mexican workers. However, after investigating, officials were convinced that Neubert broke the law only after exhausting all legal means and because he was desperate to save his tomato crop. According to authorities, Neubert was paying his workers the going rate in the area for tomato picking, around $8 to $10 per day. Neubert and the Mexican workers were released on bail to continue harvesting the tomatoes.[8]

Elsewhere, in states like New Jersey, farmers relied heavily on Puerto Rican migrant workers and southern African Americans, who ventured up to the Garden State's tomato fields annually to work the harvest. These workers lived in large migrant camps, which by the late 1960s were routinely criticized in the press for their poor sanitary conditions. In upstate New York, many farmers simply tried to out-pay their competitors in order to supply the 35,000 vegetable pickers they needed per year in the mid 1960s. As late as 1970, New Jersey growers resorted to placing ads for pickers paying them daily and offering free transportation from Philadelphia in order to entice them to come work the fields. Ultimately, the available labor proved insufficient.[9]

For California, and to a lesser extent Texas and Florida, migrant labor was much easier to be had, as long as the Bracero Program remained intact. While in 1942 a mere four thousand migrant workers were admitted under the program, this number quickly jumped to around fifty thousand per year for the remaining years of the war. Following a sharp decline in the immediate postwar years (1946–1948), enrollment in the program sharply increased, hitting 192,000 in 1951, over 200,000 in 1953, and peaking at 445,000 in 1956. By the late 1950s, however, criticism of the program was mounting, most notably by American labor leaders who argued that the program's continued existence was undermining wage levels in agricultural and industrial sectors. What had begun as a short-term solution to labor shortages caused by war had evolved into a long-term dependence by growers who wanted to expand production of labor-intensive crops. The California tomato industry stood at the top—lobbyists for the California tomato industry regularly made the trip to Washington for hearings and congressional debates over the annual extension of Public Law 78. Growers routinely argued that without Bracero labor, the California tomato crop would be ruined. Even with sufficient domestic labor, which growers claimed Americans refused to do, the Braceros, as they were known, were considered superior workers because they "specialize in 'stoop work'" required for harvesting crops like tomatoes and sugar beets.[10]

Most California growers placed almost all of their faith in continued migrant labor. The idea of a mechanized solution was one most tomato growers thought little of, even as the Bracero Program was increasingly under attack. Beginning in 1961, Public Law 78 had to be renewed annually, where previously it was renewed every two years. In 1961, fewer than 300,000 Braceros were admitted into the country. A year later, fewer than 200,000 were brought in. Finally, after more than twenty years, the Bracero Program officially ended in 1964. Not surprisingly, most growers' interest in the possibilities of mechanical harvesting increased dramatically during the early to mid-1960s, as the Bracero Program was in its final stages. During the 1964 season, California tomato growers relied on the labor of just thirty thousand Mexican workers. The program that enabled the California tomato industry to explode now threatened its existence. Already, many processors were considering relocating to Mexico, where cheap labor could be more easily secured. Processors were forced to offer an incredibly high $35 per ton, $10 higher than the previous season, in order to secure contracts with farmers for the 1965 season. Even then, California farmers planted roughly 25 percent fewer acres of tomatoes (116,000 acres) than in previous seasons.[11]

The end of the Bracero Program did not spell the end of California's reliance on migrant labor. During the 1965 season, despite a significant decrease in acreage planted, the state's employment department could not secure sufficient domestic labor for the tomato harvest. Already in March, Secretary of Labor Willard Wirtz authorized six hundred workers. Once it was clear that there was a huge labor shortage for the tomato harvest, under the threat of high prices and a complete crop failure, Wirtz authorized the entry of eight thousand migrants. By the end of the season, he had authorized 18,400 migrant workers for the tomato harvest. While this number was significantly lower than the 37,000 who worked the tomato harvest in 1964, the last year that the Bracero Program was officially in effect, the state's tomato growers had clearly not rid themselves of their reliance on foreign labor. Not until 1968 could California's tomato industry boast that it had eliminated its need for migrant labor.[12]

By the mid-1960s, just as the Bracero Program was coming to an end, the mechanical tomato harvester appeared. Writing in *Seed World* in 1965, H. B. Peto argued that "in the event that U.S. Public Law 78 is not renewed for one year, the necessity of immediately changing from hand picking of tomatoes for the cannery and other commercial uses to mechanical picking will be imperative." In 1964, an estimated one hundred machines were put to use in California's tomato fields. This number increased to 250 in 1965, harvesting up to half of the state's tomato acreage. By the late 1960s, the labor crisis in the industry was overcome primarily through the introduction of the harvester, as upward of

80 percent of the state's tomato acreage was harvested by machine. However, the tomato industry had little to do with this innovation. Just a few years prior to this, the idea of mechanically harvesting such a fragile fruit as the tomato was dismissed by most as lunacy and the work to achieve such a feat was known and observed by few farmers, processors, and agricultural researchers. The emergence of the tomato harvester took place amid a critical labor shortage; in itself, this is hardly unexpected, but what is surprising is that its development was not a product of market demand but of academic interest in overcoming the many obstacles of harvesting tomatoes mechanically.[13]

THE HARVESTER IN THE GARDEN

While there were numerous early models of the mechanical tomato harvester, the most popular and successful was initiated by scientists and engineers at the University of California, Davis, and produced by Black-welder, a small agricultural firm based in California (figure 5.4). The development of the harvester required a large cast of characters, including Jack Hanna, a breeding specialist; Coby Lorenzen, an engineer; and numerous other researchers who focused on bulk handling, agronomy, and other obstacles to the successful deployment of a tomato harvester. The harvester ultimately solidified California's place as the primary canned tomato producer in the country, and it played a pivotal role in the commodification of the tomato, allowing for an efficient process for producing millions of tons of nearly identical tomatoes to be put up in cans.

Gordie C. Hanna, better known as Jack, was a University of California breeding specialist who in many ways is the father of the mechanical tomato harvester. He became interested in the tomato around 1938 when he was looking for a second crop to work on after his primary crop, asparagus, was done around the beginning of July. Already by 1938, Hanna had started work on developing a mechanical harvester for asparagus, though at this time he had little idea that he would later do the same for tomatoes.[14]

FIGURE 5.4 An early Blackwelder Harvester. "Color Harvester," Blackwelder Manufacturing Company Archives, #D-326, box 34, Department of Special Collections, General Library, University of California, Davis. Reprinted with permission.

The idea for a mechanical harvester of tomatoes, according to Hanna, originated in conversations with his friend and colleague Albert Martin Jongeneel, a California farmer and the inventor of a sugar beet harvester. They met after working together in the asparagus fields when Jongeneel was in charge of Del Monte's asparagus crop in the 1920s. During the early 1940s, their conversations often turned to the labor problems present in the tomato industry, with Jongeneel recalling that "it was impossible, at that time, to see how you would continue to get the labor to pick the big, sloppy tomato." Hanna became interested in the history of labor and agriculture, realizing that especially in California, wave after wave of immigrants and migrants had been responsible for harvesting the vast majority of California's food production. Well before the Bracero Program, then, Hanna understood that continued production of tomatoes would require a new influx of immigrant workers, and he predicted that mechanization eventually would be required to eliminate that need.[15]

Thus from the outset of Hanna's interest in developing a mechanical harvester for tomatoes, in the early 1940s, he was keenly aware of the labor crisis facing the tomato industry and sought a solution to this problem. Yet the development of the mechanical tomato harvester does not fit neatly into the pattern of other agricultural mechanization projects, including the grain harvester. The mechanical tomato harvester came into being with virtually no interest within related agricultural industries. It was instead developed almost entirely within the public sector. The tomato industry put all its faith in the continued existence of the Bracero Program, which gave it the cheap labor it was used to. By 1959, the only outside resources the harvester project had obtained were about $500 from the Tomato Growers Association, a paltry sum for a group representing California's 130,000 acre tomato industry, especially given that it promised to reduce labor costs from about $7.50 a ton to $2.00. Hanna recalled that one of the biggest problems the project confronted was a continual lack of help. In part, he believed, this was because no one believed in the project, including many of his colleagues at Davis. When asked about funding for the project, he replied rather matter-of-factly, "Well I didn't have any funds specified at all for mechanical harvesting. I had a few rows over at the side of the field which I didn't tell anybody about." The project faced a lot of resistance from canners and growers. The harvester, Hanna said,

> was the big joke of the industry for some time, when they learned we were working on the tomato. And then they had labor trouble from time to time and the evolution of their thinking when something like this: "Well, the thing is impossible." Then, after they began talking about it: "Do you think you'll ever get anywhere with it? Well, how are you getting along?" And then: "When are we going to have one?" Finally in 1959, when they had a lot of labor trouble, they said: "Well, we've got to have it! Get off your backside and go to work!"

Even after a working model was completed in the late 1950s, resistance remained among both growers and canners, as the success of the harvester required significant changes in how to produce and process tomatoes.[16]

The fact that Jack Hanna, a plant-breeding specialist, is known as the father of the mechanical tomato harvester underscores an important part of the development of the harvester: its invention required an inordinate amount of cooperation between a variety of agricultural fields. The tomato is radically different from the crops that had been mechanized before it. The tomato is a soft, fragile fruit. In its natural state, the plants often grow on long vines. To prevent the fruit from touching the ground, vines often have to be staked. Significant care was required to avoid damaging the fruit. And perhaps most difficult of all when considering mechanization, in order to maximize yields, numerous pickings of ripe fruit on the same plants had to take place over the course of several weeks or months during the harvest. All of these considerations point to how difficult tomato picking is by hand. While growers' requests for migrant labor were couched in incredibly racist terms, often referring to Mexicans adeptness at the "tiring stooping" that was necessary for pickers, they certainly understood that picking tomatoes was no easy task. In addition to the backbreaking work, it required a skilled hand and eye to spot tomatoes at the proper stage of ripeness and to pick them quickly from the densely packed vines without injuring the plant or other fruits. A machine would have to mimic this highly skilled process. Mechanization would also require a new tomato plant, one that would ripen most fruits at the same time and would be strong enough to not drop its fruits as it was wrenched from the ground. Such a task required the work of specialists in a number of agricultural fields, including breeding and engineering.[17]

In 1949, after Hanna had worked on developing new tomato varieties fit for a mechanical harvester for nearly a decade, agricultural engineer Coby Lorenzen was assigned to work with him. Later, once a prototype was created, many other individuals became involved in the project, including specialists in bulk handling of tomatoes, as well as patenting and marketing specialists. Hanna believed this was one of the first times, if not the first, that such a level of cooperation had been achieved at a university. Combining such a group of specialists was a difficult task, as

Joe Marks later observed in *Nation's Agriculture* when he wrote "to build a tomato harvester, you need the engineering ability of a genius, the horticultural background of Luther Burbank . . . and the patience of Job!"[18]

Hanna was in charge of breeding a tomato variety that could be mechanically harvested, and Lorenzen was tasked with constructing the harvester itself. Each of these was a monumental undertaking, but progress in each area had to happen simultaneously so that adjustments could be made to each side. Hanna recalled that Lorenzen taught him how to think about tomatoes from a mechanical perspective: "I think Coby gave me a concept that I never would have gotten from any horticulturalist or geneticist—the fact that a tomato wasn't necessarily a tomato with him, it was merely an object that had certain physical properties." Hanna's job, then, was to create a tomato plant with those physical properties that could be easily harvested by machine at one time. Lorenzen's task was to create a machine that could take a tomato with those qualities and harvest it successfully. Later, once they had developed a prototype, Mike O'Brien, another agricultural engineer at UC Davis, was tasked with developing a bulk handling and central sorting system for the harvester.[19]

The ideal tomato, Hanna and Lorenzen agreed, would have four key qualities, each quite difficult to obtain. It would ripen uniformly. It would be a smaller plant with fewer tomatoes. The fruit needed to "come off the vine fairly readily," though not too easily or the fruit would fall off as the plant was pulled out of the ground. Finally, the fruit would need to be sturdier than the varieties currently used, as the machine would likely abuse the tomatoes more than hand pickers did. In order for mechanization to work, then, the tomato had to be radically altered, coming to resemble wheat or corn almost as much as a traditional tomato plant. Hanna began his work on the tomato in the early 1940s, but in 1947 did not believe his research had yet produced substantial results. It required generations of crossbreeding and hybridization to get all of these qualities into a single variety. In fact, the breeding work was not completed until the early part of the 1960s.[20]

"Creating" the perfect tomato for mechanical harvesting required an immense amount of tomato germplasm, or genetic material. Hanna utilized preexisting tomato varieties developed at other USDA facilities, most notably at Beltsville, Maryland, and Geneva, New York. Through Hanna's work, Davis became home to one of the largest tomato collections in the world. In one visit to Geneva, New York, he noticed the facility's work on the development of the Red Top tomato, which was a cross between the San Marzano (also a parent of the Roma tomato) and Gem. Each of these plants had just a few tomatoes on them, but they were small plants that grew upright. "As soon as I saw those," he recalled, "I thought well, this is what I'm looking for. I can grow these very thickly and somehow or other we can mow these and shake the fruit off." Hanna had altered the tomato plant to one that emulated a corn stalk or wheat spike. One of the primary varieties he used to develop his harvester varieties was the Red Top. Another crucial development was also the discovery of new wild tomatoes. UC Davis scientist Charlie Rick, who himself started working on tomatoes in 1943, provided some of the most important germplasm. His specialty was the collection of tomato germplasm from South America. On one of his numerous research trips to the Galapagos Islands, he discovered a wild, orange tomato "about the size of a small pea" that was "of the so-called jointless type." Put simply, the jointless characteristic "prevents the fruit from separating readily from the vine." It was this characteristic that allowed Hanna to develop a tomato that would not fall off the vine as the plant was pulled from the ground. By crossbreeding, Hanna was able to isolate this characteristic and eventually insert it into tomato varieties with other useful characteristics.[21]

Hanna started with a tomato with a tough appearance, one that could fall about three feet without breaking. Using the time-honored practice of selection, and the somewhat newer practice of cross-breeding, Hanna, over a period of more than fifteen years, was able to isolate the necessary characteristics and develop a tomato that he felt would stand up to the rigors of mechanical harvesting. In 1959, the "Rube Goldberg," the first prototype, was released. It was successful. Hanna continued work to develop a superior tomato, often utilizing the different planting seasons of the Sacramento and Imperial Valleys to get two plantings in a year. In 1961, a heat wave kept many of his 248 plantings from producing, but he found one variety, line 145, that did well, and he sent some of the seeds to Mexico to be grown through the fall and winter. From Mexico, 200 pounds of the seed were sent back to California, and in the next year, this variety, known as VF145, was distributed to California growers. The VF145 tomato was a determinant variety, meaning it was bushy and grew to about 2.5 feet before stopping its growth. The fruit ripened within about a three-week window, stayed on the vine as the plant was ripped out of the ground, and could stand the beating that mechanical harvesting doled out. To top it off, it was almost entirely coreless, meaning that the plant could be canned whole without the laborious task of cutting out the core. At least by one account, the VF145 was the dominant tomato variety in California as early as 1964. Its dominance of the California canned industry continued into the 1970s, and even today, the VF145 remains in the lineage of a majority of commercial varieties planted.[22]

At the same time that Lorenzen and Hanna were trying to figure out the necessary traits of a mechanically harvestable tomato, they also discussed the mechanical requirements of a working harvester. They both understood, for example, "that we would have to have a system that would be a once-through operation, that we would not be able to build a device that would come along and find a ripe tomato on a vine and leave the vine and pick the tomato." The basic idea behind the harvester was rather straightforward: a harvester would need to pick up the plant, separate the ripe tomatoes from the vine, convey the tomatoes for further sorting and storage, and dispose of the plants and dirt.[23]

Already by 1956, Lorenzen knew the basic processes that the harvester would be able to complete: "As visualized in its final form," Lorenzen wrote in the *American Vegetable Grower*, "the harvesting is a 'once through' process, with the machine performing four principal operations— cutting the root system, lifting the vine, separating the tomatoes from the vine, and conveying the fruit to a container." Many of these lessons were learned after taking a potato digger into the field to see how it would harvest tomatoes. They noticed that it could get the tomatoes off the vine, but it destroyed them in the process. In part, as Lorenzen stated at the time, it was because the potato digger pulled the entire plant out of the ground, mixing big clods of dirt in with the tomatoes.[24]

As they learned from that experiment, the basic mechanics of the harvester they developed by the early 1960s were quite simple:

(a) a cutting device cuts the vines mainstem, preferably at root level; (b) a tine [sharp prong] pickup lifter gently elevates the vine to a shaking device; (c) at the shaking device, rubber-covered walking bar mounted in two sets on crankshafts agitate and advance the vine along the bars. Preferably, the shaking device is novelly constructed to provide a gradually increasing shaking force as the vine moves from one end of the shaker to the other; (d) the vine carried to the end of the shaking device falls to the ground through an open chute; (e) the tomatoes removed by the shaker fall directly onto a specially agitated de-leafing conveyor, which is mounted on an incline moving rearwardly and upwardly; (f) the de-leafing conveyor carries leaves, trash, and dirt up to the open chute where they fall through with the vines; (g) the tomatoes roll down the de-leafing conveyor and are cross-conveyed to sorting belts; (h) the tomatoes are visually sorted by hand at the rear of the machine, as the sorting belts move them rearwardly; (i) the sorted tomatoes are conveyed into bulk bins, preferably located on a trailer being pulled parallel to the harvester; and (j) the packed tomatoes are then hauled away in the bins by trucks.[25]

In 1959, Lorenzen and Hanna had developed an experimental model. Les Heringer, one of the few farmers that followed the progress of the harvester with enthusiasm, invited them to harvest a small section of his crop. While Hanna asked that there not be a large crowd present, they arrived with the experimental model to a crowd of farmers and a few media members. The successes of the trial were reported in major papers throughout the country. The *New York Times* reported that it was being "hailed as foreshadowing a revolution in California's 200 square miles of tomato fields." Its success was all the more important considering it wasn't even on a crop of Hanna's specially designed tomatoes. As a result of this test, the Heringer farm donated $15,000 to help create the first commercial prototype. Also in 1959, Ralph Parks of the USDA called a meeting at UC Davis to seek out companies that wanted to take

part in producing the mechanical harvester. Representatives from a total of eight firms were present, including Blackwelder and "one major
one." According to Roy Bainer, head of the agricultural engineering department, most large companies, including International Harvester and
Massey Ferguson, both of which had facilities nearby, were simply not
interested. Robert Underhill, an administrator who worked on applying
for the patents, also sought out larger companies to no avail. Even after
a successful demonstration of the harvester, these large companies, according to Bainer, simply couldn't see a big enough market for mechanization in an industry long dominated by access to cheap labor.[26]

Out of this group, only Blackwelder, a small agricultural firm, expressed interest in working with UC Davis on the harvester. By 1960, after working out an exclusive license agreement with the university, which
at this time had already proceeded with patent applications, Blackwelder
began work on the first prototype (figure 5.5). In 1961 Blackwelder produced a total of twenty-five machines, all sold under commitments for
$15,000 each. For several years, Blackwelder focused on fixing some of
the problems in the original model and didn't produce any additional
machines until 1964. But as the completion of their first generation of
changes coincided with the end of the Bracero Program, orders soon began pouring in. In 1965, the first year that the Bracero Program was to
end in California, roughly 29 percent of the tomato harvest was done
by machine. In 1967, this had ballooned to 80 percent. A year later, in
1968, roughly 90 percent of the harvest was done with mechanical
harvesters.[27]

The tomato harvester had tremendous effects on California agriculture. The most notable was a dramatic decrease in tomato farms. Many
farmers, unable to justify purchasing a harvester, simply dropped out.
Mechanization encouraged increased tomato acreage per farm: a harvester could pick at least one hundred acres per season, and as earlier
tomato varieties were produced, this number was quickly increased to
close to two hundred acres. Since tomato farmers also needed additional
equipment to complete the harvest, including trucks to transport the
tomatoes from the field, a total of three hundred acres was generally accepted in the early 1960s as a minimum amount to justify mechanization. Small-time farmers often chose to abandon tomatoes rather than

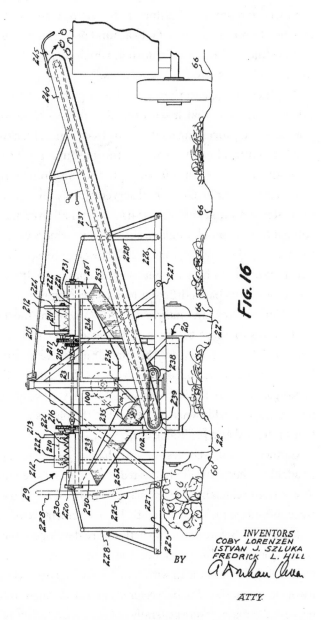

FIG. 16

INVENTORS
COBY LORENZEN
ISTVAN J. SZLUKA
FREDRICK L. HILL

BY

ATTY.

FIGURE 5.5 Drawing of original University of California Blackwelder Harvester, ca. 1960. Coby Lorenzen, Frederick L. Hill, and Istvan Szluka, Tomato Harvester, U.S. Patent #3199604a, filed Sept. 28, 1960, and issued Aug. 10, 1965.

expand their operations, especially since many of them, along with Heinz, Campbell's, and other processors, believed that the future of tomatoes could well be in Mexico. In the early 1960s, roughly 2,200 farms produced tomatoes in California. By the mid-1970s, this number had dropped by almost 75 percent, to around 600. This far outpaced the general decline in farms in California, which during the same period fell from roughly 105,000 to 55,000 farms.[28]

Another obstacle to the successful implementation of the mechanical harvester was that it required significant changes in agricultural practices and processing facilities. Indeed, Ernest Blackwelder observed that "the cultural practices were almost as important as the tomato variety and machine" in affecting production. John Lingle, writing in *American Vegetable Grower*, observed that "every grower who buys a harvester soon finds he must learn to farm all over again." In order to combat this potential problem, since many farmers were highly resistant to changing the way they farmed, Blackwelder released a variety of manuals that outlined how farmers should change their practices. Each of the six manuals had a different focus, covering topics like fertilization, irrigation, sorting, and harvest timing. One of the most difficult things for farmers to adapt to was how to decide when to harvest, since the once-over harvest used by the machine was very different from the farmers' old practice of sending workers through the fields for several pickings. Farmers initially resisted, but they eventually accepted that harvesting the fields when 80 percent of the plants were ripe would lead to a successful and profitable crop.[29]

Canneries, too, were resistant to changing their production practices to adapt to mechanically harvested tomatoes. At the outset, many canneries were reluctant to even accept mechanically harvested tomatoes since they often included a slightly higher percentage of culls than handpicked crops. Before earlier varieties were developed, mechanically harvested tomatoes also shortened the canning season. All the tomatoes from a single area came in within just a week or two, straining the capacity of the canneries. The harvester also created other problems. Machine harvested tomatoes were generally not sorted as effectively as handpicked, which necessitated increased sorting at the factory. Additionally, because the harvester kicked up more dirt and other particles, machine-harvested tomatoes needed to be cleaned more thoroughly and quickly than their handpicked counterparts. All of these steps threatened to create bottlenecks in the canneries, potentially decreasing operating efficiency. The mass production of tomato paste helped solve this bottleneck because it allowed canneries to devote most of their operations to quickly producing a concentrated product rather than have separate processes for producing many tomato products during the harvest season.[30]

At the same time that many farm operators were being chased off their land, the labor needs of tomato farms were drastically reduced, by roughly 80 percent. In the early 1960s, California's tomato harvest required around 100,000 workers, both foreign and domestic. By the late 1960s and 1970s, as few as 25,000 workers completed a much larger harvest. These were almost entirely domestic employees, many part-time, and many women.[31]

As dramatic as the changes in California were, the development of the mechanical harvester had an even more profound effect on the rest of the nation's producers of processed tomatoes, particularly as they lacked flat fields, large farms, and a dry environment, all qualities necessary to adopt the tomato harvester. Already struggling with labor shortages, droughts, blight, and suburbanization, states' canned tomato industries could not compete without the harvester. In the late 1950s, researchers at Michigan State, Cornell, and Purdue Universities all started investigating the prospects of tomato harvesters. Bill Stout, a Michigan State agricultural engineer even invented a model. But successful implementation of the harvester was confined mostly to California. Not only did the harvester require flat fields and large farms, both of which were less common in many tomato-growing states, but also a dry, even arid, environment, where irrigation largely replaced rain as a source of water. The harvester could not run on wet fields, as it would get stuck, and sorting tomatoes harvested from wet fields was a nightmare. With once-over picking, each crop of tomatoes had a short window of time that it could be harvested. Thus a single hard rain could potentially ruin the harvest of an entire field of tomatoes. In the much wetter Midwest and Mid-Atlantic, farmers simply could not take the risk of paying the cost of mechanization and then not being able to use it. As the Purdue Experiment Station director N. J. Volk argued, "the big cost in the tomato is picking it. And if we can't use a machine, we can't compete." California's stake in the nation's canned tomato supply rose from around 60 percent in the early 1960s to closer to 75–85 percent in the mid- to late 1970s. By the early 2000s, California planted around 75 percent of the nation's entire tomato harvest, processed and fresh. Already before the harvester, California was a dominant force in the canning industry, but the mechanical harvester solidified the state's position as the near-exclusive producer of processing tomatoes in the country.[32]

THE FRESH TOMATO

As in previous decades, Florida growers relied on their ability to produce fresh tomatoes for out-of-season use. Unlike California growers, however, who were able to undercut their competitors through mechanization and rationalization, Florida producers faced stiff competition from Mexican and Caribbean imports. Attempts to mechanize Florida production were limited, so Florida growers undertook a campaign to minimize the effects of cheaper Mexican tomatoes politically. At the end of the twentieth century, the Florida tomato industry continued to provide American consumers with a year-round supply of the crimson fruit. Yet these tomatoes were heavily criticized for being of poor quality, taste, and texture. Efforts made during the 1980s and 1990s to counteract the poor reputation of many fresh tomatoes by developing a genetically modified tomato stalled as well, as researchers were unable to profitably create a higher-quality, longer shelf-life tomato suitable for widespread distribution.

In 1960, as the Cold War raged, Florida tomato growers accused the Castro regime of dumping cheap tomatoes on the American markets just as they were starting their harvest. These growers, in a foreshadowing of later battles with Mexican producers, demanded action to restrict the flow of these tomatoes. Florida senator George Smathers made at least three attempts in four months to get the State Department to do something about the Cuban tomato problem. In the end, Florida growers were forced to begin mechanizing production in order to reduce labor costs. Though they could not turn to a fully mechanized solution, as the tomatoes were too fragile to be harvested by machine without making them unsellable for fresh market, they created massive "factories in the field" to make sorting and harvesting more efficient. Trucks with booms that extended as far as 165 feet drove slowly through the fields. Large work crews picked the tomatoes and placed them on conveyor belts, where they were sorted, packed, and stored (figures 5.6–5.7). These machines could not eliminate the need for large amounts of labor, as large work crews still harvested the tomatoes by hand, but they could increase the speed of production and sorting, at least reducing some of the labor costs.[33]

Over time, Mexican tomatoes emerged as the primary source of competition with Florida tomatoes, and Florida producers saw these imported tomatoes as a threat to their very existence. Throughout the 1940s, Mexican agricultural imports boomed. During the 1945–1946 season, for example, more than $50 million worth of goods traveled through Nogales, Arizona, from Mexico. In the season that followed, this number rose to more than $75 million. Tomato imports increased from 103 million pounds in 1956–1957 to 386 million pounds in 1967. By the late 1960s, Florida producers believed that without legal protection, the Florida tomato industry would be wiped off the map. On January 8, 1969, the USDA implemented new minimum-size standards on fresh market tomatoes that had the result of excluding a large percentage of Mexican tomatoes from American markets. These standards, drawn up by the Florida Tomato Committee, a group representing the interests of Florida producers, created an uproar in the press, and strained already poor relations between the United States and Latin American countries.[34]

The restrictions seem rather innocuous, as they limited acceptable sizes of fresh and fresh-green tomatoes, and they applied equally to domestic and imported tomatoes. Yet the intention behind the policy was to cut imports of Mexican tomatoes by establishing standards for fresh-ripe tomatoes that would eliminate much of Mexico's crop and ones for

FIGURES 5.6 AND 5.7 A Florida-style tomato harvesting setup. UPI photo, reprinted in "Tomato Picking Becomes a Vast Production," *Chicago Daily Tribune*, Aug. 23, 1957.

fresh-green tomatoes (which would later be gassed with ethylene to be "ripened"), Florida's specialty, that kept as many in the market as possible. Tomatoes picked green had to be at least 2 9/32 inches in diameter, while those picked ripe were required to be considerably larger, 2 17/32 inches. From the Florida producers' point of view, these regulations proved highly effective. Immediately, more than 30 percent of Mexico's tomato crop was affected, with that number expected to reach as high as 50 percent within a few months. Only 15–20 percent of Florida tomatoes were expected to be unsellable. The immediate result was three-fold: First, Florida tomatoes would have a much higher market share. Second, fresh tomato prices rose as much as 30 percent. Consumers would foot the bill for protecting Florida's tomato industry. Third, these standards threatened the viability of the Mexican tomato industry, which the United States had encouraged for decades. The United States, always eager to foster new trade ties, pushed the growth of the tomato industry in Mexico both by lending the nation agricultural experts and by persuading Mexican farmers to buy American agricultural equipment.[35]

The results of these new anti-Mexican policies were immediate. By March 1969, almost 15,000 of the 100,000 workers who picked tomatoes in Sinaloa and Sonora, the primary tomato-producing states in Mexico, had been laid off. Mexican farmers were enraged. Raul Batiz, a farmer and president of the 20,000 member Confederation of Agriculture Associations of Sinaloa, argued that "the U.S. encouraged us to grow a big crop, using machinery bought in the U.S., and now they're trying to keep us from selling it." Since the 1920s, Mexican growers had been persuaded by U.S. interests to increase their tomato production. These efforts were led by periodic visits by American agricultural experts and spurred by American investment that helped fund a large irrigation project that opened up hundreds of new acres to tomato cultivation in Sinaloa. These efforts had helped nearly quadruple Mexican tomato production in a mere decade. Yet the goodwill fostered by these actions was actively undermined by the new tomato policies. As the *Wall Street Journal* noted, the new rules were being perceived by many in Latin America as another attack on Latin American interests and threatened to worsen "already shaky relations" between the United States and its southern neighbors. One editorial argued that after prohibiting Braceros from entering the United States, this was a second U.S. attack regarding tomatoes.[36]

Most observers rejected Florida growers' attempts to explain why such regulations were necessary. Jack Peters, manager of the Florida Tomato Committee, argued that "if the restrictions were removed, we would have a demoralized, chaotic market in the U.S. within a week. . . . What we're doing is good for the entire industry, in Florida and in Mexico." The *Wall Street Journal* rejected this explanation, arguing that "because tomatoes are sold by the pound, not the dozen, a difference of 1/32 inch or so is of little concern." The editors continued, "the rules discriminate against tomatoes grown in Mexico and in favor of those produced in Florida." The *New York Times* noted that these restrictions were a direct response to the previous season, when Florida tomatoes were undercut by a market glutted with Mexican tomatoes, leading many Florida growers to dump their crops in abandoned lots and fields. William Rose, writing for the *Chicago Tribune*, likened the new rules to "cut[ting] [Mexican growers] off at the vine and let[ting] them rot just like their tomatoes."[37]

And as these observers frequently noted, the end result was a net loss for consumers. Not only did this policy result in many consumers only having access to lower quality Florida tomatoes, but they now would pay substantially more for them. One consumer wrote in to the *New York Times* and argued that the tomatoes available in the New York City area, almost all from Florida, "dropped to an all-time low in quality and climbed to an all-time high in price." When traveling in the West, he argued, he found Mexican tomatoes to be both cheaper and better. His conclusion: "I believe the end loser in this tug of war and attempt to protect the Florida tomato growers is the consumer, and this hardly seems justified."[38]

Florida's attempt to limit Mexican imports was ultimately defeated. A federal judge in Dallas issued a restraining order on the USDA's restrictions, effectively eliminating them. Despite this defeat, the Florida tomato industry has continued its strategy of appealing to the USDA and the State Department to protect its interests against Mexican tomatoes.

The implementation of NAFTA in 1994 threatened Florida producers yet again, and the industry has spent much of the last twenty years trying to find ways to protect itself against increasing supplies of Mexican tomatoes. In 1996, Florida growers fought for, and won, a deal that set a minimum price for imported tomatoes. In more recent years, Florida growers abandoned support for this agreement, as they determined that the minimum prices set in it were much lower than Mexican costs of production. In 2012, again focusing on eliminating competition rather than increasing the quality of tomatoes, fears of a trade war led to a new agreement that raised minimum prices substantially on several types of tomatoes, including an increase from 21 to 31 cents a pound for basic winter tomatoes and even higher prices on greenhouse and other specialty tomatoes. Unlike the canning industry, which faced less foreign competition, the fresh tomato industry in the United States has relied on lobbying to protect its crops from price undercutting by cheap foreign producers.[39]

PLAYING GOD: THE FLAVR SAVR TOMATO

As the quality of fresh tomatoes languished through the 1970s and 1980s, new breakthroughs in gene-altering technology seemed to promise the possibility of higher-quality out-of-season tomatoes. The field of biotechnology had advanced significantly, and scientists were hopeful that they could soon begin to bioengineer new and better crop varieties by altering plants' DNA. As scientists at Monsanto and elsewhere began research on making corn, soy, and other plants resistant to herbicides or to produce their own pesticide, Calgene, a small biotechnology company located just down the road from the University of California, Davis, had a completely different plan. It would create the world's first genetically modified tomato, eventually dubbed the Flavr Savr. Calgene's goal was to produce a tomato that would stay firm enough to be vine-ripened and still be transported to distant markets. This breakthrough would not just benefit the Florida industry; scientists hoped to develop varieties suitable for cultivation anywhere, producing a higher-quality year-round supply of fresh tomatoes. Unlike efforts to protect the Florida tomato industry, the Flavr Savr project attempted to address a persistent demand: a USDA study in the 1990s found consumers ranking the tomato the least satisfactory of thirty-one vegetables available. The problem was that the supermarket tomato was picked green, flavorless, and hard. Ethylene gas was used to turn the tomatoes red (at least on the outside), but it did little to change the inadequate flavor and texture of tomatoes. Calgene's hope was that its GMO tomato would have "that back-yard flavor" and "summertime taste" by keeping it on the vine until the ripening process had begun. In short, Calgene's goal was to make the ultimate twelve-month tomato.[40]

The origins of the Flavr Savr date back as far as 1985, but by 1988, it had become one of Calgene's top priorities. To develop the Flavr Savr, Calgene scientists, led by Bill Hiatt, isolated a gene that released an enzyme (polygalacturonase, or PG for short) that was part of the ripening process. Scientists soon discovered that when the gene was re-inserted backward and upside down it blocked the release of the PG enzyme and thus slowed down the rotting of the fruit. This discovery contained a marketable bombshell. As a former Calgene scientist reported, company scientists and executives were optimistic that if their genetically modified tomato stayed "firmer than their nonengineered counterparts during the ripening process, then they could be picked 'vine ripe' and still survive shipment to market."[41]

Calgene faced numerous obstacles in developing the Flavr Savr tomato. First was competition from other groups, including scientists at both UC Davis and the University of Nottingham. In order to protect their progress, Bill Hiatt and his Calgene team hurriedly filed patent number 4,801,540, "PG Gene and Its Use in Plants," on January 2, 1987 (it was approved in 1989). A second obstacle was the unclear regulatory process for genetically modified foods. As no genetically modified whole foods had yet been released on the market, there were no clear standards for how they were regulated by the FDA and USDA. Despite having no legal requirement to do so, Calgene CEO Roger Salquist saw FDA and USDA approval as a crucial step in overcoming potential public resistance to GMOs and an important good faith effort on the part of the biotech industry. Within a year of filing for the patent, Calgene began preparations for seeking USDA approval for the Flavr Savr tomato.[42]

A third, and relatively minor, obstacle facing Calgene was growing concern among consumers about genetically modified foods. After Calgene filed a request for advisory opinion to the FDA in August 1991 (which was later approved on May 18, 1994), the American public submitted few written comments. While most, coming from agricultural companies, scientists, and academics, were positive, a few, led by environmental groups like the Environmental Defense Fund and, especially, Jeremy Rifkin's Pure Food Campaign, expressed concern and cited a need for more research, arguing that there simply was not a public demand for such a product. Instead, Rifkin insisted, the trend was toward organic and natural products. Others were concerned that future biotech products would not be reviewed with the same rigor.[43]

Critics were certainly right that the Flavr Savr tomato set a precedent for future GMOs. The dozens of genetically modified plants already in the pipeline, as well as those yet to be developed, all faced a much less vigorous review process. The FDA's findings on the Flavr Savr tomato became a model for future genetically altered plants—these plants were no longer subject to review, with the developer given the leeway to decide whether the variety should be deemed "generally regarded as safe" (GRAS), which meant that no FDA review would be required. Former Calgene scientist Belinda Mertineau sees this as an inappropriate precedent, especially given that the anti-sensing technology used by Calgene—whereby a preexisting tomato gene was reinserted into the plant (backward and upside down) in an effort to prevent the release of an enzyme a tomato naturally releases—is radically different from most of the GMO offerings available today, where gene modification leads to the release of proteins completely foreign to the plant, and in many cases, the plants themselves are considered pesticides.[44]

A final obstacle, and one that proved fatal to the Flavr Savr tomato, was that it did not adequately fulfill its purpose. It was not a marketable, good-tasting, vine-ripened tomato. From its inception, scientists understood that the Flavr Savr gene reduced (but did not stop) the release of PG into a ripening tomato, but they could not demonstrate that this would prevent ripening tomatoes from getting too soft for efficient long-distance transport. Continued testing, while showing some improvement, nonetheless produced mixed results. Calgene Fresh CEO Danny Lopez was left to admit that the Flavr Savr technology worked "at the back end," preventing the tomato from rotting once it was very ripe, but it did not make the tomato significantly firmer through the early—from green to ripe—stages. When Flavr Savr tomatoes were released in limited quantities in 1994, they flew off the shelves, even though they commanded a premium price of $2 a pound and up (around $0.70 more than other premium tomatoes). Yet because the tomatoes were much more fragile than those picked green, they required increased handling and suffered from high shrinkage. Through 1994, the cost of growing and distributing them was around $10 per pound, $8 more than they were selling for. While these costs were reduced in 1995, they remained well above their selling price.[45]

Despite the increased costs, the Flavr Savr also did not deliver on flavor. Just as other tomato farmers picked their tomatoes green in order to lower shrinkage, Flavr Savr tomatoes were harvested as soon as they developed a hint of color, preventing them from inheriting the "summertime" taste that Calgene was after. Numerous taste tests revealed mixed results. In one held by the San Francisco Chronicle, tasters preferred organically grown tomatoes to the Flavr Savr by a healthy margin. And while the New York Times found the Flavr Savr "plump and juicy," it still concluded that it was "no replacement for the tomatoes of summer."[46]

Calgene continued to market the Flavr Savr tomato until Monsanto acquired the company in January 1997 and eventually removed the product from the market. The Flavr Savr gene increased shelf life by more than a week, but it failed to produce a tomato that could be vine-ripened, and even when picked partially ripe, it required much higher transportation and handling costs due to its fragility. Consumers were willing to pay a premium for Flavr Savr tomatoes, yet many felt that their quality was still lacking. In the end, the cost of producing a higher-quality and longer-lasting tomato was simply too high. The Flavr Savr's failure represents the continued struggle by industry to produce a high-quality fresh tomato. As discussed in the next chapter, the inability to create an industrial fresh tomato with "homegrown" flavor has played a major role in a resurgence of alternative means of producing fresh tomatoes.[47]

THE TOMATO AND FOOD CULTURE

While Florida growers secured their markets with government help and expanded production of fresh tomatoes through partial mechanization, the mechanical harvester had a still greater impact on how tomatoes entered the American diet. Fresh tomatoes remained popular, especially in salads, but the bigger trend during the postwar period was the introduction of a variety of heavily processed goods. The harvester was at the center of this transformation. Not only did it transform production by reducing the need for scarce labor, but it also played an important part in the revolution in food processing and encouraged the proliferation of tomato paste as a raw ingredient in tomato production. After the war, American food habits changed dramatically with the introduction of new convenience foods. Fresh tomatoes and canned whole tomatoes gave up market share to more heavily processed tomato products, including prepackaged tomato sauce and paste, and even prepackaged meals like pizza, canned spaghetti, and many frozen foods. Thus, while the tomato helped lead America into the canning age during the late nineteenth and early twentieth century, it was even more in the vanguard of culinary innovation after 1945.

This was a complex story. To be sure, culinary changes included increased consumption of fresh and frozen vegetables and a more diversified diet. But it also included the use of heavily processed foods. Many Americans ate more vegetables, tried new and interesting ethnic foods, and overall had access to a much wider range of foods at all times of the year. However, they also ate more junk food and other highly processed goods, which over time brought about a deskilling of American cooking, encouraged unhealthy eating trends, and led most Americans to know very little about where their food comes from or how it is made.

Historians have paid particular attention to the rise of certain convenience foods during the late nineteenth and early twentieth centuries, specifically the emergence of ketchup and condensed soup. These products, while important, were only a small part of the food culture of this period. Most housewives continued to rely on traditional cookery with a mix of modern products in the kitchen. Of greater importance in the long term was the revolution in kitchen design and appliances that took place during the first half of the century and reduced the work of home-prepared foods, fostering more elaborate meals. For example, the introduction of new cooktops, both gas and electric, made cooking multiple dishes far easier. Most important, however, were the home refrigerator and freezer, which enabled cooks to keep perishable products longer and to store leftovers. The electric refrigerator was a late introduction to the household appliance industry. It required the invention of new motors and Freon gas to make refrigerators more affordable. By 1937, however, around half of all electrified homes had refrigerators. Between 1929 and 1935, amid the Great Depression, sales actually increased by more than 700 percent. The immediate effect of the technological revolution in the American kitchen was to enable cooks to practice traditional cooking habits more efficiently. By the postwar period, however, these technologies served a new purpose: the introduction of convenience and heat-and-serve meals. While early refrigerators were quite small, with freezers often only large enough for a tray of ice, by 1950 the average refrigerator size had doubled, leaving much more space for prepackaged refrigerated and frozen goods. By 1965, between thirteen and fourteen million American households had purchased standalone freezers. Mountains of advertising and promotion advanced the trend toward convenience foods, and the success of these new foods served the interests of producers. As Paul Willis, president of the Grocery Manufacturers of America, stated in 1962, "The development of new convenience food products serves to increase total consumption of the product category." In the case of tomatoes, he argued that "the introduction of new processed tomato products, along with the growth of existing ones, has helped lift annual consumption from 2,500,000 tons to more than 5,000,000 tons since World War II."[48]

Tomato paste was also a critical ingredient in the development of the new heavily processed foods. This tomato concentrate could be further processed into a wide variety of products, including juice and sauce. The increase in consumption of canned tomato paste and sauce was a long process. In 1924, the first year in which the USDA estimated any consumption of these products, it estimated that the average American consumed a mere fifth of a pound of tomato paste and sauce per year, compared to more than six pounds per person of canned whole tomatoes and twelve pounds of store-bought fresh tomatoes. By 1945, no doubt influenced by the shortage of tin during the war, and the fact that tomato sauce and paste were concentrated and thus material-saving products, consumption of tomato paste and sauce had risen to almost three pounds per person while the consumption of canned whole tomatoes was on the decline. By 1961, the consumption of paste and sauce continued to grow, reaching almost four pounds per person.[49]

Yet much of the tomato paste that was produced was not meant to be sold directly to consumers but was instead used for the production of more heavily processed tomato products. By the 1950s, Heinz revolutionized its production by processing all of its tomatoes into paste immediately after the harvest, storing them in large tanks, and converting the paste into ketchup throughout the year. By the 1960s, Heinz had installed massive 125,000 gallon tanks for tomato paste storage in its Tracy, California, plant. The company also experimented with storing paste in large, 300-gallon flexible aseptic bags and using railroad car tanks to transport them. At the same time, a wide variety of companies introduced preflavored tomato sauces. As early as 1950, one specialty shop in Manhattan began selling ten different sauces imported from Brussels in the "French style." One choice was Sauce Piquante, made with pickles, meat stock and tomato puree. Selling for between $0.90 and $1.25 for a seven-ounce container, these early sauces were definitely for the upper-end market. A few years later, prices began to drop as Macy's offered eight-ounce jars of tomato sauce, flavored with onions, parsley, basil, garlic, and oregano for $0.42. Produced by Charles Olla, an Italian immigrant living in Union City, New Jersey, these jars failed to reach a mass audience, but they set the stage for a major transformation in American cuisine by the 1960s.[50]

At the same time that tomato paste was gaining in popularity as an industrial ingredient, companies such as Del Monte and Hunt's used tomato paste to produce canned and jarred versions of pre-spiced tomato products, including sauces and stewed tomatoes. Del Monte started selling canned tomato sauce around 1945, and by the early 1950s, Hunt's had emerged as a serious competitor. Hunt's hired Ernest Dichter, the well-known consumer pollster and marketing expert, to help market their tomato sauce. Dichter advised the company, which he claimed had "created new users and taken them from [users of] paste, soup and canned tomatoes," to use advertisements to appeal to the creativity and hard work of the cook. Dichter urged Hunt's to make tomato sauce appear as a continuation of the minimally processed tomato products of the first half of the century. Dichter argued that tomato sauce, despite being much more heavily processed, simply made the housewife's cooking duties "easier," and he urged Hunt's to give credit to the cook for both the recipe and the cooking. As he found in numerous other campaigns while working for can-makers and canneries, many American consumers were still reluctant to use canned foods, in large part because homemakers and cooks deemed them a lazy practice. For Dichter, however, consumers simply needed reassurance allowing them to "relax and feel safe that the food company is taking over [their] chores." This trend of new products and sauces was not limited to the canned food industry. Others, such as Lawry's, came out with a spaghetti sauce mix by the mid-1950s, allowing a cook to add a package of seasoning to a can of plain tomato sauce to produce what they deemed to be an acceptable spaghetti sauce.[51]

By the early 1970s, the transformation of the tomato-processing industry was complete: tomato paste had become a dominant enough commodity that beginning in 1971, the New York Cotton Exchange opened the Tomato Products Associates, which traded futures in tomato paste. This signaled the completion of a huge transformation in tomato production, from an industry based on providing consumers with minimally processed tomato products for home cooking to an industry based on giving consumers ready to eat, factory-made meals.[52]

The postwar increase in tomato consumption was also due to new uses of the red fruit, including new products like pizza, and new sites of consumption, including the hamburger joint. As one tomato processor noted, people "are eating a lot of French fries and hamburgers, and what are they putting on French fries and hamburgers? Ketchup. And, they're being introduced to pizza, and what's the basic ingredient of pizza? It's tomatoes."[53]

Although Italian food was already popular among many Americans during the first half of the century, pizza truly became a national staple during the 1950s and 1960s as more Americans experimented with various ethnic foods. Americans of all ethnic backgrounds flocked to Pizzeria Uno in Chicago when it opened in 1943. Within a decade, the *New York Times* suggested that there might be more pizzerias in the United States than in Italy. A few years later, the paper declared that pizza rivaled the hot dog in popularity. In that article, the *Times* reported that a pizza bar in a Manhattan department store attracted thousands of hungry shoppers each week. One of the three offerings, a pizza bagel, suggests that pizza owed some of its popularity to its adaptability and its easy integration into pre-established American cuisine. Soon, several new products offered Americans the ability to make pizza at home. By far the most popular of these was the frozen pizza, for which the first related patent was issued in 1954. In 1950, a New York City baker named Leo Giuffre had opened a factory on Long Island producing refrigerated pizzas that were sold in local shops. After only ten days in business, demand rose to around three thousand pizzas per day. A similar factory opened around the same time in Boston. The frozen pizza industry, which today grosses as much as $1 billion annually, took advantage of two trends present in American cuisine during the 1950s and 1960s: the prevalence of convenience foods and the growing popularity of ethnic foods.[54]

For many Americans, however, their first taste of homemade pizza was with another product introduced during the early 1950s, a dry goods kit. These packages generally came in three parts: a packet containing the flour and other dry ingredients, a second packet containing yeast, and finally, a can of tomato sauce. Consumers could then add cheese and other desired ingredients at home. For many housewives still used to making their own bread, this was a relatively easy introduction to the art of pizza making.[55]

The popularity of the classic American meal of a hamburger and French fries also helped drive tomato consumption. The dramatic rise of the fast food industry and the suburban outdoor cookout popularized tomatoes both as a fresh ingredient—a thick slice of tomato tucked neatly underneath a hamburger bun—and as ketchup both for the burger and the fries. The hamburger, which originated in the late nineteenth century, was already an American institution by the 1920s. In the mid-1920s, for example, White Castle had locations in St. Louis, Omaha, and Kansas City and served more than eighty thousand burgers a year. By 1931, White Castle had more than 130 locations, and by 1935, in the midst of the depression, the company was selling 40 million burgers a year. In addition to numerous other fast food chains, the introduction of the diner helped propel the hamburger's popularity to new heights. As Andrew Smith notes, already by the 1930s, "virtually every medium sized city in America had drive-ins, roadside stands, diners and coffee shops—all of which served hamburgers." Most of these shops did not, however, sell French fries. Already growing, the industry exploded after World War II, and with the introduction of safer frying equipment during the 1950s, burger joints, diners, and the like made possible the widespread consumption of French fries and ketchup. Obviously, the most notable burger restaurant from the 1950s and 1960s was McDonald's, the California-based burger chain bought out by Ray Kroc, who eventually revolutionized the industry and turned the casual fast food diner into a factory. But there were numerous other chains born during this period, including In-N-Out (1948), Jack in the Box (1950), Carl's Jr. (1956), and Tommy's (1946) in California; Burger King (1953) in Florida; Whataburger (1950) in Texas; and Wendy's (1969) in Ohio.[56]

The popularity of the hamburger, French fries, and pizza, along with the successes of the fast food and pizza industries during the postwar period, propelled tomatoes, already one of the country's most popular vegetables, into an important place in American cuisine. Radical changes in both where and how tomatoes were produced enabled the near-complete industrialization and commodification of the tomato by the 1960s. Each year, the fruits of California's tomato fields were transformed into a sea of millions of gallons of crimson tomato paste, which was then transformed again into a wide variety of convenience foods. The changes made the process cheaper and more efficient, but it came at the expense of a homogenization of the American diet. Even where new ethnic foods were introduced, they were quickly and drastically altered to become "Americanized" for mainstream consumption. The American pizza, for example, differs radically from what most Italians eat. Large multinational corporations have swallowed up entire industries, spanning from the field to the shopping cart. A handful of California companies currently control almost all domestic, processed-tomato production, which itself has led to a "hypercompetitive" industry with numerous investigations into corruption, bribery, and price setting. To many observers, American culinary culture (and Americans' health) has been the primary victim of these changes.[57]

Yet there remains a variety of ideas about the tomato's place in our lives. The diverse culture of the first half of the twentieth century was not eliminated with the invention of the mechanical harvester and the rise of tomato-based convenience foods. Despite the growing power of the tomato industry, and individual companies within it, individual consumers and gardeners continue to influence how the tomato is grown, prepared, and consumed. From the cooperative movements of the 1960s to the organic, "natural" movements of today, alternative views of the tomato have taken shape, and many remain popular. These views, and their effects on tomato production, consumption, and American culinary culture, are the subject of the next chapter.

6

MEET THE FARMER
OR BECOME ONE

Challenging Commercial Food Culture

The efforts to industrialize the tomato industry during the postwar period were largely successful. Beginning in the early twentieth century and continuing through the postwar era, significant efforts were made to mechanize agricultural production, increase yields through expanded chemical use, and create a national food economy with the emergence of a national network of interstate highways and the subsequent development of the long-haul trucking industry. While sometimes facing significant opposition, America's agricultural and food-processing industries, including those for both fresh and processed tomatoes, by the 1970s were highly centralized, efficient enterprises, increasingly able to shape and control American food. Yet the culture of the tomato, and American food culture in general, remains diverse, and while corporate ideas of food rank among the most persuasive, other competing views of American food remain prominent among American consumers. In order to understand recent changes in the uses and meanings of the tomato, we need to consider more generally these competing concepts of what food means.

Two of these alternative approaches, farmers' markets and home gardening, are counterpoints to the claim that American food culture is an entirely corporate vision. Other examples could be mentioned as well—the slow food movement, the growing popularity of street carts and food trucks, community supported agriculture (CSA) programs, and numerous others. But several things stand out in these two examples. First, both farmers' markets and home gardening directly address a critical question that arises in contemporary times: where does our food come from? And both challenge the corporate answer (anywhere it is profitable) with their own (nearby and if possible under our control). In each case, a growing number of consumers demand increased knowledge of the origins of their food and participation in the production of the food they consume. And both entail a rejection of the tasteless "anonymous" corporate tomato.

Second, despite shared values, both home gardening and farmers' markets attract a diverse group of people: there are few restraints on who can be a gardener or a farmers' market consumer—poor or affluent, rural or urban, liberal or conservative—both farmers' markets and home gardening are popular with wide segments of the population, and both thus represent in themselves many different ideas about food, how it should be grown, and how it should be consumed. Third, each of these examples has an important communal element to it—farmers' markets are indeed communal spaces, where conversation and the exchange of ideas are often encouraged. Farmers' markets, in the words of T. A. Lyson, "provide opportunities for producers and consumers to come together to solidify bonds of local identity and solidarity." But home gardening, too, carries with it important social elements that help further the exchange of ideas about gardening and food in general. These ideas are communicated and formed differently than corporate ideas of food are—which is to say they are rarely advertised and always up for debate.[1]

Finally, while there is no guarantee that either farmers' markets or gardeners ultimately will produce radically different foods than commercial agriculture, both represent a rejection of the century-long quest to transcend the seasonality of the tomato, and of food more broadly. Farmers' markets routinely report consumers asking for foods out of season, and gardeners still try to produce foods for as long a season as possible, obvious signs that modern Americans still want to transcend the seasonality of fresh food. These alternatives point to willingness, on the part of at least some, to abandon the notion that you can have food "your way" and opt instead for returning to nature's clock. While neither farmers' markets nor home gardening represents a potential replacement of commercial agriculture and commercialized food, they nonetheless provide environments for meaningful resistance to dominant ideas about food production and consumption.[2]

Farmers' markets and home gardening are alternative iterations of food culture that at least at times run counter to the dominant idea of food espoused by major food companies and often encouraged by government policies. These two examples serve as a reminder of the limits of corporate and government influence, forces historian Harvey Levenstein has misleadingly argued had already "standardized" American culinary culture by the 1930s. Contesting Levenstein have been scholars like Warren Belasco, who has documented challenges to the dominant food culture from the 1960s onward. Belasco stresses the countercultural roots of alternative food movements and their difficulties "struggling alone against the tide." While Belasco outlines numerous ways the counterculture and other progressive groups challenged food companies and helped increase concern among American consumers over food health and safety, home gardening and farmers' markets included not only 1960s critics of the American mainstream but actually included many from mainstream society, crossing ideological boundaries. Just as Adam Rome places much of the impetus for environmental concern in the postwar suburbs, much of the interest in home gardening arose from the backyard garden plot. Interest in both home gardening and farmers' markets remains an organic and democratic activity—from hippies in Berkeley's People's Park and recent immigrants to Brooklyn to suburban moms and dads, many of whom were members of Nixon's so-called silent majority—these activities provide diverse, often competing, groups the opportunity to seek out and practice their own ideas about food. By influencing millions of Americans to find other means of acquiring and preparing their food, both alternatives challenge the power and influence of industrial food.[3]

Most important, by viewing both home gardening and farmers' markets as significant players in the continual development of American food culture, we correct a common perception—that of the increasing passivity of the American consumer. In recent decades, scholars often have viewed American food and consumer culture with significant pessimism, and on occasion disdain. The primary concern has been on the growing power of commerce in American life: the individualizing effects of mass consumption, the ability of advertising and marketing to influence consumer behavior, and the impact of centralized production and processing on limiting consumer options. Home gardening and farmers' markets, however, demonstrate that despite the growing power of commercial culture over the course of the twentieth century, serious alternatives continue to exist. At the root of these alternatives is a demand for increased knowledge of where our food comes from and a desire on the part of consumers to play a more significant role in the productive process. This broad objective challenges the common dichotomy between the active producer and the passive consumer that is at the root of most characterizations of modern consumer society.[4]

The tremendous growth in popularity of farmers' markets and home gardening, however, needs to be tempered with the reality that it remains miniscule in economic terms compared to commercial agriculture. According to Eric Berrenson, perhaps 1 percent of all produce in California is purchased at farmers' markets despite California ranking among the most popular states for direct marketing of food. A multitude of economic and bureaucratic barriers continue to dissuade institutions—including colleges, hospitals, and other large buyers of food—from purchasing directly from local food producers. Despite the upsurge in home gardening over the previous several decades, most gardeners produce only a small portion of their household food needs. Yet they do represent continued resistance to and growing discontent with commercial agriculture and the dominant food culture.[5]

POPULARITY OF FARMERS' MARKETS AND HOME GARDENING, 1945–PRESENT

The rise of farmers' markets and home gardening is a complex, even surprising, story given the economic forces that drove the food industry. In fact, during the decades following World War II, both farmers' markets and home gardening went into decline. Farmers' markets began their decline as early as the 1930s, as the Great Depression wreaked havoc on small farmers throughout the country. Providing an accurate count of farmers' markets in the United States over time is a difficult task. Numerous scholars have attempted to complete such a project, but with varying definitions of what a farmers' market is and with inadequate regulations and reporting of farmers' market activity, providing an accurate count of farmers' markets has proven illusory. Nevertheless, scholars agree that the postwar period saw a continued decline in farmers' markets, as the dual forces of suburbanization and centralization of agriculture formed serious impediments to the existing local market tradition in the United States. Resellers rather than farmers most often populated urban markets that survived, hawking goods bought on the wholesale market, often produced hundreds, if not thousands, of miles away.[6]

The tenuous position of farmers' markets in the 1950s and 1960s represents more than a half-century of "progress" in American agriculture, fueled by the forces of economic and geographic centralization. As historian Jane Pyle noted rather pessimistically in her 1971 "Farmers' Markets in the United States: Functional Anachronisms": "A prescient person of the 1890's could have foreseen that the public market was doomed by a changing society. The railroads connected eastern population centers with distant open lands, where favorable climate and cheap labor joined forces to stock the urban larder." Where the steam locomotive sounded the death knell for many local agricultural economies in the late nineteenth century, during the middle of the twentieth century, as Shane Hamilton has argued, a wave of centralized distribution was made possible by the emergence of the trucking industry and the interstate highway system. New agricultural technologies and large government-funded irrigation projects in the western United States threatened the existence of local and regional foodways.[7]

Unlike farmers' markets, home gardening remained popular throughout World War II, but by the late 1940s, and continuing at least through the 1960s, it, too, declined. In 1950, for example, agricultural experts reported that Rockland County, New York, home to around nine thousand Victory Gardens during World War II, had seen a 40 percent decline in home gardens and a 50 percent decrease in garden size. A look at popular gardening magazines such as *Better Homes and Gardens* indicates a much greater interest in lawn care and other yard beautification rather than home food production during the 1950s and 1960s. Even as Secretary of Agriculture Charles F. Brannan announced the establishment of the "Liberty Gardens" program in 1951, which focused on maintaining the popularity of vegetable and fruit gardens, a survey found that only 6.9 percent of New York City residents, and just over 30 percent of New York suburban and rural residents, planted gardens. Flower gardening, however, saw an uptick, with over 20 percent of New York City residents, and more than 65 percent of suburban and rural residents, practicing some form of flower growing.[8]

Ironically, then, just as many Americans escaped the cities for the suburbs, giving them more space to garden, vegetable gardening became less common. Already by the 1950s and 1960s, as Gary Cross notes, much of the American workforce was sold on the idea of working longer hours as a tradeoff for higher wages and thus fuller participation in the emerging consumer culture (including entry into suburbia itself). This tradeoff, for many, left little time for home gardening. Consumer culture, with products like frozen TV dinners, Spam, and Campbell's Soup, was designed around the appeals of convenience. Suburbanization, too, has been linked with a desire to construct the home as a purely domestic space, physically separated from the productive sphere. And, as often observed in the many critiques of postwar suburbia, new home owners were more interested in displaying and meeting middle-class standards (growing the "perfect" lawn or holding backyard patio barbeques) to find time for the rigors of gardening. Finally, the rise of the automobile and the interstate highway system made long summer vacations accessible for the vast majority of American suburbanites. With significant stretches of the summer spent away from home, it was harder for people to provide the constant maintenance gardens required throughout the growing season. For many Americans still interested in outdoor life and growing plants, the result was increased attention on domestic activities like lawn care and flower gardens at the expense of home vegetable gardening.[9]

Yet the early 1970s provided an impetus for the revival of both the farmers' market and home vegetable gardening. It was at this time that a host of new concerns and values came together to lead many Americans to look for new means of food acquisition. A widely recognized motivation for many Americans was a rejection of the "artificial." Many in the counterculture, along with other groups, while having practical concerns regarding health and the environment, also had serious ideological conflicts with an emerging American society that, in their view, was based on conformity and standardization. From Stewart Brand's *Whole Earth Catalog* to Andy Warhol's Campbell's Soup cans, cultural critics used food as a means to comment on American society more broadly. These critiques, as Warren Belasco has argued, led to significant battles over food. Home gardening and farmers' markets were two grounds on which such battles were fought. Environmental alarm was at an all time high. Beginning with Rachel Carson's *Silent Spring* (1962) and a wave of environmental legislation during the late 1960s that culminated in 1970 with Richard Nixon's establishment of the Environmental Protection Agency, Americans across the board became concerned with environmental issues, including pesticide, insecticide and fertilizer use in food production. A second popular worry was the rising price of fresh produce. Inflation initially brought on by the Vietnam War became a full-on recession by the early 1970s as OPEC members declared an oil embargo. The energy crisis shocked an already unstable economy: unemployment rose from just under five percent in 1973 to a postwar high of 8.5 percent in 1975. From 1972 to 1973, food prices spiked across the board, with the price of eggs increasing almost 50 percent, poultry 40 percent, meat 25 percent, and fresh vegetables 18 percent.[10]

These conditions created an opening for farmers' interest in direct marketing and in new efforts for home food production. During the late 1960s and early 1970s, farmers' markets made a remarkable comeback, fueled less by radical elements than by mainstream Americans. In no small part, this was because farmers' markets stood in stark contrast to the industrial model of centralization and long-distance food networks that had become dominant by the 1960s. Passage of the Farmer-to-Consumer Direct Marketing Act in 1976 lent legitimacy to a revival in direct marketing efforts by farmers. By 1979, just three years after legislation allowed farmers' markets to become "certified" by proving their products were being sold direct by farmers, twenty-four certified farmers' markets had popped up across the state of California. Also, nearly four hundred farms in California allowed consumers to come to the farm and "pick your own" fruits and vegetables. Elsewhere the growth was equally remarkable. In the 1970s there were twenty markets in the state of New York. By 1985, in no small part due to the success of New York City's Greenmarket program, this number had swelled to more than 115. In 1979, New York City's Greenmarkets, a coordinated effort by the city's Council on the Environment, operated eight locations and did a total of $1 million in sales. This program expanded to eighteen locations in 1985, where more than 130 farmers provided fresh food to customers at Union Square, across the street from the World Trade Center, and in neighborhoods across the five boroughs. In 2006, this number rose to forty-five when ten new Greenmarkets opened, a single-year record. Many years the city actually has difficulty finding enough farmers to fill all of the locations as demand for fresh produce outpaces the ability of local and regional farmers to supply it. Connecticut also saw a substantial increase in farmers' markets during the 1970s and 1980s. Between 1981 and 1985, the number of farmers' markets there rose from seventeen to twenty-eight. As these markets opened to the public, they were often met with great fanfare. When a farmers' market opened in Burbank, California, in 1983, for example, more than two thousand consumers showed up on the first day, more than 50 percent above expectations. The revival of farmers' markets, particularly in California and the Northeast, led many supermarkets to try to compete by creating a farmers' market–like atmosphere in their stores, replacing the sterile metal shelving with wooden crates and creating outdoor open-air festivals during the harvest months.[11]

High food prices coupled with rising gas prices that kept many families from taking yearly summer vacations also gave Americans a greater incentive to garden. Already by 1971, W. Atlee Burpee and Co., one of the nation's largest seed houses, reported greatly increasing sales, many outlets reporting between 25 and 50 percent increases in seed sales from the previous year. Greenhouses across the country experienced record sales, as well; one nursery in New York City, the Farm and Garden Nursery, had its highest sales in its 35 years of operation in 1971, even higher than during the Victory Garden years. In 1972, an estimated 42 percent, or 28 million households, had a vegetable garden. By 1973, 46 percent, or 31 million households, planted vegetable gardens. In the same year, Americans spent an estimated $100 million on seeds alone (though not specifically on vegetable seeds). Seed companies were largely unprepared for the dramatic increase in sales. Many ran out of catalogs to distribute, and seeds flew off of shelves faster than they could be restocked. The growing trend was recognized by the USDA, which devoted its 1977 *Yearbook of Agriculture* entirely to the topic of home gardening.[12]

The popularity of both farmers' markets and home vegetable gardening outlived the contentious period in which they became popular. Both of these alternatives to the corporate tomato have increasingly drawn interest from diverse segments of the American population. In the case of farmers' markets, they have enjoyed a continuous increase in popularity from their roots in the 1970s through today, where according to Cheryl Brown and Stacy Miller, they have become the "historical flagship of local food systems." From around 340 farmers' markets in 1970, by 1994, the USDA counted 1,775 farmers' markets operating nationwide. In 2006, this number had grown to 4,385, a 247 percent increase in twelve years. Likewise, total sales at farmers' markets continue to grow: in 2000, the USDA estimated total sales at farmers' markets at $888 million; by 2009, this number had risen to over $1 billion. As a whole, direct marketing to consumers has expanded on all fronts, including farmers' markets, farm stands, and community supported agriculture programs. From their formal beginnings in the 1980s when only a handful of successful CSAs, by 2006 there were more than 1,100 CSAs operating throughout the United States, providing consumers with local, fresh produce. On the whole, demand for locally grown food continues to intensify. In 2009, the USDA estimated that total direct-to-consumer sales totaled $1.2 billion. The USDA further estimates that farmers do a total of $4.8 billion in sales of locally grown foods using both direct-to-consumer methods and "intermediated marketing channels" including supermarkets, regional distributors, and direct sales to restaurants.[13]

In addition to the difficulties in accurately counting farmers' markets, defining their total economic importance and effect on American food culture has also been met with great challenges. Farmers' markets and other direct-sales methods are often seen as skirting the line between formal and informal economies, where full-time, part-time, and non-farmers often participate in producing and selling products. With thousands of farmers' markets across the United States and many thousands more farm stands and ad hoc markets, complete record keeping has proved an illusory goal. For their part, the grocery industry has sought to downplay the influence and significance of farmers' markets and other sources of direct marketing by farmers. *Supermarket News* reported in 2012 the findings of a W. K. Kellogg Foundation study, which found that 95 percent of shoppers had bought produce at a supermarket in the last year, and defensively declared that "consumers turn to supermarkets for the majority of their produce purchases" with only "a small percent rel[ying] on alternative retailers . . . for the bulk of their produce." The same report, however, indicated that 14 percent of consumers did the majority of their produce shopping at farmers' markets, a sizable number given the state of farmers' markets just a few decades before.[14]

Academic studies have produced similar results. Marianne McGarry Wolf, Arianne Spittler, and James Ahern found in a 2005 study that 95 percent of consumers had frequented a supermarket in the previous month. The *New York Times*'s Timothy Egan, on the other hand, found that upward of three million Americans purchase produce from farmers' markets each week. Between 1997 and 2002, estimated income to farmers from all forms of direct sales increased from just under $600 million to more than $800 million. Similarly, between 2002 and 2007, these sales increased to $1.2 billion annually. While farmer income from farmers' markets is relatively meager—in 2000, the USDA estimated that 29 percent of farmers earned less than $1,000 per year selling at farmers' markets—total direct sales increased from $5,349 in 1997 to $6,958 per farm in 2002. The direct economic impact of farmers' markets and other forms of direct sales is thus quite small compared to the multibillion dollar commercialized food, yet it is nonetheless a sizable—and growing—factor.[15]

The promise of farmers' markets in the 1970s served as a counter to the food production practices of modern American agriculture, with its focus on mechanization, increased chemical use, and, above all, concentration. In addition to growing consumer demand, farmers also saw direct marketing as a potentially fruitful avenue to pursue. The crisis among small farmers during the second half of the twentieth century is well documented, and this problem did not end abruptly in the 1970s when farmers' markets began their comeback. From 1993 to 2000, for example, 33,000 farms with sales of less than $100,000 stopped operating, with that land either lying fallow or, more often, becoming swallowed up into larger, industrial farms. Yet throughout this period, farmers' markets and other sources of direct sales have proven a vital part of keeping small farmers afloat. In a study conducted in 2007, Alan Hunt reported that 36 percent of farmers surveyed at farmers' markets considered higher profit margins a significant motivator for selling at those markets. In 2000, an estimated 19,000 farmers sold exclusively at farmers' markets, up from 6,648 in 1994. USDA senior marketing representative K. Earl Gordon put it succinctly in 1989 when he wrote, "Farmers markets are a way for smaller farmers to make a living."[16]

Despite the continued tenuous economic position of small-time farming, over the past twenty years there has been an upsurge in non-farmers becoming small-time farmers. Urbanites, often fed up with city living, have returned to the land in large numbers. These farmers are a second generation of back-to-the-landers. While their interests remain in the environment, health, and food quality, they, unlike many earlier ex-urbanites and suburbanites, remain wedded to capitalism, willing to participate in alternative marketplaces in order to provide consumers with better quality, better tasting food. Some, such as Tim Stark, a Pennsylvania farmer who sells mostly tomatoes and hot peppers at the Greenmarket's Union Square location, have become quite well known among food critics, chefs, and consumers. Hundreds, if not thousands, of others operate much more anonymously, including Tracie Sturgis, who bought a farm in Beaver County, Pennsylvania, with her husband in 1989, operating the farm almost entirely on their own and selling their goods at nearby markets. These green farmers have been drawn to farm for a number of reasons, including a desire to return to the land, a love of food, environmental or health concerns, and a desire to make a difference. Their contributions, along with those of already established small farmers, have helped farmers' markets maintain and expand their popularity and have strengthened their appeal as an alternative to modern industrial agriculture.[17]

The growth in vegetable gardening, likewise, extended through the 1970s, and continued at least into the mid-1980s. A Gallup poll indicated that 47 percent of American households had a vegetable garden in 1981. Overall, as one *Christian Science Monitor* reporter extolled, more Americans were planting vegetable gardens than were watching professional sports on TV. In 1983, a poll produced for the National Gardening Association reported that 42 percent of American households had some form of vegetable garden. In 1985, home gardeners produced an estimated $9.2 billion worth of homegrown vegetables. By 1987, with improved economic conditions, the number of households estimated to have vegetable gardens dropped off to 33 percent, yet farm and garden centers reported a 20 percent increase in sales for lawn and garden supplies, as the average American spent $250 on her lawn and garden.[18]

During the 1990s, vegetable gardening continued to be a popular outdoor hobby, even as it remained significantly less popular than its peak during the 1970s. A relatively poor year in 1993, where only 26 percent of American households had gardens, was countered in 1994 with a strong comeback, with 35 percent planting gardens. After leveling off at the beginning of the decade, in 1993 the gardening supplies and products industry experienced a 10 percent growth rate, in part driven by increased interest in new gardening gadgets and specialty supplies, and more gardeners purchasing seedlings rather than planting from seed. According to the National Gardening Association, seed sales dropped from $169 million in 1992 to $20 million in 1993 as consumers increasingly purchased more expensive, pregrown seedlings. Throughout the 2000s, home vegetable gardening has had less popularity, with between 22 and 27 percent, representing between 25 and 31 million households, planting vegetable gardens. The recession that wreaked havoc on the global economy in 2009, much like in the 1970s, spurred Americans to plant vegetables at home again, with 2009 seeing the decade's highest vegetable gardening participation rate. As consumers also became weary of the limited selection of varieties available for purchase as seedlings, seed sales have made a comeback, with Burpee reporting an increase of 20–25 percent in sales in 2008, and a similar increase in 2009.[19]

These data suggest several things about changes in home gardening from the early 1970s until the present. First, the popularity of home vegetable gardening is related to the national economy. A poor economy influences at least some decisions to take up vegetable gardening. More important, however, is that close to one-third of American households plant vegetable gardens regardless of the state of the national economy. Indeed, a variety of other factors play a significant role in influencing diverse groups to participate in vegetable gardening, including a desire "get back to nature," to ensure a healthy food supply, or to grow exotic and otherwise difficult-to-find foods; a belief that homegrown vegetables taste better; an intention to engage in gardening as a form of exercise; or a competitive spirit prompting people to grow the first or biggest tomatoes on the block.

Thus, the popularity of home gardening and the proliferation of farmers' markets during the 1970s share many common elements, including a desire for more affordable food, environmental and health concerns, and even a general concern for the loss of individuality and control in postwar America. Yet, in both areas, different actors and groups were attracted to these alternative food cultures for different reasons. The variations in the motivations for shopping at farmers' markets or planting a vegetable garden, and how diverse groups went about doing so, illuminate their complexities and show how they have changed since their 1970s origins.

DIVERSITY IN FARMERS' MARKETS

Beyond the stories of thrifty gardeners, organic-produce-seeking consumers, and diverse truck farmers is a still more complex web of motivations and players. Farmers' markets reflect the diversity of the communities they serve and the wide range of ideas about food production and cuisine that exist in the United States. However, the picture usually painted is of a community of counterculturalists, many of whom have become yuppies. Historian Lisa Hamilton, for example, argues that while farmers' markets "grew organically from their communities," reflecting their urban, suburban, and rural origins, markets that cater to foodies, offering artisan breads, heirloom vegetables, and the like, have come to dominate our perception of what farmers' markets are. Hamilton contends that, aided by lifestyle magazines such as *Gourmet* and *Sunset*, the dominant perception of the farmers' market in the United States has become one filled with "fresh-faced suburban moms collect[ing] bright green and perfect eggplants in wicker baskets; where a street musician or clown is always on call to entertain; where four ounces of organic herb chevre fetch five green dollars." For many observers, the success of the modern farmers' market is predicated on its transformation from a commercial space to a social and cultural experience, one dominated by the youthful, progressive, and affluent. Yet from their inception in the 1970s, farmers' markets have appealed to the working poor along with urban professionals, the elderly, and the newer wave of young foodies that have become popular in America during the past two decades.[20]

The success of farmers' markets geared toward serving this diverse demographic has in some important ways influenced our food culture, increasing the popularity of organic and "natural" foods. At the same time it has pushed American cuisine toward an appreciation of the homemade, the ethnic, and the interesting. In the past several decades, retailers such as Whole Foods and farmers through community supported agriculture and farm stands have drawn on the popularity of farmers' markets in their own independent ventures, bolstering the image of the affluent foodie as the leading driver of culinary change.[21]

Consider how exclusive restaurants have contracted with local farmers, often through farmers' markets, for their produce needs. One example of this is Tim Stark, who quickly made a name for himself among the high-end restaurateurs and chefs that regularly frequent the Union Square market in search of the best tomatoes. By the mid-1990s, well before he published a memoir describing his transformation from a government consultant in New York City to a tomato farmer in rural Fleetwood, Pennsylvania, Stark had secured the support and business of numerous chefs, including that of Charles Kiely, the chef at the Knickerbocker, who maintained a standing order and regularly bought cases of heirloom tomatoes for use in his sauces. In Kiely's words, "Within a week of Tim's coming here, all the chefs knew about him." Stark's memoir reads as a manifesto for the foodie movement: it quickly becomes food with a story, with Stark narrating the trials and tribulations of operating an organic tomato farm. After describing the neat rows and perfect-looking fruits produced by industrial agriculture, Stark said of his own harvests: "The eye for smooth-sailing symmetry ran aground at my renegade tomatoes, chilies, and eggplants. Planted by hand and never abetted by herbicide, my rows were woefully crooked and lost in a sea of run-amok weeds." Not surprisingly, the tomato that Stark describes—the ugly, nonindustrial, and artisan tomato—has come to represent the foodie ideal.[22]

Yet this picture excludes much. The growth of foodie culture, and of organic and "natural" food, is not a phenomenon exclusive to American urban centers. Its reach extends into small towns and suburbs throughout the country, including Paso Robles, California, a small town of thirty thousand situated roughly halfway between Los Angeles and San Francisco, where a farmers' market in the city park has become, according to the *Los Angeles Times*, the "center of the city." There, "a small but passionate group of organic farmers, food artisans and restaurateurs has come . . . determined to transform the local steak-and-potato mentality into something . . . higher up on the food chain." Even the farmers' markets surrounding rural State College, Pennsylvania, cater heavily to this crowd, with Amish farmers selling a variety of wares including locally produced honey and raw milk.[23]

Despite the prevailing images of farmers' markets as hotbeds of progressive politics and lifestyle, farmers' markets remain diverse institutions and continue to reflect a variety of ideas about food. The media attention garnered by the most popular markets, including the Union Square Greenmarket, has led to innovation and change among other farmers' markets as they fight to remain successful commercial ventures, but they have also led to an overstatement of these markets' (and the foodie demographics') influence. Markets throughout the country follow a variety of models in order to serve farmers and their local communities. Farmers' markets and their customers, as one observer argues, represent many "variations on urban life."[24]

One of the leading motivations behind the resurgence of farmers' markets in the 1970s, and one that continues to be of great importance today, is the goal of providing the poor with access to affordable, high-quality food. As *New York Times* writer Peter Applebome remarked, not all farmers' markets are "the new omnivore's playland of the Union Square Greenmarket," with their "artisanal cheeses, heirloom tomatoes, $8 organic breads, grass-fed beef, spinach/goat cheese quiches or local musicians singing James Taylor songs." Markets geared specifically toward the poor take many forms: in Roosevelt, New York, a farmers' market consists of a simple setup of three tables of fresh produce. In Camden, New Jersey, a new program began in 2011 for a mobile farmers' market that also includes "vision screening, blood-pressure testing, even needle exchanges." During the late 1970s, when the revival of farmers' markets was in its infancy, the Community Revival Team in Hartford, Connecticut, organized programs designed to increase access to food among the city's poor, including starting an urban garden, a year-round canning facility, and opening a farmers' market. Farmers' markets are often used to increase access to food in underserved, impoverished areas. In 1981, a market opened in Compton, California, a city of seventy thousand with only five grocery stores. In addition to providing easier access to fresh produce, the market was also meant to bring money back into the community and region, since residents previously were forced either to shop at the few chain supermarkets in town or to travel outside the city to purchase food. This is not an isolated case: as late as

2000, with only one supermarket in Chester, Pennsylvania, a relatively poor town of thirty thousand several miles west of Philadelphia along the Delaware River, the farmers' market remained a vital venue for area consumers to purchase fresh produce.[25]

From the beginning of the movement, the elderly and the poor figured heavily in plans to open new farmers' markets across the nation. In 1985, a market opened in San Pedro, California, with the stated purpose, according to manager Dale Whitney, of bringing "good, healthy produce at reasonable prices to residents of San Pedro, particularly its low-income and elderly population." When a market opened in nearby Long Beach in 1980, farmers were met with "thousands of senior citizens in straw hats with shopping bags and carts in hand." Agricultural and marketing exports routinely examined the cost savings of farmers' markets compared to supermarkets and grocers. In addition to purchasing fresher, more locally produced food, these experts routinely determined that farmers' markets throughout the 1970s and 1980s remained significantly cheaper than the same food at supermarkets. One study produced at the University of California, Davis, in 1979 argued that farmers' markets provided a 71 percent savings to the consumer, a number that most analysts concluded was too high. A study of the farmers' market in Pasadena, California, indicated that consumer savings was about 34 percent, a much lower, but still substantial, figure.[26]

The ability of farmers' markets to aid the poor increased in 1992, when for the first time Congress passed a farm bill that included provisions for farmers' markets to be a part of Women and Infant Children (WIC) and other food aid programs. Already before this, a few states such as New Jersey had experimented with providing vouchers for use at farmers' markets. In 1991, residents of Cumberland and Salem Counties were eligible to receive ten dollar vouchers for use at farmers' markets. Proponents of the program, including New Jersey WIC director Deborah Jones, hoped that the next farm bill would include measures to expand this program nationwide. The Farmers Market Nutrition Program (FMNP), included in the 1992 farm bill, did exactly this, providing low-income families with "fresh, unprepared, locally grown fruits and vegetables." This program has provided hundreds of thousands of participants with vouchers for use exclusively at farmers' markets. In 1993, the first full year of the program, almost 350,000 people from eleven states received benefits. The following year, the program expanded to twenty-four states, with more than half a million participants receiving $5.6 million in benefits. In 2000, 58 percent of farmers' markets accepted WIC payments. By 2012, this program had expanded to thirty-six states and 1.7 million households. In 2001, the USDA established an additional program, the Seniors' Farmers Market Nutrition Program (SFMNP), aimed at providing vouchers for the low-income elderly population. In 2012, almost 900,000 seniors received vouchers through this program.[27]

These programs not only increased access to farmers' markets among the poor but also provided state and federal support for farmers' markets, injecting much-needed money into the markets and into farmers' pockets. Richard McCarthy, executive director of the Crescent City Farmers Market in New Orleans, observed that helping more than five thousand seniors enroll in the program provided the market with over $100,000 in sales. These same seniors, McCarthy said, often spent their own money as well, after seeing how much high-quality food they could get at the market. Moreover, by increasing access to the poor, farmers' markets have become more dependent on spending by these groups, forcing farmers' markets to appeal more to these groups. McCarthy continued, arguing that the program "helps bring the farmers' market out of the froufrou foodie confines and makes it a healthier experience for the whole community." In other words, these programs help ensure that farmers' markets continue to adapt and appeal to a wide variety of groups, not simply the young, affluent crowd that pervades our perceptions of farmers' markets.[28]

Farmers' markets, too, often reflect the culinary curiosity and ethnic heritages of the communities in which they serve. In the mid-1970s, for example, just a few miles away from the Greenmarket's Union Square market, a farmers' market emerged in Jamaica, a predominantly African-American neighborhood in Queens. What was once an overgrown lot was transformed into a fair, offering residents inexpensive foods, many of which were otherwise unavailable. One farmer made a weekly trek to his family farm in Georgia and returned with "okra, black-eyed peas, watermelon and collard greens," drawing on the southern roots and culinary style of many of New York's African-Americans and perhaps playing to racial stereotypes.[29]

THE FARMERS' MARKET, AMERICAN FOOD CULTURE, AND THE TOMATO

While farmers' markets have become economically and socially diverse, most share common appeals. On its face, although the farmers' market represents a minor challenge to industrial food in terms of market share, this local institution has challenged the values and methods of the industrialized product. There are many reasons for consumers frequenting farmers' markets, including cost and variety of food available, but two motivations stand out. First, the farmers' market is often seen as "the historical flagship of local food systems," offering consumers local alternatives to the national food network most readily represented by supermarket chains. While supermarkets and other outlets increasingly stock fresh, local, and organic foods, the farmers' market, for many consumers, more fully embodies their philosophical and aesthetic demands. For these consumers, a desire for local, fresh, and healthy food is the foundation of the farmers' market. Second, farmers' markets provide a critical link between agriculture and the kitchen table. Farmers and consumers sometimes want to share stories, ideas, and recipes, especially in an age of the impersonal market. Even in the Internet era, when information is democratized by instant access, farmers' markets provide sources of information and an invaluable social setting that has largely disappeared from buying and selling. These interactions—of food and people—both represent and perpetuate the growing diversity in American food culture.[30]

Although it remains on the fringe, the demand for "fresh" and local food has increased in the past several decades.[31] *Gourmet News* declared in 2007 that "the days when organic consumers were the hippies among us are over." Those interested in local, natural, and organic foods increasingly "are parents and those focused on lifestyle and values." Consumers regularly indicate a stronger desire for locally produced foods than "organic," despite the overall increase in demand for "organic" and "natural" foods as well.[32]

Though some studies suggest that consumers may have an inherent affinity toward "local" food, most cases studies find that consumer preferences for local food are based primarily on extrinsic factors: a desire to support their local community, decreasing transportation costs and fossil fuel reliance, and in most cases, a *perception* that local food is healthier, fresher, and tastes better. For example, in her study of consumer preferences for local produce in southeast Missouri, Cheryl Brown found that while 82 percent of consumers considered quality and freshness to be of primary concern, only 1 percent listed the origin of food as the most important factor in their purchasing decisions. Nonetheless, 73 percent of consumers believed that the quality of food available at farmers' markets was superior to food at supermarkets. Likewise, a study of North Carolina farmers' markets found that 88 percent of respondents frequented farmers' markets for fresh produce, while only 64 percent indicated that they went for local products. In general, as Marianne Wolf and her colleagues have argued, many consumers consider farmers' market produce to be "fresher looking, fresher tasting, a higher-quality product, a better value for the money, and more reasonably priced than supermarket produce." Ultimately, then, for many consumers, the appeal of local food stems not simply from its being grown nearby but by the assumption (correct or not) that it is fresher, healthier, and sometimes costs less.[33]

These ideas that local food is fresher and healthier frame the appeal of the homegrown and locally produced tomato. For many, as much as the pink, tasteless winter tomato represents some of the worst effects of commercial agriculture, the tomato also most fully represents the superiority of local, fresh produce. For Ronni Lundy, author of *In Praise of Tomatoes*, "the tomato is the best way to demonstrate why you want to patronize local farmers. . . . The closer to the source, the better taste you're going to have. People who don't have to be fretting about early production, ease of picking or shipping long distances can concentrate on flavor." Consumers flock to farmers' markets for the opportunity to find the perfect tomato: Fritz Sanders, of Chambersburg, Pennsylvania, remarked upon a visit to a local farmers' market in 2010, "Man, I could eat a good tomato." Likewise, in 1976, soon after a Greenmarket location opened on E. 59th Street, consumers flooded the market for fresh produce, finding beefsteak tomatoes unlike any available at a supermarket. Market observers have regularly advised consumers to "take a drive into the country or visit your local farmers market" to find the "best" tomatoes. Julio Guridy, executive director of the Council of Spanish-Speaking Organizations of the Lehigh Valley, put it simply, following the organization's creation of a farmers' market in Bethlehem, Pennsylvania: "Everyone likes a tomato that tastes like a tomato."[34]

There is substantial evidence to suggest that consumers identify local tomatoes as more valuable than other local produce. A study concerning direct marketing of produce in Delaware in 1997, for example, found tomatoes to be among the most popular fruits or vegetables purchased by consumers at both farmers' markets and roadside stands, the latter a far more popular venue for fresh produce purchases in Delaware. Almost 50 percent of consumers reported visiting direct farm markets such as roadside stands every month, compared to less than 20 percent for farmers' markets. At roadside stands, nearly 70 percent of consumers reported that they were very likely to buy tomatoes at farm stands (ranking second behind sweet corn) compared to 30 percent at farmers' markets (ranking first). A study of the statewide "Jersey Fresh" brand also indicated a strong affinity among New Jerseyans for their state's tomatoes compared to other local products.[35]

The increased demand for local tomatoes is in part due to higher dissatisfaction with supermarket tomatoes than other produce. A study in Knoxville, Tennessee, for example, indicated that around 30 percent of Knoxville consumers were dissatisfied with the out-of-state tomatoes they found at retail markets and found local tomatoes a far superior alternative to the out-of-state tomatoes offered in supermarkets. Overall, around 60 percent of Knoxville area consumers believed that local tomatoes had better freshness and taste than out-of-state tomatoes, almost 40 percent believed the local tomatoes had a better appearance, and just under 50 percent of consumers believed that local tomatoes were more nutritious. These numbers were much higher for tomatoes than for other locally produced foods.[36]

The success of farmers' markets as "flagships" of local food depends in part on the continued consumer *perception* of high quality and local offerings at farmers' markets. "It is there," declared Gerald Etter of the *Philadelphia Inquirer*; at the farmers' market "you generally find fresh, home-grown and quality foodstuffs. For the most part, you can select your own produce and do not have to be concerned with the likes of pre-packaged goods." In a review of farmers' market policies, however, the USDA found in 2000 that fully 63 percent of farmers' markets permitted processed foods to be sold, 52 percent allowed prepared foods, and 58 percent of markets also let vendors sell crafts. Similarly, 45 percent of farmers' markets allowed crops from outside of the local area to be sold and 40 percent permitted items to be resold at markets. Thus, despite the perception of high quality and fresh, local food at farmers' markets, many markets have lax regulations allowing for processed and non-local foods to be sold alongside fresh, local produce.[37]

Efforts to limit what is sold at farmers' market to locally grown or produced products not only benefit local farmers by ensuring fair competition and benefit consumers by ensuring high quality products, but they also provide an important marketing tool for the markets themselves, helping them (accurately or not) continue to be seen as superior sources for fresh and local foods. Many markets have increased their regulations in recent years, limiting how far products can be transported, allowing vendors to only sell foods that they (or their neighbors) grew, and controlling the types of products available for sale. New York City's Greenmarkets are among the most stringent farmers' markets, requiring that all farmers be located within the mid-Atlantic region, which they define as 120 miles to the south, 170 miles east and west, and 250 miles north of New York City. These regulations, whether imposed by government or the markets themselves, have helped reinforce an image of farmers' markets as premiere locations for healthy, local food.[38]

Perhaps even above their reputation for having fresh and local produce, farmers' markets can serve as important social spaces for interactions between farmers and consumers. While undoubtedly a commercial space, farmers' markets are more often viewed as community-friendly places where farmers' and consumers' interactions and conversations about food are held in higher esteem than the necessary monetary transactions. For many critics of American foodways, the farmers' market serves as an important bridge, a nexus between food production and consumption that is too often obscured by "the sanitized uniformity" of supermarkets and the physical distance and bureaucratic layers necessary for the production of industrial food. Alan Hunt, an agricultural policy analyst, found that 62 percent of farmers selling at Maine farmers' markets were motivated by a strong desire to have a direct relationship with customers. Likewise, William Lockeretz found in 1986 that consumers value dealing with farmers "face to face," turning the "abstract idea of 'support your local farmer' into a tangible reality." As Ann Vileisis argues in *Kitchen Literacy*, our food supply "derives not only from an obscured nature but also from behind-the-scenes tractors, gasoline, laser-leveled fields, fertilizers, irrigation ditches, pesticides, combines, migrant workers, laboratories, sanitized factories, stinking feedlots, semi trucks, and highways." For many customers of farmers' markets, conversing with farmers themselves and knowing that the food they buy was picked nearby, and recently, help reconnect them to the food that they put in their bodies.[39]

In 2004, *Pittsburgh Post-Gazette* writer Sarah Billingsley declared, "At the heart of any gustatory ramble is a simple truth: When the streets are filled with people, the streets are filled with food." While Billingsley's focus is on the growth of food carts in the Pittsburgh area, she relates an important truth. Food is a critical part of our communities and our social lives. Food is the stuff of festivals, of celebrations, and of mourning. Historically, food is also an essential subject of conversation: consumers barter at markets and seek out information about where their food came from or how to cook it properly. In the past half century, the farmers' market has played a pivotal role in restoring these questions and conversations about food in many Americans' lives.[40]

These interactions, while important, are undoubtedly often awkward. In his reporting for the *New Yorker* on the Greenmarkets during the 1970s, John McPhee observed numerous encounters between farmers and consumers that indicated how poor the average consumer's knowledge of food was. They were constantly obsessed with knowing the weight (and thereby the price) of the products they were browsing. They regularly requested items that were not in season. Even today, the Greenmarket website explains why peaches are unavailable in the winter and why oranges are never available. McPhee also reported that these early Greenmarket consumers needed to touch the food, often to the point of damaging it. "You people come into the market," he wrote, "and you slit the tomatoes with your fingernails. With your thumbs, you excavate the cheese. You choose stringbeans one at a time. You pulp the nectarines and rape the sweet corn. You are something wonderful, you are . . . and we, who are almost without exception strangers here, are as absorbed with you as you seem to be with the numbers on our hanging scales." For McPhee, then, these early experiences were marked with the awkwardness of two completely foreign cultural groups—food producers and consumers—coming together and meeting for the very first time.[41]

For some, the atmosphere of the farmers' market is filled with a sense of "nostalgia and romance" for a time long past, but at the core of this appeal is a desire for "social networking," a chance for consumers to meet "the people who grow their food." "Wander the makeshift stalls and striped awnings" at farmers' markets in the greater New York City area, reported *New York Times* reporter Joseph D'Agnese, "and you will spot community activity seldom found in supermarkets. Customers visit with neighbors. . . . Farmers sell produce, chatting, unloading, tidying and occasionally muttering about the lack of rain. And through it all, bunches, pints, quarts of Jersey-grown produce disappear into brown bags." As Paul Steinke, the manager of the Reading Terminal Market, observes, "People don't talk in supermarkets. But farmers markets are like community centers. It's a democratic space." Moreover, many consumers report enjoying the farmers' market experience: one study conducted of Maine farmers' markets found that 98 percent of farmers' market consumers had fun during their shopping trip, 84 percent reported conversing with vendors, and nearly 81 percent met people they knew (other than vendors) at the market. For many consumers, according to Lockeretz, the social space of farmers' markets, often with a "festive and neighborly atmosphere," has developed into "a pleasant way to shop."[42]

The farmers' market, then, is a constructed environment in some ways designed to counter the primacy of commercially dominant spaces like the shopping mall. On crowded streets and sidewalks, with makeshift tables and stands filled with colorful displays, and with consumers often expected to barter with and get information from farmers, these spaces encourage the exchange of information as much as they facilitate the exchange of goods. Unlike supermarkets and shopping malls, with their appeals toward order, cleanliness, and a sense of individualized experiences in public spaces, farmers' markets, at least in the minds of organizers, encourage community building, cross-cultural interactions, and a constant buzz of activity. The growing popularity of farmers' markets suggests that many consumers have found these qualities lacking in supermarkets and other methods of food shopping.[43]

THE BACKYARD GARDEN PLOT: SUBURBAN ROOTS

The revival of home gardening during the 1970s, much like the growth in farmers' markets, was fueled by trends broader than the expansion of a counterculture. Gardeners from diverse backgrounds shared common motivations: concern over food health and safety as well as rising food prices. Yet the diversity of home gardeners suggests that a variety of motivations affected different demographic groups. These groups include middle-class suburbanites, the urban poor, and a growing cohort of affluent urbanites. These groups were inspired to garden for different reasons. From discontent with suburban sprawl and the domestication of American masculinity to confronting the problems of urban decay and community alienation, gardeners approach the soil from their own unique perspectives.

The backyard garden, with its succulent greens, beans, and bright red tomatoes, is nearly as pervasive an image of suburbia as the white picket fence. Home gardening was an outgrowth of post-1945 suburbia. Yet it was not until the 1970s, when large numbers of Americans grew disenchanted with Wonder Bread, Velveeta, Jell-O, and even commercial canned tomato paste, that gardening became a popular activity again. Though suburban gardeners share a love for the tomato, its beautiful fruit and large yields, much of the appeal of gardening in the suburbs is drawn from the unique experience of suburbia itself. In the years following World War II, as Americans rushed out of the city, a great appeal of suburban life, as Adam Rome argues, was a desire to get back to nature and to experience life in the outdoors. Suburban homeowners, according to Rome, provided a significant impetus for the growing environmental movement as they watched prized environmental amenities disappear in their own backyards. Home gardening, for many suburban residents during the 1970s, evolved into a new environmental amenity. It provided a desired connection to nature by allowing and compelling gardeners to experiment with nature in a private, domestic space.[44]

At the same time, suburban gardening has a social element that also grew out of the postwar suburban experience: the competition among neighbors, emulation, and even jealousy so often documented by the sociology of the 1950s and 1960s suburb. David Riesman, William Whyte, Vance Packard, and many others found that the breakdown of traditional family and communal bonds that emerged following the mass exodus to the suburbs created an environment of social dislocation and disruption. These social conditions promoted a culture that valued individual consumption over communal interests while at the same time encouraging emulation and a loss of creativity. Home vegetable gardening in some ways reflects this in the desire for social status and recognition among gardeners. Gardeners routinely tried to grow the earliest or biggest tomatoes and shared their stories and their tomatoes with their neighbors.[45]

The vegetable garden offered still another extension of the postwar suburban ideal: it was one of the primary ways in which suburban residents interacted with nature in a controlled, safe environment. The *New York Times* cited "spiraling food prices and a yen to return to the land" as fueling an increase in gardening on Long Island in the mid-1970s, when garden plots big and small popped up across Nassau and Suffolk counties. Gardening provides suburban America with a connection to its agricultural past, helping turn backyards into a Jeffersonian world filled with carefully carved-out plots of vegetables and fruits.[46]

Through the act of gardening, gardeners were invited to explore and experiment with nature's rules, even if in a sanitized environment. Despite the numerous scientific advancements during the second half of the century, including new varieties, chemicals, and techniques that make gardening easier, it remains an activity where experience largely determines success. In this way, home gardening was not only a result of the social and cultural conflicts taking place in suburban America, but it was also a key response to these crises: it was a primary extension of the do-it-yourself movement that blossomed in the 1950s as especially men were encouraged to develop and display domestic skills. These skills required time, effort, and accumulated experience, all in contrast to the immediate gratification promoted by popular consumer culture.[47]

The USDA was quick to provide training and a proper attitude for the home gardener. One of its popular publications stressed that amateurs ought to "obtain all possible scientific background for their garden work . . . [but] it cannot take the place of experience." The only way to succeed in the backyard garden is to get your hands dirty, to learn nature's lessons from season to season, and to treat gardening as an art form. Experts were careful to warn gardeners not to start too big in their quest to build the perfect garden, as "it is better to have a small garden well maintained than a large one neglected and full of weeds." Gardeners were warned not think of gardening as an "all or nothing" affair; instead they were advised to start small and expand as they learned more, determined their food needs, and were confident they had the time and energy to take care of an entire garden.[48]

This advice was surely hard for many gardeners to follow, but it challenged the packaged satisfactions of TV and TV dinners. The late 1970s saw a flood of books, guides, and manuals for home gardening. Gardening was also featured on a weekly PBS show, *Crockett's Victory Garden*, later renamed *The Victory Garden*, which entered its thirty-fifth season in 2014. *The Victory Garden* and a host of other shows aired by HGTV (established in 1994) and other networks presented gardening on a large scale. Bob Thomson, for example, the second host of *The Victory Garden*, maintained a huge garden at his Boston-area home and instructed viewers on the importance of staggering plantings, "so that I don't suddenly find myself with 50 crookneck squash in their prime, or 100 lettuce plants ready for pulling." Many of the gardening experts also offered advice on maximizing the amount of plants one could plant in a given space. This was especially the case with Mel Bartholomew's Square Foot Gardening Method, first introduced in 1981 and still popular today. Bartholomew, a retired engineer from New Jersey, argued that instead of planting in rows, like traditional farming, backyard gardens should be as compact and compressed as possible. He divided his garden into one-foot squares and planted as many plants as possible in each of them. While his overall message was to shrink the amount of space a garden needed to take up, for many Americans with large backyards and visions of a bountiful harvest, the likely result was overplanting. Such is the case with gardener William Alexander, who after planting a huge backyard garden with his wife, wrote a memoir that he aptly subtitled "how one man nearly lost his sanity, spent a fortune, and endured an existential crisis in the quest for the perfect garden."[49]

More important, gardening on a large scale appealed to many suburban gardeners because it enabled them to stand out among their neighbors. One source of pride was growing the earliest, biggest, and most produce, especially tomatoes. One gardener, Frank Reichstein, gave tips in *Better Homes and Gardens* for how to "get the jump on the neighbors and show them really early tomatoes." *The Victory Garden's* Bob Thomson admitted that "one of my goals with tomatoes is to be the first kid on the block with red, ripe fruit." For many, producing early homegrown tomatoes, when neighbors were still forced to buy lower quality supermarket tomatoes, was a great source of pride.[50]

For others, achieving the largest harvest is a great motivation. Rocklin, California, gardener Jerry Bell, whose garden has been featured on HGTV several times, routinely harvests 50–60 pounds of tomatoes per week during the height of the season. Bill Pennington, an Atlanta-area gardener, harvested more than 150 pounds of tomatoes a week during the peak of the harvest in 1990. For many, a large crop enabled them to supply their neighbors with the surplus as both an act of kindness and as a source of pride. Lynette Evens, writing for the *San Francisco Chronicle*, posed the inevitable and difficult question: "Do I give away my best produce or my second-best, and save the best for myself?" The tradition of sharing the harvest with neighbors is not an isolated one: one study in Knoxville, Tennessee, found that as many as 70 percent of consumers receive tomatoes from a neighbor's garden, a far higher number than other homegrown foods. The tomato, then, has served as a means for suburban residents to measure their own success while also giving neighbors a view of that success (an important theme of the period for consumer researcher Ernest Dichter). Suburban gardeners with access to enough space for a large garden often place significant value on the social side of gardening, even if the activity itself and the environment in which they practice it, remains in the private sphere.[51]

Finally, while many gardeners placed great value in growing the most tomatoes, others tried to grow the largest tomato among their peers. In the spirit of agricultural fairs, farmers' markets, tomato clubs, and other groups routinely host contests for the largest homegrown tomato, and winning such an award generates great pride, even if the monetary reward is often minimal. This trend is evident by the success of the beefsteak tomato and other large varieties. In 1987, the *Houston Chronicle* reported that despite the fact that smaller fruited tomatoes are more successful in the area due to the extreme heat of late summer, the beefsteak tomato was the overwhelming favorite among most gardeners who want the largest tomatoes that they can grow. Stern's Miracle-Gro, a chemically produced plant food, recognized the popularity of large tomatoes and made a contest of it in 1993, offering gardeners $100,000 for any tomato produced using Miracle-Gro that topped the world record tomato of seven pounds, twelve ounces by the end of 1995. That record had been set just a few years before, breaking a previous record set in 1987 by Oklahoma gardener Gordon Graham, who, through intensive watering, cultivated a fifteen-foot-tall plant. At one point, the plant was so tall that wind knocked it over. At the end of the season, after leaving it for dead, Graham was surprised to find that the plant had grown a single tomato, weighing in at a world record six pounds, five ounces. The desire to grow the earliest, biggest and most tomatoes helps give suburban gardening, a largely private experience, a social element that fits into the American suburban experience. The desire for the "best" tomatoes, however one defines it, can produce a spirit of emulation and friendly competition among neighbors and help bring social experiences into the private sphere of the suburban backyard.[52]

THE URBAN GARDEN

The suburban garden was hardly the only American setting for tomato cultivation. The urban garden offers a very different picture. It is defined by its primary difficulty: a lack of space. By necessity, gardening in an urban environment takes place in locations that differ greatly from the backyard garden plot: on balconies, rooftops, empty lots, and in community spaces. While urban gardeners often have similar motivations for gardening to their suburban counterparts, the unique experience of city living and the demographics of urban America provide other motivations for gardening as well. Ethnic Americans and the urban poor often take advantage of community gardens, vacant lots, and other open space in urban America to grow food in order to save money, practice traditional food habits, and as a means of community revitalization. At the same time, the gentrification of the American city has led new groups—yuppies, hipsters, and foodies—to experiment with growing specialty foods, often organic or heirloom, in order to support their culinary habits.

COMMUNITY GARDENS

The Victory Garden movement during World War II was the heyday of the community garden. Community gardens existed in every large city and many smaller cities and towns across the country. After waning interest during the 1950s and 1960s, community gardens made a resurgence in the early 1970s, as high food prices and city revitalization efforts peaked. Community gardens continued to sprout up through the 1980s, and in 1985, New York City could boast 450 community gardens providing 156 acres for more than 11,000 gardeners to cultivate. In nearby Newark, 153 vacant lots had been converted into urban gardens, with more than 3,700 participants in 1987. This movement was aided by the USDA's formation of the Urban Gardening Program in the early 1970s, which was designed to provide support and gardening advice to America's urban centers. In 1978, the program had offices in sixteen cities, and by 1985, it had expanded to twenty-one cities. The results of this program were substantial: in 1978, the program supported almost 28,000 New York City residents. By 1980, the program had served almost 200,000 urban gardeners. In 1985, gardens in Boston, Cleveland, Jacksonville, Memphis, New York, Los Angeles, and Philadelphia all produced more than $1 million in produce. Community gardens played a critical role in providing food for the poor and offering a sense of community to areas devastated by urban decay. As Laura Lawson argues, community gardens provide individuals and local groups with a means of "resiliency to deteriorated social and physical infrastructure," making community gardens a place of "physical and social reclamation."[53]

For many urban gardeners, gardening held the potential for significant savings in food costs. As Peter Tonge reported in the *Christian Science Monitor*, "it pays, often quite handsomely, to grow your own." For Tonge, investing in his garden amounted to a "pay raise." The USDA estimated in the 1970s that a family could save as much as $300 per year on food by gardening. The *New York Times* recounted a "well publicized projection" in 1973 that claimed up to $100 in savings from $3.10 spent on seeds for a ten-by-fifteen-foot garden. Even as late as the mid-1980s, Auburn University horticulturalist Dave Williams estimated that a gardener could expect a tenfold return on the costs of seed and fertilizers. In some cases, urban gardeners have located space to grow enough produce to sell at farmers' markets. One family in eastern New York, for example, cultivated four plots at community gardens and ended up selling more than

$3,000 in produce. While not all gardens are successful, and even fewer gardens make a profit for their cultivators, urban gardens throughout the country serve an important function in most cities by enabling urban residents to provide a substantial amount of their family's food needs.[54]

Increased access to affordable food is not the only reason urban gardening became popular in the 1970s. For many, the primary appeal of urban gardening was the need for new avenues of community formation and revitalization. During the 1970s and 1980s, the urban gardening movement was often a grassroots effort to combat urban decay and blight. As many federal and state revitalization projects focused on tearing down blighted neighborhoods, community gardens were often placed on recently razed lots at the request of the local community. The creation of an urban garden often brought communities together to clean up the area, removing trash and other materials. Urban gardens were often a democratic experience, with members voting to establish rules, create expectations regarding land and water use, and determine how costs would be paid. The urban garden also emerged as a social space, much like the farmers' market, where gardeners could exchange information and advice and talk about the local community. Judy Elliot, education coordinator for the Denver Urban Gardens, observed that one of the crucial benefits of urban gardens was "getting to talk to all of these old-timers who have all of these crazy little tricks." This is especially true for many immigrant groups who often use urban gardens not only to grow foods not available at supermarkets but also to "retain a tie to the earth" and to practice traditional food growing. In much the same way as suburban gardens, many see the urban gardening movement as providing integral benefits on both a personal and community level, giving residents the ability to provide some of their own food while also aiding community development and revitalization.[55]

URBAN FOODIES

Urban gardening has also appealed to groups other than recent immigrants and the urban poor. Loosely defined groups such as yuppies, hipsters, and foodies, who share some intellectual roots concerning food with the 1960s counterculture, have more recently become involved in the gardening movement. These groups are less interested in gardening in order to save money, and are more motivated by the perceived health benefits and taste of the food they grow. Many of these gardeners fit the description of bourgeois bohemians described by David Brooks, with "one foot in the bohemian world of creativity and another foot in the bourgeois realm of ambition and worldly success." For these "bobos," obtaining high quality, tasty food is a middle-ground position, fulfilling a need for productive, culturally significant creativity. While these groups are often more partial to frequenting farmers' markets, being members of CSAs, and shopping at upscale retailers like Whole Foods, they nonetheless represent a significant demographic of gardeners in urban areas. Their urban gardening efforts often consist of utilizing available patios, rooftops and other domestic space for the production of heirloom, organic, and other more artisanal foodstuffs.[56]

In addition to community gardens, urban gardeners of all types routinely make use of any available sunny space to plant gardens, including patios, rooftops, and small yards. As early as the 1970s, Jack Kramer suggested that city residents could utilize the newest dwarf plant offerings to create container gardens on balconies and in doorways. In more recent years, as the foodie movement has taken hold, gardening experts have offered extensive advice on planting a garden where space is a luxury. Alex Mitchell notes that in addition to planting gardens on rooftops and in window boxes, utilizing fire escapes to plant small container gardens is becoming an increasingly popular, if potentially hazardous, activity. In his words, for urban residents "your own little bit of outdoor space has always been something to covet, but now more than ever we're embracing the chance to green up our environment." Employees of the *San Francisco Chronicle* recently started a garden on the rooftop of the newspaper's headquarters, and they have reported on their experiences growing all sorts of edible plants. Many urban gardeners can also now grow food inside their homes, as a host of products, from self-watering potted tomato plants to full-on artificially lit hydroponic systems such as the Aerogarden have become available in recent years (figure 6.1).[57]

FIGURE 6.1   AeroGarden Indoor Home Gardening Unit. From AeroGarden.com (accessed July 13, 2014). Reprinted with permission.

While urban home gardeners do not have a monopoly on growing organic, heirloom, or specialty crops, their lack of available space and particular interests in high quality food and unique cuisine generally lead them to focus more on quality than quantity. Food and health enthusiasts throughout the country, in suburbs, cities, and the countryside have in recent decades become interested in healthier, more specialized food. The organic movement that grew out of the environmental movement of the 1960s and 1970s, of course, was not a new idea during that period. It owed its existence to traditional agricultural techniques and, more specifically, to the late-nineteenth-century biodynamic movement led by Austrian philosopher Rudolf Steiner, which focused on organic fertilizers, companion planting, and new irrigation techniques. Though the organic movement had maintained some popularity since its origins in the 1970s, it did not gain widespread attention until the 1980s and 1990s, when a growing economy and renewed concern about both the environment and public health convinced many consumers to look for organic produce and many gardeners to abandon their time-honored chemical fertilizers and pesticides for more natural products. The gardening industry has followed suit, with big chemical companies such as Pennington and Ortho introducing organic gardening additives and gardening retailers offering a host of organic products, including seeds, potting soils, and additives.[58]

Much like with organic food, the popularity of heirloom vegetables has in recent years received significant attention, with the tomato at the helm of this movement. Several thousand specific tomato varieties have been identified as heirlooms, generally meaning that they have existed for at least fifty years and are open-pollinated rather than hybrid varieties. Some, such as the Rutgers or Bonny's Best, were initially developed as commercial cultivars with qualities similar to commercial tomatoes produced today. Others, such as the Brandywine or Cherokee Purple, are celebrated by food enthusiasts for their superior taste, color, and texture. Some heirlooms are "gnarly looking, old-fashioned tomatoes, the kind Grandpa and Great-Grandpa grew," and a growing number of Americans consider the flavor of the best of these to be "superior to the best modern hybrid tomatoes." For many gardeners, growing old and rare tomato varieties has become a lifelong passion. Bill Ellis, while teaching English and American Studies at Penn State, enjoyed growing an old Polish variety that was smuggled into the United States during the Cold War because he felt he was "back fighting the battle against communism." Kent Whealy, after receiving the seeds of a pink tomato from his grandfather as a wedding gift, ultimately started an organization, the Seed Saver's Exchange, devoted to the saving and swapping of heirloom vegetable seeds. Created in the mid-1970s, by 1993 there were 7,000 members swapping seeds with fellow gardeners. In the same year, Burpee capitulated to consumer interest in heirloom varieties, devoting one page to heirloom seeds. By the early 2000s, interest in heirloom varieties in the Sacramento area had grown enough so that master gardeners representing the University of California Cooperative Extension Service conducted an heirloom tomato trial. Elsewhere in California, food enthusiasts could see more than 160 tomato varieties displayed at Tomato Day 2004 in Vacaville, more than 300 at TomatoFest 2004 in Carmel, and more than 120 homegrown tomatoes at the Homegrown Tomato Challenge. The rejection of commercial tomato varieties has forced retailers to offer better selections of heirloom varieties. Still, the proliferation of the Internet has opened up avenues for dozens of new firms, often part-time, family-owned ventures, to participate in the marketplace and to challenge the supremacy of major seed companies, gardening superstores, and agricultural experts.[59]

TOMATOES—THE "KING OF THE VEGETABLE PLOT"

If farmers' markets created a lexicon of locality and authenticity across class and culture, gardeners, despite diverse backgrounds, also shared a common language of taste. Well before World War II the tomato had become one of the most popular vegetables for the home garden. This popularity continued during the second half of the twentieth century. Numerous polls from the second half of the century indicate that at least 80 to 85 percent of home vegetable gardeners grow tomatoes. In 1987, for example, one poll indicated that the next highest planted crop was peppers, with 58 percent, followed by 50 percent for onions and cucumbers. Even the ever-popular lettuce was only planted in 42 percent of home gardens. Many gardeners, often with little space to plant or little time to cultivate an extensive plot, choose to plant only tomatoes.[60]

The popularity of tomatoes can be traced to the ease with which they are grown, their suitability for nearly any American environment, and their comparatively high yields. As George Haegel reported in 1956, "tomatoes are certainly the crop most likely to succeed anywhere. The plants are adaptable to various soils and most climate peculiarities." Just as commercial tomato production was spread out across nearly every region in the country during the first half of the twentieth century, the tomato's unique qualities enabled home gardeners from nearly any climate and in nearly any soil type to successfully enjoy one of nature's most beautiful and tasty treats. As numerous experts and observers indicated, tomatoes are also well suited to compact growing environments, in small plots and in containers.[61]

And just a few plants can produce an astonishing number of tomatoes with little effort on the part of the gardener. With regular watering and staking (if the gardener subscribes to the opinion that staking is the best method), tomato plants will grow reliably. Experts never agreed on the exact amount a grower could expect to get from a single plant, but one tomato booster asserted that a single plant could yield as many as "50, 75, 100 or more large tomatoes"—an unlikely high yield. But these predictions only offered further reassurance to the potential tomato gardener.[62]

Homegrown tomatoes also have the benefit, in most gardeners' eyes, of tasting far better than their supermarket counterparts, which Wayne McLaurin dubbed "10 mph tomatoes" for the amount of shock they are expected to be able to endure as they are mechanically harvested, transported, and processed. Richard Langer put this succinctly when he argued in 1977 "grow your own tomatoes and chances are you'll rarely again buy the tasteless cue balls passed off as the vegetable at the local supermarket." Francis Coulter, writing for the *New York Times*, argued that tomatoes were best suited to be grown at home, in part because "no tomato ever has the flavor of one eaten, like an apple, right off the vine." William Evans, writing in *Organic Gardening*, agreed: "If summer had a taste, it might be flavored like a fresh, homegrown tomato. . . . [T]omatoes take the best that summer has to offer—long hot days, warm nights, and a smattering of afternoon showers—and turn it into juicy fruit." A 1994 survey suggested that gardeners agreed, indicating that 77 percent of gardeners cultivate vegetable plants because they desired fresher, tastier produce.[63]

Another writer urged gardeners to try to produce the earliest tomatoes because "no matter how you slice it, nothing quite compares to that first bite of your first homegrown tomato of the season." "After that," Harold Faber reported, "the deluge. Once the tomatoes start to ripen, there is an anthology of tomatoes. Tomatoes for breakfast, tomatoes for dessert, tomatoes for dinner." And these tomatoes, Faber continued, are far superior to their supermarket siblings, which "have turned red more in embarrassment than in pride." Food expert James Beard argued that most commercially produced tomatoes "stink. They have practically no flavor and a wooly texture." One New York City cookbook writer and gardener grew 150 plants annually to avoid eating supermarket tomatoes, which he described as "like eating a blotter." Several explanations for this could be given: the fresher the tomato, the better the taste, but home gardening also gives consumers the choice to grow varieties more known for their flavor than for their high yields and capability for long-distance shipping.[64]

Yet another reason for the tomato's popularity, one more difficult to document, is the aesthetic advantages of the tomato plant. Many gardeners awaited the arrival of the seed catalogs in the dead of winter to be inspired by "bright days to come," and their "visions of red, plump, juicy and flavorful vine-ripened tomatoes" continued on their minds as they broke ground in the spring. This joy repeated itself, according to Lynette Evens, "with the thrill of a first fruit set and the kiss of the first bite of ripe tomato." The joy of seeing the first red-tinged tomatoes on the vine in July or August is, to the gardener, a most welcome site, a preamble to the harvest. The contrast of the large, crimson globes on a backdrop of brown dirt and green foliage underscores the reward for a season of hard work and patience under nature's watch. As Harold Faber reported in 1971, just as home gardening was making its resurgence: "The most glorious product of the home vegetable garden is a work of art. Thriving in the hot sun, the tomato reddens gradually against a background of deep green leaves and blushingly beckons to an orgy of taste."[65]

The resurgence of farmers' markets and home gardening during the second half of the century points to a growing resistance to commercial food culture in the United States, even as growers, farmers, and gardeners continued to rely on commercial producers of seeds, fertilizers, and other supplies and equipment. Despite the increasing influence that agricultural conglomerates, food processors, supermarkets, and other entities have on our food options, and the significant expansion in advertising and marketing efforts aimed at influencing our choices, American food remains diverse. Farmers' markets and home gardening represent merely two challenges to this trend, of which there are many more, including a renewed interest in ethnic foods, CSA programs, food co-ops, and a growing number of food trucks in many metropolitan areas. Each of these examples reflects the vibrancy, diversity, and popular initiative of American food culture, despite the significant power of corporations, lobbyists, and government regulators to influence public policy and culture.

In part, the continued resistance to the dominance of consumerism lies in the fact that these alternatives share a long history, which extends well before the postwar period. Farmers' markets, a modern invention that draws on a long tradition of farmer direct-marketing, saw a decline during the depression and immediately following World War II, but it remained less than a generation removed from the vibrant market culture of the early twentieth century. Likewise, despite a significant decline in the popularity of home gardening during the early postwar period, gardeners could rest assured that their efforts matched those of their parents and grandparents just a few decades before. Thus, in both cases, these alternatives were not "radical" but simply a return to the not-so-distant past, a nostalgia, real or imagined, for when food was local, fresh, healthy, and tasted good.

These alternatives also benefited from casting a wide net, drawing in diverse socioeconomic, cultural, and ethnic groups. While they shared certain ideological beliefs with the counterculture of the 1960s and 1970s, both farmers' markets and home gardening have proven to have lasting, widespread appeal. This was in part because they attracted diversity at the same time that they reflected the shared values of increasing access to higher quality food. Another such shared value was and is a quest for food that is local and that provides perceived social benefits in contrast to the universal and impersonal food offered by commercial agriculture. Gardeners and farmers' market consumers also demand increased participation in the process of creating nature's "miracle," either by growing it themselves or by taking a more active role in shopping. For many, unique and high-quality tastes are demanded over quick, convenient sources of nutrition.

The tomato, for its part, plays a pivotal role in each of these food alternatives. As one of the nation's most popular foods, and one that consumers demand be fresh and tasty, the tomato represents, for many, both the worst aspects of American consumerism and the promise of rejecting that culture. After nearly two centuries of efforts to transcend the seasonality of tomatoes and insist on the ready accessibility of both fresh and preserved tomatoes, a new culture has emerged celebrating nature's limited harvest. This culture, to a certain degree, also rejects the standardization of tomato varieties and the qualities they contain, instead extoling genetic and culinary diversity. And with its emphasis on supporting local farmers and encouraging home gardening, it is a rejection of the doctrine of "natural advantage" and the implied supremacy of geographically concentrated production that dominates commercial agriculture today. In its place, these alternatives imagine a world in which the tomato favorites of yesteryear, from New Jersey, Texas, and even Gibson County, Tennessee, could all be celebrated in their season and on their merits. These alternatives have had a limited effect on commercial agriculture, but they nonetheless represent competing voices that have forced agricultural companies, retailers, and farmers to consider some of the growing demands of American consumers.

CONCLUSION

The story of the tomato in America is an unlikely one. The tomato was not present in most areas of the United States until the end of the eighteenth century, and it was highly perishable, ripening at a time when other, less bothersome, foods were readily available. Yet, since the middle of the nineteenth century, the tomato has stood as one of America's most popular vegetables: in sauces that turn bland pasta and meat into popular dishes and as the jewel of the salad, as the red stuff in the can or jar but also as the trophy of the suburban gardener. Stretching across the widest range of food forms, both canned and fresh, industrial and homemade, the history of tomato (and more broadly food) culture cannot be reduced to the historical triumph of industrialization, standardization, and commodification.

The tomato offers a much more complex narrative. It is a story of culinary change, of the transition from a near-complete reliance on hard and root vegetables in the early colonial diet toward the adoption and popularization of soft fruits and vegetables such as tomatoes beginning by the nineteenth century. During the nineteenth century, both farmers and cooks sought to expand the usefulness and attractiveness of the tomato by introducing new cooking methods and culinary styles and by expanding the growing season of the tomato. By the early twentieth century, the tomato had surpassed traditional American vegetables such as squash, pumpkins, and rutabagas in popularity. During the early twentieth century, continued efforts at expanding access to the tomato, especially out-of-season, were paralleled by a culinary revolution in America. New middle-class reform movements aimed at decreasing meat consumption fueled tomato consumption and led to the fresh tomato becoming an integral part of salads. Similarly, the influx of immigrants, especially Italians, during the late nineteenth and early twentieth century brought new culinary traditions and ideas to the United States. Despite numerous efforts to curb their appeal, Italian-American and other immigrant cuisines significantly influenced American culinary culture, with the tomato playing a leading role. Pizza and pasta grew in popularity among non-Italian Americans during the 1920s and 1930s, and by the postwar period these foods had become popular dishes on American dinner tables. The development of tomato culture in the United States during the past two centuries parallels a significant trend in food culture in general: the diversification of the American diet, supplementing and challenging the dominance of the traditional diet of meat and potatoes. These efforts have provided American tables with new ingredients, new culinary techniques, and ethnic inspirations.

On its face, the rise of the tomato in America appears to be a success story of industrial America, where standardization of varieties and products and improved agricultural and industrial technologies laid the groundwork for a revolution in American food. The end result, too, was a near-complete commodification of the tomato, with processed tomatoes being planted, harvested, and processed by machine, with minimal human contact and fresh tomatoes planted in sand, covered in plastic, and fed a controlled dose of nutrients. The products that resulted were usually very standardized products, often requiring very little skill or effort on the part of the cook to prepare. Yet the story of the tomato in America is not simply a story of the "march of industrialization."

The tomato serves as an important counterexample to the traditional model of industrialization offered by historians. First, from the beginning, local forces—farmers, cooks, agricultural researchers, plant breeders, and small-scale canneries—have played an important role in innovations in tomato production and consumption. The primary problems facing efforts to integrate the tomato fully into the American diet during the nineteenth century—its seasonality and perishability— were largely solved not by the burgeoning food industry but by farmers, canners, cooks, and local agricultural extension workers. Thus the tomato industry during the late nineteenth century looked starkly different from the meat and grain trade, where production and processing had already become largely streamlined and concentrated in the name of rationalization.

This pattern continued during the early twentieth century and highlights a second point: as the tomato industry grew into its own, it continued to defy centralization and product differentiation (branding). Thousands of small farmers and canneries operated across the country, helping to produce a relatively stable supply of both canned and fresh tomatoes throughout the year. The decentralized nature of the industry was fueled by the desire to transcend the seasonality of tomatoes, making them available across the country throughout the year.

Third, tomato consumption became more diverse in the early twentieth century. Despite the existence of prominent companies like Heinz, Campbell's, and Hunt's, the tomato industry during the early twentieth century was largely dominated by small and medium sized firms that produced relatively standardized but also highly customizable products like canned whole tomatoes as middle-class and immigrant diners fueled a revolution in tomato cookery, popularizing tomato dishes ranging from fresh tomato salads to spaghetti. Not until the second half of the twentieth century, just as tomato production came increasingly under the control of large corporations, did tomato consumption become more homogenized with the introduction of frozen TV dinners, frozen pizza, and premixed pasta sauce, all of which lacked the customizability of earlier standardized tomato products.

Fourth, there is a disconnect between corporate images of the tomato and popular tomato culture. Despite the popularity of corporate offerings like canned tomato soup (immortalized by Andy Warhol's pop art painting) and premixed tomato sauce, the homegrown and hand-picked tomato, red and ripe right off the vine, remains firmly planted in the

American imagination. The financial success of the industrial tomato does not necessarily indicate consumer satisfaction or preference, but in many cases it represents a shortage of viable alternatives. Indeed, as the resurgence of farmers' markets and home gardening beginning in the 1970s show, the image of the red, ripe, and tasty tomato remains influential, and under the right conditions, this image has shaped many consumers' purchasing decisions.

Alternative methods of food acquisition, including farmers' markets, home gardening, and community supported agriculture programs, remain limited in their impact and their economic success. Despite their tremendous growth in recent decades, they still account for only a small fraction of total food purchases. Nonetheless, these countercultures illustrate the persistence of popular images of the tomato with their emphasis on quality, freshness, and taste above the corporate promise of year-round access, price, and aesthetic and genetic uniformity. Further, these alternative food cultures influence corporate decision making. Consider, for example, the packaged tomato on the vine.

Scholars have traditionally focused on the expansion of corporate food. But, the growing dissatisfaction with American food culture displayed by the popularity of Michael Pollan's *Omnivore's Dilemma*, Eric Schlosser's *Fast Food Nation*, and numerous documentaries and films such as *Food, Inc.* demonstrates resistance to branded, processed, and packaged nourishment. Consumer dissatisfaction with supermarket tomatoes often becomes a symbol of consumer resistance to corporate food offerings.[1]

The innovators in resolving the key problem of seasonality and perishability turned out to be not corporate but popular actors. To be practical for large-scale consumption, cooks adapted existing preservation methods for the tomato, a soft, highly perishable fruit that naturally ripened during the peak of the harvest. Likewise, farmers used various techniques to expand the growing season, making fresh tomatoes accessible for longer periods of the year. The culmination of these efforts was not simply the development of the tomato canning industry but a decentralized geography of production that, by the early twentieth century, transformed the tomato into a year-round commodity. While in the long run these innovations were co-opted by Big Food, Americans, from immigrants to WASPish foodies, began to resist the twelve-month tomato as a prime example of the ills of modern industrial agriculture and to promote the local, in-season tomato.

✕✕✕

This history of the tomato is part of a larger story of American food culture: the modern shift in the American diet toward a wider range of soft and perishable vegetables. The difficulty in mechanically harvesting and industrially processing fruits and vegetables—broccoli, grapes, and small-scale, specialty products like kale—produced solutions similar to those we have found with the tomato. While historians have focused on "hard" and less perishable crops, we need to expand the field of food history to consider this wider group.

Moreover, the tomato counters the standard story of progressive farmers and businesses creating new technologies to deal with labor shortages and costs. This narrative often begins with the likes of Cyrus McCormick and his reaper, which began to solve the age-old need for legions of harvest workers. The tomato story once again offers a different scenario: first, it long continued to be cultivated and harvested by local farmers and laborers in relatively small gardens; second, when the scale of production increased, large-scale farmers continued to seek large groups of migratory harvest workers, often using political means. It was not the corporate farmer but a land-grant university that found long-term solutions to labor shortages by designing effective harvesting machines and new breeds of tomatoes adapted to those machines.

On the consumption side of the equation, imported ideas have shaped American food. Italian American cuisine in particular has deservedly been the focus of much discussion of how ethnic groups maintained their cultural practices, including cuisine, long after they arrived in America. In a few cases, including Jeffrey Pilcher's 2012 *Planet Taco*, scholars have sought to examine how ethnic cuisines have been adapted to a global, corporate food industry. In such works, the emphasis has largely been on the trend toward the bland, packaged imitation of indigenous foods. New emphasis, however, should be placed on how ethnic cultures, from Italian to Japanese, Mexican to Indian, have shaped and diversified American food culture, not just how they were homogenized into the American cooking pot.[2]

The influence that countercultures have on the industrial food system also demands continued examination. A much larger portion of the population than just countercultural foodies participates in alternative food cultures, even as many also continue to shop at supermarkets and eat at fast food restaurants. While Big Food has resisted critiques such as those issued in *Food, Inc.* by publishing long responses dismissive of the motives and facts used by its critics, food manufacturers have also become increasingly active in producing organic food, free-range chicken, and many other products. This tension between dismissing criticisms and adopting new products and new ideas will likely continue for many years.[3]

The history of the tomato in America represents the diversity and complexity of American food culture. On the one hand, much like many other agricultural products and commodities, the story of the tomato is one of industrialization. Following more than a century of experimentation and advancement led by rural cooks and farmers, by the early twentieth century a tomato industry emerged in the United States defined by a decentralized geography and diverse forms of production. By the second half of the century, with new mechanization technologies and a burgeoning consumerism that emphasized convenience over quality, the tomato industry reversed course, becoming highly centralized economically and geographically. Increasingly, too, tomato products became highly homogenized and offered less freedom for culinary creativity.

Yet the history of the tomato is also a story of culinary diversity, creativity, ethnic influences, and entrepreneurial innovation. Beginning with nineteenth-century cooks and farmers, the development of tomato culture in the United States was focused on expanding and transcending the seasonality of the tomato but, in so doing, creating an amazing variety of uses of preserved and fresh tomatoes. This trend continued into the twentieth century as farmers, agricultural researchers, and canners created a uniquely decentralized industry designed to maximize access to the twelve-month tomato. The products produced by these efforts, including canned whole tomatoes, were highly malleable, allowing cooks to use tomatoes in a wide variety of dishes. Increased access to the tomato and tomato products also helped fuel a revolution in tomato cookery, as the tomato became a significant part of both middle-class reform cookery and immigrant cuisine.

Today, tomato production and processing has become highly mechanized and standardized. The majority of the tomatoes produced in the United States are sent to canneries where they are processed into pulp and paste and later reprocessed into sauces, juice, and other tomato products. Most of the remaining tomatoes are picked green and artificially ripened just before being sold. Yet consumers and food activists have offered alternatives, symbolic in ways, which challenge the industrial tomato and the larger industrial food system. Only time will tell whether these countercultures can compete with industrial food, or whether industrial food will reinvent itself and the industrial tomato.

NOTES

INTRODUCTION

1. Botanically, the tomato is a fruit. It is often referred to as a vegetable, however. The U.S. Supreme Court even took up this question in *Nix v. Hedden* (1893) and ultimately decided that, for the purposes of collecting customs, the tomato was a vegetable. As this is a cultural rather than scientific work, I generally refer to the tomato as a vegetable.

2. For information on the potato, see, for example, John Reader, *Potatoes: A History of the Propitious Esculent* (New Haven, CT: Yale University Press, 2008), 79–171.

3. The literature on tomatoes has addressed a number of issues raised by the increasing power of the corporate tomato industry, including the growing economic strength of processing companies, the cultural symbols of tomatoes provided by advertising and marketing, factory and field workers' attempts to organize and the transnational implications of migrant labor in tomato fields, and finally, the physical reconstruction of the tomato to serve the needs of the processed-tomato industry. See Barry Estabrook, *Tomatoland: How Modern Industrial Agriculture Destroyed Our Most Alluring Fruit* (Kansas City, MO: Andrews McMeel, 2011); Andrew Smith, *The Tomato in America: Early History, Culture, and Cookery* (Columbia: University of South Carolina Press, 1994); Andrew Smith, *Souper Tomatoes: The Story of America's Favorite Food* (New Brunswick, NJ: Rutgers University Press, 2000); Daniel Sidorick, *Condensed Capitalism: Campbell Soup and the Pursuit of Cheap Production in the Twentieth Century* (Ithaca, NY: ILR/Cornell University Press, 2009); Arthur Allen, *Ripe: The Search for the Perfect Tomato* (Berkeley: Counterpoint Press, 2010); Deborah Barndt, *Tangled Routes: Women, Work, and Globalization on the Tomato Trail* (New York: Rowman and Littlefield, 2002). On the importance of canning, see Daniel Boorstin, *The Americans: The Democratic Experience* (New York: Random

House, 1973), 309. "The annihilation of time, space, and taste" is a turn on a phrase first used by Karl Marx in *Outlines of the Critique of Political Economy* (New York: Penguin, 1973), 524. Some of the best works on other modern food industries include William Cronon, *Nature's Metropolis: Chicago and the Great West* (New York: Norton, 1991); Steven Stoll, *The Fruits of Natural Advantage: Making the Industrial Countryside in California* (Berkeley: University of California Press, 1998); John Soluri, *Banana Cultures: Agriculture, Consumption, and Environmental Change in Honduras and the United States* (Austin, TX: University of Texas Press, 2005). For the centralization and standardization of lettuce, see Gabriela Petrick, " 'Like Ribbons of Green and Gold': Industrializing Lettuce and the Quest for Quality in the Salinas Valley, 1920–1965," *Agricultural History* 80, no. 3 (2006): 269–95. For more general works on the homogenization of American food culture and food industries, see Susan Strasser, *Satisfaction Guaranteed: The Making of the American Mass Market* (Washington, DC: Smithsonian Institution Press, 1989); Harvey Levenstein, *Revolution at the Table: The Transformation of the American Diet* (New York: Oxford University Press, 1988); Ann Vileisis, *Kitchen Literacy: How We Lost Knowledge of Where Food Comes from and Why We Need to Get it Back* (Washington, DC: Island Press, 2008).

4. Sidney Mintz, *Sweetness and Power: The Place of Sugar in Modern History* (New York: Viking Penguin, 1985), 42.

5. Production of numerous crops remained geographically diverse as late as 1939, including cantaloupe, celery, carrots, and eggplants. The tomato industry, however, had the highest degree of decentralization of these examples. See, for example, U.S. Census Bureau, *1940 Census of Agriculture*, vol. 3, part 8 (Washington, DC: Government Printing Office, 1942): 804–9.

6. Richard Osborn Cummings, *The American and His Food* (New York: Arno Press, 1970), 12; Waverley Root and Richard de Rochemont, *Eating in America: A History* (New York: William Morrow, 1976), 10.

7. Vileisis, *Kitchen Literacy*, esp. 3–29.

8. Alan Trachtenberg, *The Incorporation of America: Culture and Society in the Gilded Age* (New York: Hill and Wang, 1982); Cronon, *Nature's Metropolis*, 97–147, 207–59; Roger Horowitz, *Putting Meat on the American Table: Taste, Technology, Transformation* (Baltimore: Johns Hopkins University Press, 2005); Soluri, *Banana Cultures*, 18–74; Douglas Cazaux Sackman, *Orange Empire: California and the Fruits of Eden* (Berkeley: University of California Press, 2007); Stoll, *Fruits of Natural Advantage*, esp. 63–123; Petrick, "Like Ribbons of Green and Gold."

9. Strasser, *Satisfaction Guaranteed*, esp. 29–57; Roland Marchand, *Advertising the American Dream: Making Way for Modernity, 1920–1940* (Berkeley: University of California Press, 1985), 1–24; Pamela Walker Laird, *Advertising Progress: American Business and the Rise of Consumer Marketing* (Baltimore: Johns Hopkins University Press, 1998); Kathleen Parkin, *Food Is Love: Food Advertising and Gender Roles in Modern America* (Philadelphia: University of Pennsylvania Press, 2006); T. Jackson Lears, *Fables of Abundance: A Cultural History of Advertising in America* (New York: Basic Books, 1994), esp. 2–3.

10. Harvey Levenstein, *Revolution at the Table: The Transformation of the American Diet* (New York: Oxford University Press, 1988), 103.

11. *Canners Directory 1925* (Washington, DC: National Canners Association, 1925). The 1925 directory listed more than 1,500 companies producing tomato products, most of which produced canned whole tomatoes. With many canneries going unreported due to limited production, this number could easily be much higher.

12. The changes in American food culture during the postwar period are consistent with broader changes in the history of consumer culture and consumption. Scholars have long pointed to the postwar period as one in which consumption and the "right" to participate in the marketplace became prevailing ideas in American society. See, for example, Lizabeth Cohen, *A Consumers' Republic: The Politics of Mass Consumption in Postwar America* (New York: Knopf, 2003), esp. 112–29, and Meg Jacobs, *Pocketbook Politics: Economic Citizenship in Twentieth-Century America* (Princeton, NJ: Princeton University Press, 2007).

13. A classic exposition on the link between labor shortages in the United States and American technological innovation is Nathan Rosenberg, *Technology and American Economic Growth* (New York: Harper and Row, 1972).

14. For one of the best works on the importance of the early twentieth century to the industrialization of agriculture, see Deborah Fitzgerald, *Every Farm a Factory: The Industrial Ideal in American Agriculture* (New Haven, CT: Yale University Press, 2003). For other works on the rise of industrial agriculture in the United States, see J. L. Anderson, *Industrializing the Corn Belt: Agriculture, Technology, and Environment, 1945–1972* (De Kalb: Northern Illinois University Press, 2008), and Bruce L. Gardner, *American Agriculture in the Twentieth Century: How It Flourished and What It Cost* (Cambridge, MA: Harvard University Press, 2002).

15. Much of the literature on challenges to the food industry during the postwar period focuses on the counterculture. See, for example, Warren Belasco, *Appetite for Change: How the Counterculture Took on the Food Industry* (Ithaca, NY: Cornell University Press, 2006).

1. THE EARLY AMERICAN TOMATO

1. Waverly Root and Richard de Rochemont, *Eating in America: A History* (New York: William Morrow, 1976), 61–62; Andrew Smith, *The Tomato in America: Early History, Culture, and Cookery* (Columbia: University of South Carolina Press, 1994). Smith's *The Tomato in America* sought to rewrite the history of the tomato by rejecting two key assumptions about tomatoes in early America: First, he challenged the commonly held belief that tomatoes were not present in the United States until close to the turn of the nineteenth century. Second, he contested the idea that even after its introduction into the United States (and until close to the turn of the twentieth century) most American believed the tomato to be poisonous or otherwise unhealthy. In this way, Smith successfully demonstrated that the tomato was much more

common in eighteenth- and nineteenth-century America than had been previously accepted.

2. J. A. Jenkins, "The Origin of the Cultivated Tomato," *Economic Botany* 2, no. 4 (1948): 379–92. For other main sources in the debate on the origins of the tomato, see A. P. de Candolle, *Origins of Cultivated Plants* (New York: D. Appleton, 1885); J. Sabine, "On the Love Apple or Tomato," *Royal Horticultural Society Transactions* 3 (1819): 342–54; C. H. Muller, "A Revision of the Genus *Lycopersicon*," USDA Misc. Publication 382 (1940); and C. H. Muller, "The Taxonomy and Distribution of the Genus *Lycopersicon*," *National Horticultural Magazine* 19 (1940): 157–60.

3. Petrus Andreas Matthiolus [Mattioli], *Di Pedacio Dioscoride Anazarbeo libri cinque della historia, et material medciciale tradotti in lingua volgare Italiana* (Venice, 1554); Jenkins, "Origin of the Cultivated Tomato," 380.

4. Jenkins, "Origin of the Cultivated Tomato," 380; Smith, *Tomato in America*, 17; Rudolf Grewe, "The Arrival of the Tomato in Spain and Italy: Early Recipes," *Journal of Gastronomy* 3 (Summer 1987): 67–68, 74–75. For the discussion around the healthfulness of tomatoes in eighteenth-century Europe, see Smith, *Tomato in America*, 18–19.

5. Jenkins, "Origin of the Cultivated Tomato," 389; Smith, *Tomato in America*, 16–17.

6. David Gentilcore, *Pomodoro!: A History of the Tomato in Italy* (New York: Columbia University Press, 2010), 25, 41, 48, 55; "Love-Apple, or Tomato Berry," *Times* (London), Sept. 22, 1820.

7. The story of Robert Gibbons Johnson is well documented in Smith, *Tomato in America*, 3–10, and Andrew Smith, "The Making of the Legend of Robert Gibbon Johnson," *New Jersey History* 108 (1990): 59–74. See also Adrianna Morganelli, *The Biography of Tomatoes* (New York: Crabtree, 2007), 15, and Joan R. Callahan, *50 Health Scares That Fizzled* (Santa Barbara, CA: Greenwood, 2011), 97–101. On Thomas Jefferson's introduction of the tomato in Lynchburg, see *Saga of a City, Lynchburg, Virginia, 1786–1936* (Lynchburg, 1936), 58–59.

8. William Salmon, *Botanologia: The English Herbal; or, History of Plants* (London: I. Dawks for H. Rhodes and J. Taylor, 1710), 29. Linguistic evidence supports the idea that tomatoes went from Europe first to the Caribbean and then to the United States, as the term *tomato*, as opposed to *tomate* or *love apple*, appears to have originated in the Caribbean. As opposed to European countries, which tended to use *tomate* or *love apple*, the American colonies, especially those in the South, typically used the term *tomato*. See Smith, *Tomato in the America*, 26.

9. Thomas Jefferson, *Notes on the State of Virginia* (Paris, 1782), 165; Peter J. Hatch, "Thomas Jefferson's Favorite Vegetables," in *Dining at Monticello: In Good Taste and Abundance*, ed. Daniel Lee Fowler (Charlottesville, VA: Thomas Jefferson Foundation, 2005), 57; Fowler, *Dining at Monticello*, 122; C. Margaret Scarry, "Plant Remains from Fort Matanzas" (unpublished paper, Feb. 1991), 7; John Lee Williams, *A View of West Florida* (Philadelphia: H. S. Tanner and the Author, 1827), 67; John Williams, *The Territory of Florida: Sketches of the Topography, Civil and Natural History* (New York: A. T. Goodrich, 1837), 24; Smith, *Tomato in America*, 27, 45.

10. Smith, *Tomato in America*, 29–36.

11. See C. F. Volney, *View of the Climate and Soil of the United States of America* (London: C. Mercier, 1804), 323–24, for a scathing indictment of New England cuisine, claiming their "turnips and potatoes swim in hog's lard, butter, or fat."

12. Massimo Montanari, *Food Is Culture*, trans. Albert Sonnenfeld (New York: Columbia University Press, 2006), 14; Thomas Hine, *The Total Package: The Secret History and Hidden Meanings of Boxes, Bottles, Cans, and Other Persuasive Containers* (New York: Little, Brown, 1995), 28; Gary Cross and Robert Proctor, *Packaged Pleasures: How Engineering and Marketing Revolutionized Desire* (Chicago: University of Chicago Press, 2014), chap. 2; Anna Revedin et al., "Thirty Thousand-Year-Old Evidence of Plant Food Processing," *Proceedings of the National Academy of Sciences of the United States of America (PNAS)* 107, no. 44 (2010): 18815–19; Alexander Young, *Chronicles of the First Planters of The Colony of Massachusetts Bay, from 1623 to 1636* (Boston: Charles C. Little and James Brown, 1846), 267, 477, quoted in Richard J. Hooker, *Food and Drink in America* (New York: Bobbs-Merrill, 1981), 9; Hooker, *Food and Drink in America*, 30; David Hackett Fischer, *Albion's Seed: Four British Folkways in America* (New York: Oxford University Press, 1989), 137.

13. Bernard M'Mahon, *The American Gardener's Catalog* (Philadelphia: B. Graves, 1806), 319. One hundred days is a very rough estimate of the minimum amount of time from planting until harvest. Seed catalogs and other sources did not begin to identify this period until the end of the nineteenth century. At that point, a particularly early variety would be one that yielded tomatoes within eighty or ninety days. In 1806, on the other hand, there were not even established varieties, meaning that most tomatoes would be considered "main crop" as specialization within the seed industry had not yet begun. The hundred-day estimate, then, should be seen as a minimum amount of days rather than a prediction of the exact time frame until tomatoes could be harvested.

14. Israel Acrelius, "A History of New Sweden," in *Memoirs of the Historical Society of Pennsylvania* 11 (1876): 151.

15. Printed in Henry Stephens Randall, *The Life of Thomas Jefferson*, vol. 1 (New York: Derby and Jackson, 1858), facing 44.

2. THE TOMATO ON THE FARM

1. Untitled article, *Atkinson's Saturday Evening Post* (Philadelphia), Aug. 8, 1835, 2; "Farmers' Department," *Western Christian Advocate* (Cincinnati), Aug. 3, 1838. See also "Virtues of the Tomato," *New England Farmer, and Horticultural Register* (Boston), Sept. 2, 1835, 62; "Miscellanies," *Genesee Farmer and Gardener's Journal* (Rochester, NY), Sept. 9, 1835, 304; "Part III. Miscellaneous Intelligence," *Southern Agriculturist and Register of Rural Affairs* (Charleston, SC), Oct. 1835, 557; "Is the Tomato a Medicine or an Aliment?" *Graham Journal of Health and Longevity* (New York), Oct. 13, 1838, 321; "Virtues of the Tomato," *Christian Register and Boston Observer*, Aug. 22, 216; and "Tomato, or Love Apple," *American Magazine of Useful and*

Entertaining Knowledge (Boston), Sept. 1835, 29. For a longer discussion on the importance of Bennett to the rise of tomatoes during the 1830s, see Andrew Smith, *The Tomato in America: Early History, Culture, and Cookery* (Columbia: University of South Carolina Press, 1994), 102–6.

2.   Sugar was considered a medicine (as were soda water and, of course, distilled alcoholic beverages) before they were treated as recreational food and drink. David Courtwright, *Forces of Habit: Drugs and the Making of the Modern World* (Cambridge, MA: Harvard University Press, 2001), 18, 72, 74; Wolfgang Schivelbusch, *Tastes of Paradise* (New York: Vintage, 1992), 159; Wendy Woloson, *Refined Tastes: Sugar, Confectionery, and Consumers in Nineteenth-Century America* (Baltimore: Johns Hopkins University Press, 2002), 26–49; John Riley, *A History of the American Soft Drink Industry: Bottled Carbonated Beverages, 1807–1957* (Washington, DC: American Bottlers of Carbonated Beverages, 1958), 26.

3.   Fearing Burr Jr., *The Field and Garden Vegetables of America* (Boston: J. E. Tilton, 1865), 628.

4.   For a discussion of the influence of numerous ethnic traditions, especially German and Dutch, on the formation of American cuisine, see Waverly Root and Richard de Rochemont, *Eating in America: A History* (New York: William Morrow, 1976), 303–12.

5.   "The Gardener's Manual," *Genesee Farmer and Gardener's Journal* (Rochester, NY), Sept. 5, 1835, 282.

6.   Launcelot Sturgeon, *Essays, Moral, Philosophical, and Stomachical* (London: G. and W. B. Whitaker, 1823), 80–81. For a lengthier discussion of the origins of tomato ketchup, see Andrew Smith, *Pure Ketchup: A History of America's National Condiment* (Washington, DC: Smithsonian Institution Press, 2001), 12–23.

7.   James Peterson, *Sauces: Classical and Contemporary Sauce Making*, 3rd ed. (Hoboken, NJ: John Wiley and Sons, 2008), 3, 5, 12; Ivan Day, *Cooking in Europe, 1650–1850* (Westport, CT: Greenwood Press, 2009), 2, 11–12.

8.   Sturgeon, *Essays, Moral, Philosophical, Stomachical*, 83; Smith, *Pure Ketchup*, 8; C. Anne Wilson, *Food and Drink in Britain: From the Stone Age to the 19th Century* (Chicago: Academy Chicago Publishers, 1991), 221–22.

9.   E. Smith, *The Compleat Housewife* (London, 1739), 80–99; Elizabeth Raffald, *The Experienced English Housekeeper* (Manchester, 1769), 316–68; Amelia Simmons, *American Cookery; or, the Art of Dressing Viands, Fish, Poultry and Vegetables* (Albany, NY, 1796), 64; Hannah Glasse, *The Art of Cookery Made Plain and Easy* (Alexandria, VA, 1805), 145ff, esp. 216–17.

10.   James Mease, *Archives of Useful Knowledge*, vol. 2 (Philadelphia: David Hogan, 1812), 306, cited in Andrew Smith, *Pure Ketchup*, 19; Maria Eliza Rundell, *A New System of Domestic Cookery* (London: John Murray, 1808); Rundell, *The American Domestic Cookery* (New York: Evert Duyckinck, 1823); William Kitchiner, *The Cook's Oracle* (New York: Evert Duyckinck, 1825); Mary Randolph, *The Virginia Housewife; or, Methodical Cook* (Mineola, NY: Dover, 1993), 201.

11.   Smith, *Pure Ketchup*, 25.

12.   Untitled article, *Farmer and Gardener's Journal* (Rochester, NY), Aug. 17, 1833, 258; "Household Affairs," *Cultivator* (Albany, NY), Oct. 1834, 105; *Cultivator*, "To Make

Tomato Catsup," *Farmer's Register* (Richmond, VA), Dec. 1834, 427; L. E. Landon, "Miscellaneous," *Farmer and Gardener, and Live-Stock Breeder and Manager* (Baltimore), Nov. 4, 1834, 215; "Preserving Apples for Hogs," *New England Farmer, and Horticultural Register* (Boston), Oct. 7, 1835, 101; "An Experienced House-Keeper and a Father," "Farmers' Department," *Western Christian Advocate* (Cincinnati), Sept. 23, 1836, 87.

13. "To Make Tomato Ketchup," *New England Farmer, and Horticultural Register* (Boston), Sept. 11, 1829, 59; "Recipes," *Southern Planter* (Richmond, VA), Sept. 1844, 203; Lydia Marie Francis Child, *The Frugal Housewife*, 2nd ed. (Boston: Carter and Hendee, 1830), 33; "Tomato Catsup," *Ohio Cultivator* (Columbus), Sept. 1, 1850, 271; Edward James Hooper, *The Practical Farmer, Gardener and Housewife* (Cincinnati: Geo. Conclin, 1840), 493.

14. "Virtues of the Tomato," *Christian Register*, 216; "Tomato Sauce and Butter," *Maine Farmer* (Augusta), Sept. 5, 1850, 1. See also "Tomato Sauce," *New England Farmer, and Horticultural Register* (Boston), Dec. 19, 1828, 174; "Love Apple—Tomato," *Genesee Farmer and Gardener's Journal* (Rochester, NY), Apr. 7, 1832, 107.

15. Kitchiner, *Cook's Oracle*, 345. See, for example, "A Boston Housekeeper," *The Cook's Own Book* (Boston: Munroe and Francis, 1832), 222–23; Eliza Leslie, *Directions for Cookery* (Philadelphia: Carey and Hart, 1840), 223; Thomas G. Fessenden, *The New American Gardener* (Boston: J. B. Russell, 1828), 291; Eliza Leslie, *Miss Leslie's New Cookery Book* (Philadelphia: T. B. Peterson, 1857), 400.

16. Untitled article, *Cincinnati Mirror, and Western Gazette of Literature, Science, and the Arts*, Sept. 6, 1834, 375; untitled article, *Valley Farmer* (St. Louis), Sept. 1855, 400; "Cookery," *Tennessee Farmer* (Jonesborough), Sept. 1837, 128; untitled article, *New England Farmer, and Horticultural Register* (Boston), Nov. 13, 1829, 133; "The Tomato," *Farmers Cabinet and American Herd Book, Devoted to Agriculture, Horticulture, and Rural and Domestic Affairs* (Philadelphia), Sept. 15, 1843, 44; Landon, "Miscellaneous," 215; "Family Receipts," *Genesee Farmer and Gardener's Journal* (Rochester, NY), Aug. 30, 1834, 35; H. L. Ellsworth, "Tomato Figs," *American Farmer, and Spirit of the Agricultural Journals of the Day* (Baltimore), July 10, 1841, 97; "Household Affairs," *Southern Agriculturist, Horticulturist, and Register of Rural Affairs* (Charleston, SC), Sept. 1841, 503; American Farmer, "Tomato Figs," *New England Farmer, and Horticultural Register* (Boston), Sept. 1, 1841, 66; "For Housekeepers," *Saturday Evening Post*, Sept. 22, 1849, 4. Ellsworth's article on tomato figs was reprinted across the country, including in the *Southern Planter*, the *Maine Farmer*, and the *New Genesee Farmer and Gardeners' Journal*.

17. "A Female Reader," "Domestic Economy," *Cultivator* (Albany, NY), June 1844, 198; "A Female Reader," "To Preserve Tomatoes," *Southern Planter* (Richmond, VA), Aug. 1844 186.

18. "Method of Preserving Tomatoes," *Workingman's Advocate* (New York), Sept. 26, 1835, 1. See also untitled article, *New England Farmer, and Horticultural Register* (Boston), Sept. 6, 1837, 67.

19. Untitled article, *New England Farmer, and Horticultural Register* (Boston), Oct. 14, 1835, 109; D., "Turkish Preparation of Tomato," *New York Farmer*, Oct. 1836, 299;

"Tomato," *New England Farmer, and Horticultural Register* (Boston), Oct. 14, 1835, 106.

20. H., "The Best Way of Preserving Fruits and Vegetables," *Horticulturalist and Journal of Rural Art and Rural Taste*, Sept. 1, 1851, 417; Ploughman Mars, "Keeping Tomatoes," *Maine Farmer* (Augusta), Oct. 6, 1853, 1. See also "Preserving Tomatoes," *Valley Farmer* (St. Louis), Sept. 1855, 400.

21. "Tomatoes," *Workingman's Advocate* 4, no. 3 (1832): 2; "Family Receipts," 35; untitled article, *Baltimore Monument*, Oct. 15, 1836, 16.

22. "Pickles, Tomatoes, Etc.," *Godey's Lady's Book and Magazine*, Aug. 1855, 174; "Tomatoes," *Christian Watchman and Reflector* (Boston), Aug. 12, 1852, 132; "To Cook Tomatoes," *New England Farmer, and Horticultural Register* (Boston), July 30, 1845, 36; "Domestic Receipts," *Maine Farmer* (Augusta), Aug. 25, 1853, 1; untitled recipe, *Cincinnati Mirror, and Western Gazette of Literature, Science, and the Arts*, Aug. 8, 1835, 332; "For Housekeepers," 4.

23. Hooper, *Practical Farmer, Gardener and Housewife*, 496; Putnam, *Mrs. Putnam's Receipt Book*, 67; Hale, *Ladies' New Book of Cookery*, 251.

24. Advertisement, *Genesee Farmer and Gardener's Journal* (Rochester, NY), July 20, 1833, 227; untitled article, *New England Farmer, and Horticultural Register* (Boston), July 19, 1837, 14.

25. Advertisement, *New England Farmer, and Horticultural Register* (Boston), Aug. 7, 1833, 31; "Boston Faneuil Market, Aug. 14, 1833," ibid., Aug. 14, 1833, 39; advertisement, ibid., Aug. 21, 1833, 47; "Faneuil Hall Vegetable Market," ibid., July 29, 1835, 23; "Faneuil Hall Market," ibid., Sept. 9, 1835, 71.

26. Edmund Morris, *Ten Acres Enough* (New York: James Miller, 1864), 118–20.

27. Thos. D. Baird, "The Garden: The Tomato," *National Stockman and Farmer*, June 13, 1889, 173; "Varieties of Tomatoes," *Michigan Farmer*, Feb. 15, 1890, 3; N. Hallock, "Experiences with Tomatoes: Results of a Large Experiment," *American Garden: A Monthly Illustrated Journal Devoted to Garden Art*, May 1890, 292.

28. "Hurrying up the Tomatoes," *Maine Farmer* (Augusta), Aug. 26, 1852, 1; James M. Garnett, "Culture of the Tomato and the Indian Pea," *Farmer's Register* (Richmond, VA), Oct. 31, 1841, 589; William Chorlton, "Culture of the Tomato," *Horticulturist and Journal of Rural Art and Rural Taste*, Mar. 1, 1855, 130; "Gardening for the South," *Southern Cultivator* (Atlanta), Mar. 1850, 39.

29. For catalogs listing only a single variety, see G. Thorburn and Son, *Catalogue of Kitchen Garden, Herb, Flower, Tree and Grass Seeds* (New York: Clayton and Van Norden, 1825), 14, in Henry G. Gilbert Nursery and Seed Trade Catalog Collection, Manuscript Collection #120, National Agriculture Library, Beltsville, MD (hereafter STCC); John B. Russell, *Catalogue of Kitchen Garden Herb, Tree, Field and Flower Seeds* (Boston: New England Farmer Office, 1827), 15, STCC; Joseph Breck and Co., *Catalogue of Vegetable, Herb, Tree, Flower and Grass Seeds* (Boston, 1840), 12, STCC; and Charles H. B. Breck, *Catalogue of Vegetable, Herb, Tree, Flower and Grass Seeds* (Boston: Tuttle and Dennett, 1842), 8, STCC. For early varieties listed for sale, see David Prouty and Co., *Catalogue of Garden, Flower, Field and Grass Seeds* (Boston,

1851), 95, STCC; Comstock, Ferre and Co., *Descriptive Catalogue of Garden Seeds Cultivated and Sold at the Wethersfield Seed Garden* (Wethersfield, CT, 1852), 42–43, STCC; and James M. Thorburn, *Thorburn's Catalogue of Kitchen Garden Seeds* (New York: William S. Dorr, 1853), 6, STCC. The National Agriculture Library's seed catalog is extensive. I examined all of the available seed catalogs from prior to 1870. From 1870 through 1957, I selected boxes covering the letters *L* through *O*, typically in five-year increments. This allowed me to focus on several seed houses that were of great importance to the tomato trade, including Livingston and Co., while also tracing the offerings of numerous other seed houses over time.

30.   Henry A. Dreer, *Dreer's Garden Calendar, 1861* (Philadelphia, 1861), 19, STCC; Benjamin K. Bliss, *Descriptive Catalogue of a Choice Collection of Vegetable, Agricultural, and Flower Seeds . . . 1865* (Springfield, MA, 1866), 83, STCC. See also David Landreth and Son, *Descriptive Catalogue of the Garden Seeds Cultivated at Bloomsdale, the Seed Grounds of David Landreth & Son* (Philadelphia, 1865), 19, STCC.

31.   Washburn and Co., *Washburn & Co.'s Amateur Cultivator's Guide to the Flower and Kitchen Garden, 1869 Catalogue* (Boston, 1869), 124, STCC; Burr, *Field and Garden Vegetables of America*, 643–52; Edward J. Evans and Co. catalog (York, PA, 1868), STCC.

32.   W. F., "Tomatoes—Varieties and Culture," *Cultivator and Country Gentleman*, Sept. 25, 1884, 796; A. W. Livingston, *Livingston and the Tomato* (Columbus, OH: A. W. Livingston's Sons, 1893), 9–15, 20–23.

33.   Livingston, *Livingston and the Tomato*, 24–26; E. S. Goff, "Mr. A. W. Livingston," *American Garden: A Monthly Illustrated Journal Devoted to Garden Art*, Mar. 1, 1887, 75; "Care in Selecting Seed," *New England Farmer, and Horticultural Register* (Boston), Jan. 26, 1884, 1; "Obituary," *American Gardening*, Nov. 26, 1898, 812.

34.   Livingston, *Livingston and the Tomato*, 28, 31–32, 42, 64–65.

35.   "Hurrying up the Tomatoes," 1; "Cultivation of Tomato," *American Farmer, and Spirit of the Agricultural Journals of the Day* (Baltimore), Aug. 30, 1843, 117.

36.   Untitled article, *Cultivator* (Albany, NY), Mar. 1835, 8; "Hot Beds," ibid., Feb. 1844, 69; "Hot Beds," *Genesee Farmer and Gardener's Journal* (Rochester, NY), Mar. 28, 1835, 98.

37.   "Work for March," *Western Farmer and Gardener* (Cincinnati), Mar. 1844, 190; untitled article, *Cultivator* (Albany, NY), Mar. 1835, 8; "Art. VIII: On the Cultivation of Tomatoes; (Solanum Lycopersicum); by the Editor," *Southern Agriculturist and Register of Rural Affairs* (Charleston, SC), Feb. 1829, 79; Livingston, *Livingston and the Tomato*, 70–77.

38.   "Hot Beds," *Southern Planter*, 52; "Raising of Early Tomatoes," *Genesee Farmer and Gardener's Journal* (Rochester, NY), Feb. 8, 1834, 45. See also G. W. P. Jerrard, "Early Tomato Plants," *Maine Farmer* (Augusta), Mar. 20, 1884, 2.

39.   W. F. Massey, "Trucking in Virginia and North Carolina—Early Tomatoes," *Southern Planter*, Feb. 1896, 59. See also "Tomatoes Under Glass," *Meehan's Monthly*, Feb. 1892), 27. For *Meehan's Monthly*, I examined a run from 1891 to 1902 in full at the University of Delaware Special Collections Library, Wilmington.

40. John Thorpe, "Fruits and Vegetables Under Glass," *American Garden*, Sept. 1, 1889, 310; W. Falconer, "Tomatoes at Christmas," *Cultivator and Country Gentleman*, Sept. 11, 1884, 756; "Winter-Grown Vegetables," *Meehan's Monthly*, Mar. 1896, 56; E. C. Green, "The Earliest Tomato," *Ohio Farmer*, Mar. 23, 1899, 247; "Forcing Tomatoes," *Meehan's Monthly*, Jan. 1893, 13.

3. A TOMATO FOR ALL SEASONS

A previous version of this chapter was published as John Hoenig, "A Tomato for All Seasons: Innovation in American Agriculture, 1900–1945," *Business History Review* 88, no. 3 (Autumn 2014): 523–44. I would like to thank Cambridge University Press for permission to reprint, as well as the editors and reviewers for their very meaningful and helpful comments.

1. The best book on both the meatpacking and grain industries becoming concentrated in Chicago is William Cronon, *Nature's Metropolis: Chicago and the Great West* (New York: Norton, 1991), 211, 235, 244. For the citrus industry, see Steven Stoll, *The Fruits of Natural Advantage: Making the Industrial Countryside in California* (Berkeley: University of California Press, 1998). For the emergence of iceberg lettuce and its centralization in California, see Gabriela Petrick, "'Like Ribbons of Green and Gold': Industrializing Lettuce and the Question for Quality in the Salinas Valley, 1920–1965," *Agricultural History* 80, no. 3 (2006): 269–95.

2. James H. Collins, *The Story of Canned Foods* (New York: E. P. Dutton, 1924), 2–5; Nicholas Appert, *The Art of Preserving All Kinds of Animal and Vegetable Substances* (London: Black Perry, 1812), 1–19; Clarence Francis, *A History of Food and Its Preservation* (Princeton, NJ: Princeton University Press, 1937), 9–11.

3. A. J. Howard, *Canning Technology* (Washington, DC: Sherwood Press, 1949), 3, 4; Earl Chapin May, *The Canning Clan: A Pageant of Pioneering Americans* (New York: Macmillan, 1938), 2, 10, 12; Collins, *Story of Canned Foods*, 10–11.

4. Collins, *Story of Canned Foods*, 16–17; American Can Company, *The Canned Food Reference Manual*, 3rd ed. (New York, 1949), 29; *The Canning Industry, Its History, Organization, Methods, and the Public Service Values of Its Products* (Washington, DC: National Canners Association, 1952), 7, Hagley Library, Wilmington, DE.

5. May, *Canning Clan*, 12, 21, 28, 87;

6. Ibid., 28–29; Howard, *Canning Technology*, 4; Edward S. Judge, "The Past, Present and Future of the Canned Food Industry," in *A History of the Canning Industry; by its most Prominent Men*, ed. Arthur I. Judge (Baltimore: Canning Trade, 1914), 55; May, *Canning Clan*, 29. For references to other important, but similar, innovations, see Stanley Macklem, interview, 1963–64, transcript 1199, p. 42, in Stanley Macklem Oral History, New York State Food Processing Oral History Project, #2378, Cornell University, Division of Rare and Manuscript Collections.

7. Howard, *Canning Technology*, 4; May, *Canning Clan*, 88–95; Macklem interview, 24; American Can Company, *Canned Food Reference Manual*, 49; George W. Cobb, "The Development of the Sanitary Can," in Judge, *History of the Canning Industry*, 94–96.

8.   May, *Canning Clan*, 23–24, 26; American Can Company, *Canned Food Reference Manual*, 31; Collins, *Story of Canned Foods*, 16, 22.

9.   May, *Canning Clan*, 42–44, 129–38.

10. John D. Cox, "The Evolution of Tomato Canning Machinery," in Judge, *History of the Canning Industry*, 82; Dean A. Doerrfeld, David L. Ames, and Rebecca J. Siders, *The Canning Industry in Delaware, 1860 to 1940+/–: A Historic Context* (Wilmington: University of Delaware, Center for Historic Architecture and Engineering, 1993), 18; Cox, "Evolution of Tomato Canning Machinery," 82.

11. Canners' Supply Company, catalog (Bridgeton, NJ; Philadelphia, ca. 1890), 66–69, Hagley Library; Cox, "Evolution of Tomato Canning Machinery," 83–84; Judge, "Past, Present and Future of the Canned Food Industry," 56.

12. Canning Trade, *1916 Almanac of the Canning Industry* (Baltimore: Canning Trade, 1916), 23; May, *Canning Clan*, 23; John G. Ruge, "The Canning Industry in the South," in Judge, *History of the Canning Industry*, 15; *Canning Industry, Its History*, 7; Judge, "Past, Present and Future of the Canned Food Industry," 56.

13. Susan Strasser, *Satisfaction Guaranteed: The Making of the American Mass Market* (Washington, DC: Smithsonian Institution Books, 1989), 26–31.

14. Douglas Collins, *America's Favorite Food: The Story of Campbell Soup Company* (New York: Harry N. Abrams, 1994), 13, 21, 24; Andrew F. Smith, *Souper Tomatoes: The Story of America's Favorite Food* (New Brunswick, NJ: Rutgers University Press, 2000), 84; "The House of Heinz," *Fortune*, Feb. 1941, 74; Robert C. Alberts, *The Good Provider: H. J. Heinz and His 57 Varieties* (Boston: Houghton Mifflin, 1973), 8–9; Eleanor Foa Dienstag, *In Good Company: 125 Years at the Heinz Table* (New York: Warner Books, 1994), ciii, 24, 26; Charles Robson, ed. *The Manufactories and Manufacturers of Pennsylvania of the Nineteenth Century* (Philadelphia: Galaxy, 1875), 383.

15. Alberts, *Good Provider*, 13–18, 28–29, 86–87, 90, 101, 119, 149; Dienstag, *In Good Company*, 31, 34, 54, 69–71.

16. Collins, *America's Favorite Food*, 13, 37, 39, 82; Smith, *Souper Tomatoes*, 87, 89.

17. Collins, *America's Favorite Food*, 109–13; Dienstag, *In Good Company*, 38, 62, 156; "In Grandpa's Shoes," *Saturday Evening Post*, June 23, 1949, 102.

18. Gary Cross and Robert Proctor, *Packaged Pleasures: How Technology and Marketing Revolutionized Desire* (Chicago: University of Chicago Press, 2014), chap. 2.

19. Alberts, *Good Provider*, 40–41; Collins, *America's Favorite Food*, 87, 97–98; Strasser, *Satisfaction Guaranteed*, 84–88, 203–4; "House of Heinz," 140.

20. Collins, *America's Favorite Food*, 49, 89; Roland Marchand, *Advertising the American Dream: Making Way for Modernity, 1920–1940* (Berkeley: University of California Press, 1985), 229–30; Gary Cross, *The Cute and the Cool* (New York: Oxford University Press, 2004), chap. 3.

21. Dienstag, *In Good Company*, 24, 154; advertisement, *Good Housekeeping*, July 1909, back advertising section; advertisement, *Saturday Evening Post*, Feb. 27, 1909, 20–21; advertisement, *Good Housekeeping*, July 1909, back advertising section; advertisement, *Good Housekeeping*, Sept. 1909, back advertising section.

22. Alberts, *Good Provider*, 119–22, 127; Dienstag, *In Good Company*, 127. For examples of Heinz advertising its "Aristocrat" tomato, see advertisements, *Good Housekeeping*,

May 1926, 116 and Apr. 1926, 240. For Campbell's advertising its own work on tomatoes, see advertisement, *Good Housekeeping*, May 1919, 75.

23. National Canners' Association, *Canned Food Pack Statistics: 1950, Part 1—Vegetables*
(Washington, DC, June 1951), 22; Collins, *America's Favorite Food*, 44–45, 47, 132–34;
U.S. Department of Agriculture (USDA), Bureau of Agricultural Economics (BAE),
Supplement for 1961 to Consumption of Food in the United States 1909–52, supplement
to Agricultural Handbook (Washington, DC, 1962), 25; USDA BAE, *Consumption of
Food in the United States, 1909–1952*, Agricultural Handbook 62 (Washington, DC,
1953), 117, 119, 121, 142; "House of Heinz," 136.

24. Canning Trade, *1918 Almanac of the Canning Industry* (Baltimore, 1918), 23; National
Canners Association, *Canned Food Pack Statistics, 1943* (Washington, DC, 1944), 18;
National Canners Association, *Canned Food Pack Statistics, 1948* (Washington, DC,
1949). There is evidence that tomato paste was imported into the United States prior
to World War I, for consumption primarily by Italian Americans. During World
War I, with trade cut off between the United States and Italy, a few American producers began producing paste. This is discussed in greater detail in the next chapter.

25. Doerrfeld, Ames, and Siders, "Canning Industry in Delaware," 18; Cox, "Evolution of
Tomato Canning Machinery," 82; Clyde H. Campbell, *Campbell's Book: A Manual on
Canning, Pickling, and Preserving*, 3rd ed. (Chicago: Vance, 1950). See also Howard,
Canning Technology, and American Can Company, *Canned Food Reference Manual*.

26. Cox, "Evolution of Tomato Canning Machinery," 82; Sprague Canning Machinery
Co., *Sprague General Catalogue of Canning Machinery and Supplies* (Chicago, ca.
1910), 129, 131, Smithsonian National Museum of American History, Washington,
DC (hereafter NMAH); Macklem interview, 42; Judge, "Past, Present and Future of
the Canned Food Industry," 56. For an example of a factory replacing all of its equipment as it expanded, see Edgar Heher, interview by Edward F. Keuchel, Aug. 16, 1963,
transcript 1226, pp. 66–67, in Stanley Macklem Oral History.

27. H. P. Stuckey and J. C. Temple, "Tomatoes: Two Parts," Georgia Experiment Station
Bulletin 96 (Atlanta: Blosser, 1911), 57; "Home Canning Outfit," *Market Growers
Journal*, Jan. 15, 1908, 19; George S. Demuth, "Canning Tomatoes on a Large Scale,"
Market Growers Journal, May 7, 1910, 5; "Gardeners' Club," *Market Growers Journal*,
Mar. 23, 1912, 12; H. S. Mill Canning Company, letter book 1905–1908, #2497, Hagley
Library, 169–70, 235, 340–41, 432; Morton Adams, interview, June 30, 1964, transcript 1219, p. 87, in Stanley Macklem Oral History. By the 1930s, as chain stores
became popular, this trend began to decline, as wholesaler and chain store brands
replaced those of individual canneries. See, for example, Heher interview, 19. I examined the *Market Growers Journal* at length, reading almost all issues from 1908
through 1945.

28. U.S. Census Bureau, *Twelfth Census of the United States*, vol. 2 (Washington, DC:
Government Printing Office, 1902); U.S. Census Bureau, *Fourteenth Census of the
United States*, vol. 5, chap. 12 (Washington, DC: Government Printing Office, 1922),
830; Henry A. James, "Tomatoes for Market and Canning," University of Maryland
Agricultural Experiment Station Bulletin 248 (Feb. 1922), 154; Frank App and Allen

G. Waller, "Costs, Profits and Practices of the Can-House Tomato Industry in New Jersey," New Jersey Agricultural Experiment Station Bulletin 353 (Apr. 1921), 6, 13–14.

29. App and Waller, "Costs, Profits and Practices," 6; USDA BAE, "Vegetables for Commercial Processing: Acreage, Production, Value; Revised Estimates, 1918–50," Statistical Bulletin 132 (June 1953); James Beattie, "Tomatoes for Canning and Manufacture," U.S. Department of Agriculture Farmers' Bulletin 1233 (Oct. 1921), 5–6.

30. *Canners Directory 1925* (Washington, DC: National Canners Association, 1925). It should be noted, too, that the *Canners Directory* did not list every cannery in operation. I discovered this omission while researching canning in northeast Pennsylvania and working on the Pennsylvania Agricultural History Project led by Sally McMurry. Often, the directory did not mention smaller canneries, especially in areas that were not dominant sites of food production.

31. C. A. McCue, "Tomatoes for the Canning Factory," Delaware College Agricultural Experiment Station Bulletin 101 (1912), 56; Charles M. Arthur, "Marketing Tomatoes in New Jersey," New Jersey State Agricultural College Extension Bulletin 1 no. 6 (1915), 1–12.

32. F. C. Gaylord and K. I. Fawcett, "A Study of Grade, Quality and Price of Canned Tomatoes at Retail in Indiana," Purdue University Agricultural Experiment Station Bulletin 438 (1939), 5, 9; F. C. Gaylord and K. I. Fawcett, "A Study of Grade, Quality and Price of Canned Tomatoes Sold at Retail in Indiana," Purdue University Agricultural Experiment Station Bulletin 495 (1944), 3, 7.

33. "The Earliest in the World" (May's Tomato Seed advertisement), *Market Growers Journal*, Feb. 5, 1908, 3.

34. W. Atlee Burpee and Co., catalog (Philadelphia, 1904), 31, and catalog (Philadelphia, 1905), 11, both in NMAH; L. G. Schermerhorn, "Scientific Breeding Gives New Jersey the Rutgers Tomato," *New Jersey State Horticultural Society News* 15, no. 6 (1934): 1. At the National Museum of American History, I was able to examine nearly a complete run of Burpee seed catalogs from the late nineteenth century through the 1990s.

35. A. W. Livingston, *Livingston and the Tomato* (Columbus, OH: A. W. Livingston's Sons, 1893), 34–35, 59. The Plant Patent Act of 1930 offered patent protect for sexually reproducing plants but did not extend protection to asexually reproducing plants, such as tomatoes. There are numerous reasons why asexually reproducing plants did not receive such protection. A big part of the explanation is that asexually reproducing plants are much harder to isolate than sexually reproducing plants, making "proving" that one variety is distinct from another and that it is stable very difficult. For a great discussion on patent protection in plants, and in particular on asexually reproducing plants, which did not receive patent protection until the second half of the century, see Jack Kloppenburg Jr., *First the Seed: The Political Economy of Plant Biotechnology, 1492–2000* (New York: Cambridge University Press, 1988), and Cary Fowler, "The Plant Patent Act of 1930: A Sociological History of Its Creation," *Journal of the Patent and Trademark Office* 82 (2000): 621–44.

36. N. Hallock, "Experiences with Tomatoes: Results of a Large Experiment," *American Garden: A Monthly Illustrated Journal Devoted to Garden Art*, May 1890, 292;

D. Landreth and Sons, catalog (Philadelphia, 1900), 30–31, Henry G. Gilbert Nursery and Seed Trade Catalog Collection, Manuscript Collection #120, National Agriculture Library, Beltsville, MD (hereafter STCC); Nebraska Seed Company, catalog (Omaha, 1905), 21–22, STCC; D. Landreth Seed Company, *Landreth's Garden Seeds* (Bristol, PA, 1915), 89–94, STCC; Leonard Seed Co., *Leonard's Seeds* (Chicago, 1920), 44–45, STCC.

37.   For consumer demand for out-of-season tomatoes, see E. V. Wilcox, "Are Vegetable Growers Meeting Consumers Half Way?" *Market Growers Journal*, Oct. 15, 1925, 5, 7. For the economic need to produce early tomatoes, see "Secrets of Success with Early Tomatoes: A Summary of the Experience of Thirty-Six Growers," *Market Growers Journal*, Mar. 9, 1912, 5, 19; C. A. U., "A Farmer's Report on Tomato Growing," *Market Growers Journal*, Feb. 5, 1908, 9; and W. H. Harris, "Earliest Crops in the Vegetable Garden," *Market Growers Journal*, Jan. 15, 1925, 32. For farmers reporting the prices received in the first two weeks of the season, see "This Week's Topic," *Market Growers Journal*, Mar. 9, 1912, 13–19, and Mar. 16, 1912, 12–19.

38.   USDA BAE, "Commercial Truck Crops: Revised Estimates of Acreage, Production and Value, 1928–1941, under New Seasonal Groupings," Statistical Bulletin (Oct. 1943), 4–5.

39.   USDA BAE, "Shipments and Unloads of Certain Fruits and Vegetables, 1918–1923," Statistical Bulletin 7 (Apr. 1925); USDA BAE "Car-Lot Shipments and Unloads of Important Fruits and Vegetables for the Calendar Years 1924–1926," Statistical Bulletin 23 (Apr. 1928).

40.   See "Mexican Vegetables for American Trade Increasing Yearly: Home Growers Should Get Busy," *Market Growers Journal*, Nov. 1, 1925, 13; "Vegetable Imports Jump $3,000,000 Over Totals of First Half of 1924," *Market Growers Journal*, Oct. 15, 1925: 3, 12; "Vegetable Exports of the United States," *Market Growers Journal*, Apr. 1, 1925, 53.

41.   "Tomato Growing in Tennessee," *Market Growers Journal*, Feb. 17, 1912, 5; S. H. Essary, "Notes on Tomato Diseases with Results of Selection for Resistance," Tennessee Agricultural Experiment Station Bulletin 95 (Jan. 1912).

42.   "Mississippi Tomatoes Have Wide Distribution," *Market Growers Journal*, July 15, 1925, 24; "Shipments and Unloads of Certain Fruits and Vegetables, 1918–1923"; "Car-Lot Shipments and Unloads of Important Fruits and Vegetables for the Calendar Years 1924–1926."

43.   Charles E. Sando, "The Process of Ripening in the Tomato, Considered Especially from the Commercial Standpoint," USDA Bulletin 859 (Sept. 1920), 2; W. F. Massey, "Timely Topics," *Market Growers Journal*, May 18, 1912, 6; James H. Beattie, "Greenhouse Tomatoes," USDA Farmers' Bulletin 1431 (Dec. 1924), 2.

44.   Wilcox, "Are Vegetable Growers Meeting Consumers Half Way?," 5, 7. Emphasis added.

45.   Beattie, "Greenhouse Tomatoes," 1–2.

46.   Ibid.; C. W. Waid, "Growing Tomatoes Under Glass," *Market Growers Journal*, Jan. 1, 1908, 8.

47.   Waid, "Growing Tomatoes Under Glass," 8; C. W. Waid, "Packages for Greenhouse Tomatoes," *Market Growers Journal*, May 18, 1912, 9.

48.   E. E. Adams, "Packages for Hothouse Tomatoes," *Market Growers Journal*, June 29, 1912, 2.
49.   "Airplane View of the Zuck Greenhouses," *Market Growers Journal*, Mar. 15, 1925, 45; "Davis Gardens, with 29 Acres Under Glass, Gives Indiana World's Biggest Range," *Market Growers Journal*, Apr. 15, 1925, 22, 35.

4. CONSUMING TOMATOES

1.   Susan Strasser, *Satisfaction Guaranteed: The Making of the American Mass Market* (Washington, DC: Smithsonian Institution Press, 1989); Harvey Levenstein, *Revolution at the Table: The Transformation of the American Diet* (Berkeley: University of California Press, 2003).
2.   U.S. Census Bureau, *Statistics of the Population of the United States at the Tenth Census* (Washington, DC: Government Printing Office, 1883), xxix–xx, 4; U.S. Census Bureau, *Twelfth Census of the United States*, vol. 1, part 1 (Washington, DC: Government Printing Office, 1901), lviii–lxii, cii.
3.   U.S. Census Bureau, *Twelfth Census*, vol. 1, part 1, cii; U.S. Census Bureau, *Statistics of the Population, Tenth Census*, 469–70.
4.   "More Beans and Less Meat," *American Food Journal*, Jan. 1913, 59–60, 66; W. O. Atwater, "The Chemistry of Foods and Nutrition, V. Pecuniary Economy of Food," *Century Illustrated Magazine*, Jan. 1888, 437–48, 442, 444; W. O. Atwater, "Foods: Nutritive Value and Cost," USDA Farmer's Bulletin 23 (1894), 10; W. O. Atwater, "What We Should Eat," *Century Illustrated Magazine*, June 1888, 257, 261; W. O. Atwater, "The Chemistry of Foods and Nutrition, II. How Food Nourishes the Body," *Century Illustrated Magazine*, June 1887, 238. The literature on Atwater, along with the nutrition and home economics movements, is extensive. For some of the most recent work, see Megan J. Elias, *Stir It Up: Home Economics in American Culture* (Philadelphia: University of Pennsylvania Press, 2008); Carolyn M. Goldstein, *Creating Consumers: Home Economists in Twentieth-Century America* (Chapel Hill: University of North Carolina Press, 2012); and Rachel Louise Moran, "Body Politic: Government and Physique in Twentieth Century America" (PhD diss., Pennsylvania State University, 2013). For a general analysis of reform efforts to change both working-class and middle-class eating habits (along with their spending habits), see Daniel Horowitz, *The Morality of Spending: Attitudes Toward the Consumer Society in America, 1875–1940* (Chicago: Elephant Paperbacks, 1992).
5.   Atwater, "Foods: Nutritive Value and Cost"; Levenstein, *Revolution at the Table*, 44–59.
6.   "The Discovery of New Vitamines," *American Food Journal*, July 1922, 24; "What Are Vitamines?—Best Described by What They Do," ibid., Jan. 1921, 24. See also Rima Apple, *Vitamania: Vitamins in American Culture* (New Brunswick, NJ: Rutgers University Press, 1996).
7.   For the shift toward reforming middle-class eating habits, see Horowitz, *Morality of Spending*, 67–84.

8. Caroline L. Hunt and Helen W. Atwater, "How to Select Foods," USDA Farmers Bulletin 808 (1917), 4, 8.

9. Levenstein, *Revolution at the Table*, 98–108.

10. Strasser, *Satisfaction Guaranteed*, 53, 91, 164–67; Jennifer Scalon, *Inarticulate Longings: The Ladies' Home Journal, Gender, and the Promises of Consumer Culture* (New York: Routledge, 1995).

11. Mary Green, *Better Meals for Less Money* (New York: Henry Holt, 1917), 21; Janet McKenzie Hill, *Canning, Preserving and Jelly Making* (Boston: Little, Brown, 1915), 162–63; Eliza R. Parker, "Seasonable Work for Housekeepers," *Good Housekeeping*, Sept. 18, 1886, 237; William V. Cruess, *Home and Farm Food Preservation* (New York: Macmillan, 1918), 140–41. I examined almost every issue of *Good Housekeeping* from the 1880s through the 1940s.

12. Emma B. Matteson and Ethel M. Newlands, *A Laboratory Manual of Foods and Cookery* (New York: Macmillan, 1917), 24; Hill, *Canning, Preserving and Jelly Making*, 10; "Cooking in a Southern Kitchen," *Good Housekeeping*, Sept. 28, 1889, 242; "Preserves and Pickles," *Good Housekeeping*, Aug. 1895, 55; Parker, "Seasonable Work for Housekeepers," 235; Elizabeth Robinson Scovil, "Tomatoes," *Good Housekeeping*, Sept. 15, 1888, 223.

13. "Half a Hundred: Recipes for James, Jellies, Preserves and Pickles," *Good Housekeeping*, July 20, 1889, 129; "A Yankee Housewife," "Good Things for the Table," ibid., Aug. 22, 1885, 21; A. M. P., "Pickles and Their Kindred," ibid., Sept. 15, 1888, 229; Mary Currier Parsons, "Fall Canning, Preserving and Pickling," ibid., Sept. 18, 1886.

14. Mary B. Hughes, *Everywoman's Canning Book*, 2nd ed. (Boston: Whitcomb and Barrows, 1918), 60; Marion Harris Neil, *Canning, Preserving and Pickling* (Philadelphia: David McKay, 1914), 165, 167, 202–3; Hill, *Canning, Preserving and Jelly Making*, 145; Parker, "Seasonable Work for Housekeepers," 235; Maria Parloa, "Many Meals for the Millions and a Few for the Millionaires," *Good Housekeeping*, Oct. 1892, 152.

15. Hill, *Canning, Preserving and Jelly Making*, 134–35, 139; Neil, *Canning, Preserving and Pickling*, 167–68; Cruess, *Home and Farm Food Preservation*, 8; "Housewife," "Good Things for the Table," *Good Housekeeping*, Oct. 3, 1885, 13.

16. While today chow chow is more commonly associated with a relish containing a green tomato base and piccalilli is more likely a pickle or pepper relish common in the Northeast and Midwest, the distinction in the early twentieth century was not at all clear. Leah Zeldes, "Eat This! Chow Chow and Piccalilli Pickle the Southern Harvest," *Dining Chicago*, Aug. 18, 2010, http://www.diningchicago.com/blog/2010/08/18/eat-this-southern-pickles-and-relishes/; Parker, "Seasonable Work for Housekeepers," 236; Green, *Better Meals for Less Money*, 20; Hill, *Canning, Preserving and Jelly Making*, 139–40; Lucy Ryerson, "Pickles and Sauces," *Good Housekeeping*, June 1893, 262; "Preserves and Pickles," 54; Neil, *Canning, Preserving and Pickling*, 172; "Pickles," *Good Housekeeping*, July 20, 1889, 129.

17. "Domestic Economy—VII. Recipes for Various Condiments," *Good Housekeeping*, Sept. 1896, 93; Angelina M. Tuttle, "The Uncertain Tomato," ibid., Aug. 1893, 71; S. M. D., "Canning Tomatoes (from a Reader)," ibid., Sept. 28, 1889, 259; Hughes, *Everywoman's*

Canning Book, 24–25; Neil, *Canning, Preserving and Pickling*, 29–30; Matteson and Newlands, *Laboratory Manual of Foods and Cookery*, 37–38.

18. There were also a number of canning recipes for mixed vegetables, often including tomatoes and okra, among other vegetables. These, however, were far outnumbered by both canned whole tomato recipes and sauce, pulp, and paste recipes. For mixed vegetables, see Hughes, *Everywoman's Canning Book*, 28. For tomato sauces, pulp, and paste, see Hill, *Canning, Preserving and Jelly Making*, 35–36; Hughes, *Everywoman's Canning Book*, 29; Cruess, *Home and Farm Food Preservation*, 177–78, 206, 239–40; E. Wagner, *Recipes for the Preserving of Fruit Vegetables, and Meat*, trans. Chas. Salter (London: Scott, Greenwood and Son, 1908), 91; "Meals for the Many of Moderate Means," *Good Housekeeping*, Oct. 1, 1887, 259; and Scovil, "Tomatoes," 223. For preparations of tomato sauces, see Christine Herrick, *Consolidated Library of Modern Cooking and Household Recipes*, vol. 3 (New York: R. J. Boomer, 1905), 198–99; Neil, *Canning, Preserving and Pickling*, 241–42; and Green, *Better Meals for Less Money*, 85. For sauces intended for meat, poultry, and fish, see McKenzie Hill, *Practical Cooking and Serving: A Complete Manual of How to Select, Prepare, and Serve Food* (New York: Doubleday, Page, 1919), 207; Emma Louise Hauck Rowe, "Soups and Soup Stocks," *Good Housekeeping*, Jan. 1899, 28; and "Housewife," "Good Things for the Table," 13. For cocktail sauces and other sauces for fish, see Green, *Better Meals for Less Money*, 17; Herrick, *Consolidated Library of Modern Cooking and Household Recipes*, 185; untitled article, *Good Housekeeping*, Mar. 1891, 122; "Good Things for the Table," *Good Housekeeping*, June 27, 1885, 16. For sauces intended for vegetables, polenta, and eggs, see "Strictly Fresh," *Good Housekeeping*, May 1896; Emily Holt, *The Complete Housekeeper* (New York: Doubleday, Page, 1917), 196; Herrick, *Consolidated Library of Modern Cooking and Household Recipes*, 71.

19. For Hamburger steak with tomatoes, meatloaf and the bean and tomato dishes, see Florence Nesbitt, *Low Cost Cooking: A Manual of Cooking, Diet, Home Management and Care of Children* (Chicago: American School of Home Economics, 1915), 87, 97, and Frances Stern and Gertrude T. Spitz, *Food for the Worker: The Food Values and Cost of a Series of Menus and Recipes for Seven Weeks* (Boston: Whitcomb and Barrows, 1917), 92, 103, 106. For examples of stewed and curried tomatoes and dessert preparations, see Herrick, *Consolidated Library of Modern Cooking and Household Recipes*, 97–99; Hester M. Poole, "Vegetables," *Good Housekeeping*, July 23, 1887, 137; Mary Currier Parsons, "Canning Vegetables," *Good Housekeeping*, Aug. 21, 1886, 193; D. H. R. Goodale, "Company Dinners for One," *Good Housekeeping*, May 30, 1885, 17; Nesbitt, *Low Cost Cooking*, 68; and Hill, *Practical Cooking and Serving*, 287.

20. For Creole influenced dishes, see Herrick, *Consolidated Library of Modern Cooking and Household Recipes*, 30–31, 80; Green, *Better Meals for Less Money*, 35. For rice and tomato soups, see Herrick, *Consolidated Library of Modern Cooking and Household Recipes*, 87; Green, *Better Meals for Less Money*, 31–32; and Margaret Burroughs, "Seasonable Menus—VIII," *Good Housekeeping*, Aug. 1899, 84. For soups combining tomatoes and vegetable proteins, including beans, see Hill, *Practical Cooking and Serving*, 184; Green, *Better Meals for Less Money*, 33; Herrick, *Consolidated*

Library of Modern Cooking and Household Recipes, 47, 75–76; Nesbitt, *Low Cost Cooking*, 52; and "The Kitchen Table: Good Soup Without Milk," *Good Housekeeping*, Dec. 1896, 270.

21. Many have credited companies like Campbell's and Franco-American with popularizing soup in the United States around 1900. But at least as early as the 1880s, American cookbooks and periodicals began printing recipes for tomato-based soups. For a discussion of the early acceptance of soups in America, see Andrew Smith, *Souper Tomatoes: The Story of America's Favorite Food* (New Brunswick, NJ: Rutgers University Press, 2000), 15–25. For examples of plain tomato soup, see "Good Things for the Table," *Good Housekeeping*, May 30, 1885, 19; Maria Parloa, "Gastronomic Thoughts and Suggestions," *Good Housekeeping*, May 2, 1885, 11; Hill, *Practical Cooking and Serving*, 181; Lenna Frances Cooper, *How to Cut Food Costs* (Battle Creek, MI: Good Health Publishing, 1917), 64–65; Hughes, *Everywoman's Canning Book*, 28; and Herrick, *Consolidated Library of Modern Cooking and Household Recipes*, 63. For winter consumption of homemade tomato soup, see Carrie May Ashton, "Two New Year's Dinners," *Good Housekeeping*, Jan. 1900, 36; "From Soup Tureen to Pudding Dish," *Good Housekeeping*, Jan. 5, 1889, 106. The quote ending the paragraph is from Helen Campbell, *The Easiest Way in Housekeeping and Cooking: Adapted to Domestic Use or Study in Classes* (Boston: Little, Brown, 1903), 126–27. For examples of cream of tomato soup or bisque, see Campbell, *Easiest Way in Housekeeping and Cooking*, 126–27; "The Kitchen Tables: Tomato Dishes," *Good Housekeeping*, June 1895, 253, reprinted from the *New York Tribune*; Holt, *Complete Housekeeper*, 152–53; Cooper, *How to Cut Food Costs*, 61; Herrick, *Consolidated Library of Modern Cooking and Household Recipes*, 37, 58; and Hill, *Practical Cooking and Serving*, 190.

22. Herrick, *Consolidated Library of Modern Cooking and Household Receipts*, 102–3.

23. Menu Collection, #6452 (hereafter Cornell Menu Coll), box 2, folder 9(a), 9(b), 9(c), Division of Rare and Manuscript Collections, Cornell University Library, Ithaca, NY.

24. Herrick, *Consolidated Library of Modern Cooking and Household Recipes*, 96. See also Mary E. Williams and Katharine Rolston Fisher, *Elements of the Theory and Practice of Cookery: A Textbook of Household Science for Use in School* (New York: Macmillan, 1913), 243.

25. Cornell Menu Coll, box 1; Herrick, *Consolidated Library of Modern Cooking and Household Recipes*, 215; "Some Seasonable Dishes," *Good Housekeeping*, July 24, 1886, 146; "Palmetto," "A Spring Breakfast," *Good Housekeeping*, Apr. 2, 1887, 257; "A Few Salad Recipes," *American Food Journal*, June 1913, 167.

26. "The Kitchen Tables: Tomato Dishes," 253; "The Best Dinner Chauncey M. Depew Ever Sat Down To," *Good Housekeeping*, May 1896, 240; Cornell Menu Coll, box 4, folder 74; box 4, folder 72; box 11, folder 3.

27. Emma Conley, *Principles of Cooking: A Textbook in Domestic Science* (New York: American Book Company, 1914), 61; Ruth A. Wardall and Edna Noble White, *A Study of Foods* (Boston: Ginn, 1914), 19; Green, *Better Meals for Less Money*, 133–34; Herrick, *Consolidated Library of Modern Cooking and Household Recipes*, 105, 218–19, 221, 236.

28. Donna R. Gabaccia, *Italy's Many Diasporas* (Seattle: University of Washington Press, 2000), 1, 5, 45, 58; David Gentilcore, *Pomodoro!: A History of the Tomato in Italy* (New York: Columbia University Press, 2010); Hasia R. Diner, *Hungering for America: Italian, Irish, and Jewish Foodways in the Age of Migration* (Cambridge, MA: Harvard University Press, 2001), 53; John W. Briggs, *An Italian Passage: Immigrants to Three American Cities, 1890–1930* (New Haven, CT: Yale University Press, 1978), xv. For information on the number of Italians that immigrated to America, see Colleen Leahy Johnson, *Growing Up and Growing Old in Italian-American Families* (New Brunswick, NJ: Rutgers University Press, 1985), 24–25; Humbert S. Nelli, *Italians in Chicago, 1880–1930* (New York: Oxford University Press, 1970); and Gabaccia, *Italy's Many Diasporas*, 69.

29. Thomas Kessner, *The Golden Door: Italian and Jewish Immigrant Mobility in New York City, 1880–1915* (New York: Oxford University Press, 1977), 72, 100, 138; Marie Hall Ets, *Rosa: The Life of an Italian Immigrant* (Minneapolis: University of Minnesota Press, 1970), 174.

30. Gentilcore, *Pomodoro*, 71, 76, 78–79.

31. Diner, *Hungering for America*, 75.

32. Deanna Paoli Gumina, *The Italians of San Francisco* (New York: Center for Migration Studies, 1978), 195; Nelli, *Italians in Chicago*, viii–ix, 176, 178; Johnson, *Growing Up and Growing Old in Italian-American Families*, 39, 90–91, 93; Diner, *Hungering for America*, 70–71, 73, 80–81; Herbert J. Gans, *The Urban Villagers: Group and Class in the Life of Italian-Americans* (New York: Free Press, 1982), 184.

33. Gentilcore, *Pomodoro*, 83, 109–119.

34. Diner, *Hungering for America*, 62–68; Gentilcore, *Pomodoro*, 105; Richard Raspa, "Exotic Foods Among Italian-Americans in Mormon Utah: Food as Nostalgic Enactment of Identity," in *Ethnic and Regional Foodways in the United States: The Performance of Group Identity*, ed. Linda Keller Brown and Kay Mussell (Knoxville: University of Tennessee Press, 1984), 186.

35. Silvano Serventi and Francoise Sabban, *Pasta: The Story of a Universal Food*, trans. Antony Shugaar (New York: Columbia University Press, 2002), 175, 192–94, 209.

36. Diner, *Hungering for America*, 64, 66; Gumina, *Italians of San Francisco*, 101, 103, 135.

37. J. H. Shrader, "The Manufacture of Tomato Paste," *American Food Journal*, Sept. 1919, 13; J. Alexis Shriver, "Canned-Tomato Industry in Italy," ibid., Aug. 1915, 360–61.

38. J. H. Shrader, "Economies in Tomato Manufacturing," *American Food Journal*, Aug. 1918, 426–28.

39. Shrader, "Manufacture of Tomato Paste," 13, 35; Shrader, "Economies in Tomato Manufacturing," 427.

40. Donna R. Gabaccia, "Italian-American Cookbooks: From Oral to Print Culture," *Italian Americana* 16, no. 1 (1998): 15–23; Maria Gentile, *The Italian Cookbook: The Art of Eating Well* (New York: Italian Book Co., 1919).

41. Niccolo de Quattrociocchi, *Love and Dishes* (New York: Bobbs-Merrill, 1950), 165, 183–85, 191–93.

42. Briggs, *Italian Passage*, xvi, 5–6, 156–57.

43. Donna Gabaccia, *We Are What We Eat: Ethnic Food and the Making of Americans* (Cambridge, MA: Harvard University Press, 1988), 99–103; *American Cooking: The Melting Pot, Supplement* (New York: Time-Life Books, 1972), 13, 59, 77–80; Quattrociocchi, *Love and Dishes*, 30; Diner, *Hungering for America*, 53–54; Gentilcore, *Pomodoro*, x, 101–2.

44. Herrick, *Consolidated Library of Modern Cooking and Household Recipes*, 23–24, 61; Stern, *Food for the Worker*, 93; Holt, *Complete Housekeeper*, 157; Parker, "Some Seasonable Dishes," *Good Housekeeping*, Aug. 21, 1886), 187; "The Kitchen Table: Good Soup Without Milk," 270; Maria Parloa, "Ten Mornings in the Kitchen," *Good Housekeeping*, July 1891, 1. For a similar argument on the failed "Americanization" of Italian immigrant food culture, see Gabaccia, *We Are What We Eat*.

45. Frank App and Allen G. Waller, "Costs, Profits and Practices of the Can-House Tomato Industry in New Jersey," New Jersey Agricultural Experiment Station Bulletin 353 (Apr. 1921), 10; W. J. Enright, "Supplies of Food Change Sharply," *New York Times*, Mar. 7, 1943, 16; "25 to 40% Cut Seen in Canned Food," *New York Times*, June 8, 1945, 16. I looked at the *New York Times* extensively using broad keyword searches on topics ranging from "tomatoes" and "farmers markets" to "Victory Gardens," "War gardens," and "home gardening." I examined a significant body of evidence from the late nineteenth century through the early 2000s. I also looked at several weekly columns in their entirety, including those written by Jane Holt (see n50 below).

46. Gabaccia, *We Are What We Eat*, 52–53.

47. Collegiate Section of the U.S. Food Administration, *Food and the War: A Textbook for College Classes* (Boston: Houghton Mifflin, 1918), 195, 201, 203; U.S. Food Administration, *Food Guide for War Service at Home* (New York: Charles Scribner's Sons, 1918), 55–56, 58–59, 60; Holt, *Complete Housekeeper*, 143; C. Houston Goudiss and Alberta M. Goudiss, *Foods That Will Win the War and How to Cook Them* (New York: World Syndicate Company, 1918), foreword.

48. Collegiate Section, *Food and the War*, 204–5; "18,000,000 Gardens Urged for Victory," *New York Times*, Jan. 22, 1943, 23; L. H. Robbins, "15,000,000 Victory Gardens," *New York Times*, Aug. 23, 1942, SM15, 25; "Victory Gardens Held Vital to U.S.," *New York Times*, Mar. 3, 1944, 12; "Big Slash in Canned Vegetables," *New York Times*, June 2, 1945, 16; "25 to 40% Cut Seen in Canned Food," 16.

49. "Cornfield Thrives in Midtown Plot," *New York Times*, June 11, 1942, 25; R. L. Watts, "Victory Garden Thoughts," *Pennsylvania Farmer*, Feb. 13, 1943, 7, 13; Francis C. Coulter, "Raising Food for a Family of Four," *New York Times*, Mar. 21, 1943, SG13; Esther C. Grayson, "Planning Those Garden Crops Eases the Burden of Canning," *New York Times*, June 14, 1942, D8. See also Robbins, "15,000,000 Victory Gardens," SM15, 25.

50. Jane Holt, "Vegetable Variety," *New York Times*, Aug. 19, 1945, SM14; Esther C. Grayson, "Especially for Salads: Out of the Victory Garden Many Good for the Big Wooden Bowl," *New York Times*, Mar. 21, 1943, SG18; Jane Holt, "Fresh Vegetables Plus," *New York Times*, Aug. 20, 1944, SM26; Jane Holt, "Warm-Weather Salads," *New York Times*, July 15, 1945, 56; Jane Holt, "News of Food: Recipes, with Tomatoes Basic Ingredient, Offered as Suggestions for Summer Meals," *New York Times*, Sept.

2, 1943, 22; Jane Holt, "Home-Made Relishes," *New York Times*, July 11, 1943, SM22. For literature on the Office of Price Controls, see, for example, Meg Jacobs, *Pocketbook Politics: Economic Citizenship in Twentieth-Century America* (Princeton, NJ: Princeton University Press, 2005).

51. "Canning Centers Opening Rapidly," *New York Times*, Aug. 25, 1943, 22; "Fruits of a Victory Garden," *New York Times*, July 2, 1943, 16; Jane Holt, "News of Food: Output of Canning Equipment Increased to Stimulate Home Processing of Foods," *New York Times*, Feb. 10, 1944, 20; Collegiate Section, *Food and the War*, 276–77.

52. Robbins, "15,000,000 Victory Gardens," 15, 25.

53. Levenstein, *Revolution at the Table*; Ernest Dichter to Charles Feldman, Young and Rubicam, Mar. 27, 1952, Ernest Dichter Papers, #2407A, box 10, 264E, Hagley Library, Wilmington, DE.

54. Gentilcore, *Pomodoro*, 131.

55. Ibid.; email correspondence between Conagra and the author, Oct. 25, 2012.

5. "A POOR TOMATO IS BETTER THAN NO TOMATO"

1. For a local study of tomato canning in Arkansas, see Tom Dicke, "Red Gold of the Ozarks: The Rise and Decline of Tomato Canning, 1885–1955," *Agricultural History* 79, no. 1 (2005): 1–26.

2. Deborah Fitzgerald, *Every Farm a Factory: The Industrial Ideal in American Agriculture* (New Haven, CT: Yale University Press, 2003), 5.

3. Carol Helstosky, *Pizza: A Global History* (London: Reaktion Books, 2008).

4. James E. Bylin, "Big Tomato Harvest in California Not Likely to Cut Consumer Cost," *Wall Street Journal*, Dec. 7, 1966; "Record Tomato Crop Forces Prices Down; Some Packers Impose Ceilings on Deliveries," *Wall Street Journal*, Oct. 15, 1962; U.S. Department of Agriculture, *2002 Census of Agriculture*, vol. 1, part 51 (Washington, DC: Government Printing Office, 2004), 477.

5. "Blight Hits Tomatoes," *New York Times*, Aug. 14, 1946; "Tomato Crop Blight Descends on Jersey," *New York Times*, Aug. 23, 1946; "Jersey Tomato Crop Hurt," *New York Times*, Oct. 3, 1946; "Crop Damage in Jersey," *New York Times*, May 13, 1947; "Tomatoes Jam Canneries," *New York Times*, Aug. 25, 1947; "Tomato Harvest Sets Record," *New York Times*, Oct. 12, 1947; "50% Loss in Tomato Crop Seen," *New York Times*, Aug 12, 1948; "Tomato Blight in Pennsylvania," *New York Times*, Aug. 26, 1948; "Record Heat Ruins $15,000 Tomato Crop," *New York Times*, Aug. 30, 1948; "Heat Hurts Crops: Local Prices Hold," *New York Times*, Aug. 31, 1948.

6. June Owen, "Food: Tomato Farmers: Family in Nassau County One of Few to Raise and Sell Crops in the Area," *New York Times*, Aug. 6, 1962; "Rockland Farmer Fleeing Bumper Crop of Red Tape," *New York Times*, Oct. 3, 1956; "$75-Million 'Town' to Rise on 640 Acres Near Miami," *New York Times*, Dec. 31, 1967.

7. Public Law 78, Pub. L. 82–78, 65 Stat. 19 (1951).

8. "Mexican Aliens Free in Bail to Pick Tomatoes," *Chicago Daily Tribune*, Aug. 22, 1945; "53 'Smuggled' Mexican Farm Hands Jailed," *Chicago Daily Tribune*, Aug. 21, 1945.

9. Ronald Sullivan, "Migrant Workers Add New Charges: Jersey Negroes Complain of Loan Rates up to 50%," *New York Times*, Aug. 27, 1967; Ronald Sullivan, "Jersey Migrant Camp Squalor Called Worst in U.S. by Witness," *New York Times*, Sept. 22, 1966; "Upstate Growers Vie for Pickers," *New York Times*, Aug. 21, 1966; "Tomato Pickers Needed," *Philadelphia Tribune*, Sept. 1, 1970.

10. Kitty Calavita, *Inside the State: The Bracero Program, Immigration, and the INS* (New Orleans: Quid Pro Books, 2010), 218; C. P. Trussell, "Braceros' Entry Sought in Senate," *New York Times*, July 29, 1963.

11. Lawrence E. Davies, "Growers Counter Loss of Braceros," *New York Times*, Feb. 23, 1964; A. I. Dickman, *Interviews with Persons Involved in the Development of the Tomato Harvester, the Compatible Processing Tomato and the New Agricultural Systems That Evolved* (Davis: University of California at Davis Oral History Office, Shields Library, 1978), introduction; Lester S. Heringer, interview, in Dickman, *Interviews*, 69, 71; Arthur Allen, *Ripe: The Search for the Perfect Tomato* (Berkeley: Counterpoint Press, 2010), 104–5; James E. Bylin, "Tomato Prices Expected to Fall This Year Due to Use of Harvesting Machines in West," *Wall Street Journal*, Mar. 21, 1966; James E. Bylin, "Lack of Workers May Limit Tomato Crops in California; Higher Retail Prices Seen," *Wall Street Journal*, Aug. 12, 1965.

12. Bylin, "Lack of Workers May Limit Tomato Crops in California"; "Lack of Workers Perils Coast Crop: Growers in California Find Domestic Help Unstable," *New York Times*, Mar. 14, 1965; Davies, "Growers Counter Loss of Braceros"; "U.S. Admits 6,000 Braceros," *New York Times*, Aug. 2, 1966; "Braceros Stream into California," *New York Times*, Sept. 5, 1965.

13. H. B. Peto, "Mechanical Harvesting of Tomatoes," *Seed World*, Nov. 8, 1963, 14–15; Davies, "Growers Counter Loss of Braceros"; Bylin, "Lack of Workers May Limit Tomato Crops in California."

14. Gordie C. Hanna, interview, in Dickman, *Interviews*, 2.

15. Ibid., 2–3; Albert Martin "Fum" Jongeneel, interview, in Dickman, *Interviews*, 22–23.

16. Hanna, interview, 9–10; Melvin P. Zobel, interview, in Dickman, *Interviews*, 106. The idea that the labor shortage did not fuel the search for mechanized tomato harvesting stands in contrast to the main historical work on tomato harvesters; see Wayne D. Rasmussen, "Advances in American Agriculture: The Mechanical Tomato Harvester as a Case Study," *Technology and Culture* 9, no. 4 (1968): 531–43. Another important perspective focuses on growers' support of the harvester by the late 1950s and early 1960s as union pressure mounted; see Dennis Nodín Valdés, "Machine Politics in California Agriculture, 1945–1990s," *Pacific Historical Review* 63, no. 2 (1994): 203–24.

17. Bylin, "Lack of Workers May Limit Tomato Crops in California."

18. Hanna, interview, 7–8; Coby Lorenzen, interview, in Dickman, *Interviews*, 43; Joe Marks, "Tomato Harvesters," *Nation's Agriculture* 40, no. 5 (1965): 12–13.

19. Hanna, interview, 8.

20. Lorenzen, interview, 44; Hanna, interview, 3–4. For a discussion of agricultural mechanization being valued above hand-picking, see Siegfried Giedion, *Mechanization Takes Command: A Contribution to Anonymous History* (New York: Norton, 1969).

10. Belasco, *Appetite for Change*. These challenges were not only reserved for the food industry. For an example of the do-it-yourself home industry in the 1970s, see Benjamin Lisle, "Thinking for Myself, Building for Myself: The 1970s Post-Industrial Homestead in Main" (presented at "A Hands-On Approach: The Do-It-Yourself Culture and Economy in the 20th Century," German Historical Institute, April 24, 2014). See also Bureau of Labor Statistics, "Labor Force Statistics from the Current Population Survey," http://data.bls.gov/timeseries/ LNU04000000?years_option=all_years& periods_option=specific_periods&periods=Annual+Data (accessed Mar. 10, 2017); U.S. Department of Agriculture (USDA), Economic Research Service, "Food Consumption, Prices, and Expenditures, 1970–1997," Statistical Bulletin SB-965 (April 1999), table 95, http://www.ers.usda.gov/publications/sb-statistical-bulletin/sb965.aspx#.UyNJBPmwLYg.

11. Brown, "Counting Farmers Markets," 657; Sandra Michioku, "Farm Markets Thrive from Eureka to L.A.," *Los Angeles Times*, Sept. 30, 1979; James Brooke, "Farmers' Markets: Fresh and Folksy," *New York Times*, Aug. 28, 1985; Neal R. Peirce, "Green Revolution Plants Seeds of Hope in Cities," *Los Angeles Times*, Sept. 2, 1979; Jane Gross, "Farmers' Market Lures Office Workers at Lunchtime," *New York Times*, Aug. 3, 1985; Kim Severson, "Greenmarket at 30, Searching for Itself," *New York Times*, July 19, 2006; Kitty O'Steen, "2,000 Shoppers Seek Bargains at Opening of Burbank Farmers' Market," *Los Angeles Times*, Sept. 4, 1983.

12. Harold Faber, "Sales of Seeds at Record as Home Gardening Gains Popularity," *New York Times*, Feb. 18, 1974; Todd Hunt, "Homegrown Vegetables Will Set a Pace for the Seventies," *New York Times*, Jan. 9, 1972; Elizabeth M. Fowler, "Home Grown: Vegetable Gardens Sprouting Anew," *New York Times*, May 21, 1972; USDA, *Yearbook of Agriculture: Gardening for Food and Fun* (Washington, DC: Government Printing Office, 1977).

13. Cheryl Brown and Stacy Miller, "The Impacts of Local Markets: A Review of Research on Farmers Markets and Community Supported Agriculture (CSA)," *Agricultural & Applied Economics Association* 90, no. 5 (2008): 1296; Allison Brown, "Farmers' Market Research 1940–2000: An Inventory and Review," *American Journal of Alternative Agriculture* 17, no. 4 (2002): 1; Hardesty, "Growing Role of Local Food Markets": 1289; Lydia Zepeda and Jingham Li, "Who Buys Local Food?" *Journal of Food Distribution Research* 37, no. 3 (2006): 2; Tim Payne, "U.S. Farmers Markets—2000: A Study of Emerging Trends," USDA Agricultural Marketing Service (2002), 11; USDA, Agricultural Marketing Service, "Farmers' Market Program Fact Sheet," http://www.ams.usda.gov/AMSv1.0/getfile?dDocName=STELPRDC5080175&acct=frmrdirmkt (accessed Oct. 20, 2014); Sarah A. Low and Stephen Vogel, "Direct and Intermediated Marketing of Local Foods in the United States," ERR-128, USDA Economic Research Service (Nov. 2011), 2–3.

14. "Shoppers Look to Supermarkets for Produce Purchases," *Supermarket News*, May 23, 2012.

15. Wolf, Spittler, and Ahern, "Profile of Farmers' Market Consumers," 193; Timothy Egan, "Growers and Shoppers Crowd Farmers' Markets," *New York Times*, Nov. 29,

2002, 29; Thilmany and Watson, "Increasing Role of Direct Marketing and Farmers Markets," 19; Payne, "U.S. Farmers Markets," 22.

16. Jennifer Wilkins, "Think Globally, Eat Locally," *New York Times*, Dec. 18, 2004; Alan R. Hunt, "Consumer Interactions and Influences on Farmers' Market Vendors," *Renewable Agriculture and Food Systems* 22, no. 1 (2007): 59; Payne, "U.S. Farmers Markets," iv; Ina Aronow, "White Plains Acts on Farmers Market," *New York Times*, May 7, 1989. Some of the major works on modern American agricultural practices, which focus on mechanization, chemical use, and concentration, include J. L. Anderson, *Industrializing the Corn Belt: Agriculture, Technology, and Environment, 1945–1972* (De Kalb: Northern Illinois University Press, 2008); Bruce L. Gardner, *American Agriculture in the Twentieth Century: How It Flourished and What It Cost* (Cambridge, MA: Harvard University Press, 2002); R. Douglas Hurt, *Problems of Plenty: The American Farmer in the Twentieth Century* (Chicago: Ivan R. Dee, 2002); John T. Shover, *First Majority—Last Minority: The Transforming of Rural Life in America* (Dekalb: Northern Illinois University Press, 1976).

17. Tim Stark, *Heirloom: Notes from an Accidental Tomato Farmer* (New York: Broadway Books, 2008); Jeanne Dutel-Martino, "Farmers Market Opens Tonight in Cranberry," *Pittsburgh Post-Gazette* (9 May 1997); Karen Kane, "For This Couple, Farming Is Worth the Long Days, Dirty Hands and Low Pay," *Pittsburgh Post-Gazette*, Aug. 19, 2001. See also Kristin Kimball, *The Dirty Life: On Farming, Food, and Love* (New York: Scribner, 2010).

18. Gallup Poll (AIPO), June 1981, retrieved Feb. 19, 2014, from iPoll Databank, Roper Center for Public Opinion Research, University of Connecticut, http://www.ropercenter.uconn.edu/data_access/ipoll/ipoll.html; Peter Tonge, "TV Series Whets the Appetite for Simple Backyard Garden," *Christian Science Monitor*, May 14, 1982; Louise Cook, "A Plan for Jobless: Plant a Food Garden," *Philadelphia Inquirer*, Mar. 20, 1983; Louise Saul, "Home Gardening Making Strides," *New York Times*, Apr. 29, 1984; Tom Hallman, "Ever Thought of 'Investing' in a Veggie Garden?—You Could Reap What You Sowed, up to Tenfold," *Atlanta Journal and Atlanta Constitution*, May 5, 1986; Peggy Lane, "Baby Boomers Have Taken to Gardening: In Record Numbers, They Are Spending Record Dollars Growing Everything from Radishes to Roses," *USA Today*, Apr. 18, 1988.

19. Glenn Collins, "Increase in Home Gardening Yields Bumper Crop of Sales: A Bumper Crop in Gardening Supplies," *New York Times*, Aug. 20, 1994; email correspondence with Bruce Butterfield, National Gardening Association, Feb. 21, 2014; Virgil Adams, "Garden Centers Doing Well, Thank You," *Atlanta Journal and Atlanta Constitution*, Jan. 21, 1990. For an example of the proliferation of store-bought seedlings, see Walter F Naedele, "Seeds Fade in Favor—Just Ask Anyone Named Burpee," *Houston Chronicle*, Oct. 7, 1994; Debbie Arrington, "As Gardening Expands, So Does Burpee Mailing List," *Sacramento Bee*, Jan. 16, 2010.

20. Lisa M. Hamilton, "The American Farmers Market," *Gastronomica: The Journal of Food and Culture* 2, no. 3 (2002): 76.

21. For examples of specialty markets and clubs, see James Kindall, "A Movement That Follows the Credo: Think Globally, Grow and Buy Locally," *New York Times*, Aug. 24,

2008, and Karen Newell Young, "Appetite for Unusual Feeds Gourmet Markets," *Los Angeles Times*, Nov. 4, 1988. For CSAs, see Bette McDevitt, "Fresh off the Farm," *Pittsburgh Post-Gazette*, Aug. 31, 2000, and Mary Klaus, "Growing Trend: Organic Produce Helps Farm Build Subscription List," *Patriot-News* (Harrisburg, PA), July 29, 2001.

22. Tim Blangger, "Berks Grower Finds Market for Heirloom Varieties in New York City," *Morning Call* (Allentown, PA), Sept. 12, 1996; Stark, *Heirloom*, 63–64.

23. Corie Brown, "A Napa Just Waiting to Happen," *Los Angeles Times*, Oct. 13, 2004.

24. Patricia Brooks, "Farmers' Markets Bring Variety to Urban Life," *New York Times*, Oct. 7, 1979.

25. Peter Applebome, "Providing Fresh Vegetables to a Community Where Fast Food Reigns," *New York Times*, Sept. 20, 2010; Tara Nurin, "Farmers' Market on Wheels: Camden Gets Much-Needed Fresh Food with Help from State, Greensgrow Farms," *Philadelphia Inquirer*, July 7, 2011; Tracie Rozhon, "Urban Farmers Develop Their Own Market," *New York Times*, Sept. 6, 1981; Virginia Escalante, "Compton Market Opens: Shoppers Save, Farmers Profit," *Los Angeles Times*, Sep. 24, 1981; Dan Hardy, "Farmers' Market Flourishes: In Chester, It Offers a Cornucopia of Benefits, from Fresh Produce to Nutritional Information," *Philadelphia Inquirer*, Aug. 13, 2000.

26. Sheryl Stolberg, "Growers Eager to Sell Their Bounty Find City Folks Wanting to Stock up at San Pedro's Farmer's Market," *Los Angeles Times*, Sept. 24, 1989; Erin Kelly, "A Bumper Crop of Customers," *Los Angeles Times*, July 17, 1980; For savings at farmer's markets, see Karen Gillingham, "Cornucopia in Gardena Parking Lot," *Los Angeles Times*, July 5, 1979; Victor M. Valle, "Fast-Growing Farmers' Market Sales in the Green," *Los Angeles Times*, July 15, 1982; Brooks, "Farmers' Markets Bring Variety to Urban Life"; and Robert Sommer, Margaret Wing, and Susan Aitkens, "Price Savings to Consumers at Farmers' Markets," *Journal of Consumer Affairs* 14, no. 2 (1980): 452–62.

27. Jenifer Naughton, "Helping the Poor Buy Fresh Fruits and Vegetables," *New York Times*, Sept. 22, 1991; Richard E. Just and Quinn Weninger, "Economic Evaluation of the Farmers' Market Nutrition Program," *American Journal of Agricultural Economics* 79, no. 3 (1997): 902–17; Christopher Bedford, "Meeting the Challenge of Local Food," *Business* 28, no. 1 (2006): 17–20; Payne, "U.S. Farmers Markets," 19. For data on the FMNP, see http://www.fns.usda.gov/fmnp/overview. For data on the SFMNP, see http://www.fns.usda.gov/sfmnp/overview. The USDA's farmers' market programs have not been without their troubles, including the difficulty in transitioning toward a paperless payment system, which has in many cases made it difficult for small farmers to accept program members. See, for example, Corby Kummer, "Less Green at the Farmers' Market," *New York Times*, May 10, 2007.

28. Johnson Pableaux, "$20 to Spend, Surrounded by Ripeness," *New York Times*, July 21, 2004.

29. "A Farmers Market in the City," *New York Times*, Aug. 13, 1976.

30. Brown and Miller, "Impacts of Local Markets": 1296.

31. There is little consensus among scholars, farmers, or consumers about what exactly "local" means. Social scientists have had great difficulty finding consistency in how consumers define "local." In some cases, consumers consider produce grown within

one's state or region to be local. In many cases, consumers limit the term "local" to mean grown within one's county or adjoining counties, thus undermining the efforts of many states to create a statewide brand for agricultural products. In a few studies, consumers abandon political and geographical boundaries altogether and instead define "local" based on driving time from farm to market. The literature on statewide branding efforts is extensive. For less successful efforts, see David B. Eastwood, John R. Brooker, and Morgan D. Gray, "Location and Other Market Attributes Affecting Farmer's Market Patronage: The Case of Tennessee," *Journal of Food Distribution Research* 30, no. 1 (1999): 63–72; Paul M. Patterson, Hans Olofsson, Timothy J. Richards, and Sharon Sass, "An Empirical Analysis of State Agricultural Product Promotions: A Case Study," *Agribusiness* 15, no. 2 (1999): 179–96. For the more successful case of New Jersey, see Adesoji O. Adelaja, Robin G. Brumfield, and Kimberly Lininger, "Product Differentiation and State Promotion of Farm Produce: An Analysis of the Jersey Fresh Tomato," *Journal of Food Distribution Research* 21, no. 3 (1990): 73–85. For studies of consumer definitions of "local," see, for example, Lydia Zepeda, and Catherine Leviten-Reid, "Consumers' Views on Local Food," *Journal of Food Distribution Research* 35, no. 3 (2004): 1–6; Cheryl Brown, "Consumers' Preferences for Locally Produced Food: A Study in Southeast Missouri," *American Journal of Alternative Agriculture* 18, no. 4 (2003): 213–24.

32.   Katie Gallagher, "Retailers Learn to Tap Into Growing Organic Market," *Gourmet News* 72, no. 8 (2007): 3–4; "How to Keep Ag Business Profitable," *Public Opinion*, Dec. 17, 2006; Suzanne Martinson, "Fresh Is Best, Produce Survey Respondents Concur," *Pittsburgh Post-Gazette*, June 13, 2002. For reasons to buy local, see "Localvore Living," *Wayne (PA) Independent*, Sept. 9, 2011; Joanna Poncavage, "Food for Thought: 'Eating Local' to Help the Environment Sounds Simple. But Is It?" *Morning Call*, June 22, 2007.

33.   Brown, "Consumers' Preferences for Locally Produced Food," 217; Susan Andreatta and William Wickliffe II, "Managing Farmer and Consumer Expectations: A Study of a North Carolina Farmers' Market," *Human Organization* 61, no. 2 (2002): 171; Wolf, Spittler, and Ahern, "Profile of Farmers' Market Consumers," 198. See also Alan S. Kezis, F. Richard King, Ulrich C. Toensmeyer, Robert Jack, and Howard W. Kerr, "Consumer Acceptance and Preference for Direct Marketing in the Northeast," *Journal of Food Distribution Research* 15, no. 3 (1984): 39. For examples of studies indicating that local food is intrinsically valued by consumers, see Kim Darby, Marvin T. Batte, Stan Ernst, and Brian Roe, "Decomposing Local: A Conjoint Analysis of Locally Produced Foods," *American Journal of Agricultural Economics* 90, no. 2 (2008): 485.

34.   Amy Culbertson, "The Big Red One: To Savor Summer, Eat 'Real' Tomato," *Patriot News*, July 14, 2004; Roxann Miller, "Farmers Markets Equal Fresh Produce," *Public Opinion*, July 10, 2010; "E. 59th St. Farmers' Market Thrives," *New York Times*, Aug. 1, 1976; Jimmy Schmidt, "Heirloom Tomatoes: A Luscious Legacy to Bring to the Table," *Philadelphia Inquirer*, Sept. 3, 1997; "Council Opens Produce Market in South Side," *Morning Call*, Aug. 30, 1990.

35.   James Gallons, U. C. Toensmeyer, J. Richard Bacon, and Carl L. German, "An Anal-
      ysis of Consumer Characteristics Concerning Direct Marketing of Fresh Produce in
      Delaware: A Case Study," *Journal of Food Distribution Research* 28, no. 1 (1997): 100,
      102; Adelaja, Brumfield, and Lininger, "Product Differentiation and State Promo-
      tion of Farm Produce," 73–85.

36.   John Brooker, David B. Eastwood, and Robert H. Orr, "Consumers' Perceptions of
      Locally Grown Produce at Retail Outlets," *Journal of Food Distribution Research* 18,
      no. 1 (1987): 100–105.

37.   Gerald Etter, "Their Approach to Food Is Fresh," *Philadelphia Inquirer*, June 20,
      1982; Payne, "U.S. Farmers Markets," 16, 18.

38.   For recommended standards of the Greenmarkets, see http://www.grownyc.org
      /greenmarket/faq#q_fresh. For Greenmarket farmer rules, and map of eligibility,
      see http://www.grownyc.org/files/gmkt/questionnaire/farmer.pdf.

39.   Emily Adams, "Fresh from the Farm: Customers at Outdoor Markets Enjoy Chat-
      ting with Growers," *Los Angeles Times*, Oct. 4, 1992; Hunt, "Consumer Interactions
      and Influences on Farmers' Market Vendors," 59; William Lockeretz, "Urban Con-
      sumers' Attitudes Towards Locally Grown Produce," *American Journal of Alterna-
      tive Agriculture* 1, no. 2 (1986): 88; Ann Vileisis, *Kitchen Literacy: How We Lost
      Knowledge of Where Food Comes from and Why We Need to Get It Back* (Washing-
      ton, DC: Island Press, 2008), 9.

40.   Sarah Billingsley, "Takin' It to the Streets: From Ethnic Lunch Trucks to the Corner
      Hot Dog Stand, the City Is Full of Flavor," *Pittsburgh Post-Gazette*, May 7, 2004.

41.   John McPhee, "Giving Good Weight," in *Giving Good Weight* (New York: Farrar,
      Straus and Giroux, 1979), 3; GrowNYC, "Frequently Asked Questions," www.grownyc
      .org/greenmarket/faq#q_available (accessed May 7, 2014).

42.   Marian Burros, "A Farmers' Market Worth Fighting For," *New York Times*, July 27,
      1988; Dianna Marder, "Sprouting in the City: Besides Good Fresh Food and Sunday
      Hours, Area Farmers Markets Offer a Chance to Meet the Folks Who Grow the
      Eats," *Philadelphia Inquirer*, Apr. 22, 2010; Joseph D'Agnese, "From the Fields to a
      Parking Lot Near You," *New York Times*, July 18, 1999; Hunt, "Consumer Interac-
      tions and Influences on Farmers' Market Vendors," 59–60; Lockeretz, "Urban Con-
      sumers' Attitudes Towards Locally Grown Produce," 88.

43.   On the emergence of shopping malls and other commercial spaces as dominant
      "public" spaces, see Tridib Banerjee, "The Future of Public Space: Beyond Reinvented
      Streets and Reinvented Places," *Journal of the American Planning Association* 67,
      no. 1 (2001): 9–24; Cohen, *Consumers' Republic*, 6.

44.   Rome, *Bulldozer in the Countryside*, esp. 124–28.

45.   Karal Ann Marling, *As Seen on TV: The Visual Culture of Everyday Life in the 1950s*
      (Cambridge, MA: Harvard University Press, 1996); David Riesman, *The Lonely
      Crowd* (New Haven, CT: Yale University Press, 1950); William Whyte, *Organization
      Man* (Garden City, NY: Doubleday, 1956); Vance Packard, *The Status Seekers* (New
      York: David McKay, 1961). For a more nuanced discussion of the sociology of the
      1950s, see Gary Cross, *An All-Consuming Century: Why Commercialism Won in*

Modern America (New York: Columbia University Press, 2000), 93–155. For a discussion of the changing role of citizenship and community in the postwar consumer culture, see Cohen, *Consumer's Republic*, 13–14.

46. Barbara Delatiner, "Food Prices Spur Gardening in Nassau and Suffolk," *New York Times*, May 26, 1974; Saul, "Home Gardening Making Strides."

47. For a discussion of the development of hobbies and masculinity during the 1950s, see Steven M. Gelber, *Hobbies: Leisure and the Culture of Work in America* (New York: Columbia University Press, 1999).

48. Victor R. Boswell and Robert E. Wester, "Growing Vegetables in Town and City," USDA Home and Garden Bulletin 7 (1951), 1; Robert Wester, "Growing Vegetables in the Home Garden," USDA Home and Garden Bulletin 202 (1972), 1.

49. Bob Thomson, *The New Victory Garden* (Boston: Little, Brown, 1987), 45; Pat Rubin, "A Garden Plan That's Strictly on the Square," *Sacramento Bee*, Apr. 5, 2008; Mel Bartholomew, *All New Square Foot Gardening* (Franklin, TN: Cool Springs Press, 2005). For an example of a gardener overplanting and facing trials and tribulations, see William Alexander, *The $64 Tomato* (Chapel Hill, NC: Algonquin, 2006).

50. Frank Reichstein, "Plant Tomatoes Now," *Better Homes and Gardens*, Apr. 1946; Thomson, *New Victory Garden*, 45.

51. Pamela Ruth, "The Perfect Tomato Plan," *Organic Gardening*, Apr. 2007; Vierria Dan, "Mr. Tomato—Retired NASA Worker's Rocklin Garden Is out of This World," *Sacramento Bee*, Mar. 23, 2002; Mark Sitth, "Three Experts Share Their Secrets for Growing Terrific Tomatoes—Enjoy a Late Harvest of Luscious Home-Growns," *Atlanta Journal and Atlanta Consitution*, July 28, 1991; Lynette Evans, "Should Gardeners Give Away the Best Produce or Keep It for Themselves?" *San Francisco Chronicle*, Aug. 25, 2007; Brooker, Eastwood, and Orr, "Consumers' Perceptions of Locally Grown Produce at Retail Outlets," 100–101; John A. Starnes Jr., "Lots of Tomatoes," *St. Petersburg Times*, Jan. 20, 2001; "Beginner Tomato Preservation," *Organic Gardening*, Aug.–Oct. 2007; Ernest Dichter, *Handbook of Consumer Motivations* (New York: McGraw-Hill, 1964).

52. William D Adams, "Get Your Veggies in a Row—Tomatoes Lead the Field of Spring Favorites," *Houston Chronicle*, Feb. 28, 1987; Mimi Fuller Foster, "Killer Tomatoes—'Mater Mania's Taken Hold, in a Humongous-Is-Best Quest That's Just Ripe—for Competition," *Atlanta Journal and Atlanta Constitution*, June 11, 1993.

53. Laura J. Lawson, *City Bountiful* (Berkeley: University of California Press, 2005), 26, 206; William Bryant Logan, "Community Garden Experts: Tending the Green City Lots," *New York Times*, Aug. 15, 1985; Robert J. Salgado, "Lots Once Strewn with Rubble Are Becoming Urban Farms," *New York Times*, Aug. 9, 1987.

54. Peter Tonge, "Grow Your Own Food and Bank the Savings," *Christian Science Monitor*, Jan. 8, 1982; Lawson, *City Bountiful*, 215; Harold Faber, "A Good Season Is Predicted for Home Vegetable Gardens," *New York Times*, May 13, 1973; Hallman, "Ever Thought of 'Investing' in a Veggie Garden?"; Tracie McMillan, "Urban Farmers' Crops Go from Vacant Lot to Market," *New York Times*, May 7, 2008.

55. Lawson, *City Bountiful*, 206, 18–20; Douglas Brown, "No Garden? No Problem— Community Plots, Other Yards Await Tilling," *Denver Post*, Apr. 11, 2008; Peirce, "Green Revolution Plants Seeds of Hope in Cities."

56. David Brooks, *Bobos in Paradise: The New Upper Class and How They Got There* (New York: Simon and Schuster, 2000), 11.

57. Jack Kramer, *Basket Bounty: Growing Vegetables, Fruits, and Herbs in and Around the House* (New York: Charles Scribner's Sons, 1975), 2–27; Alex Mitchell, *The Edible Balcony: Growing Fresh Produce in Small Spaces* (New York: Rodale, 2011), 8; Jim Tunks, "Bounty from Our Rooftop," *San Francisco Chronicle*, Sept. 27, 2009. See also, Anne Raver, "Hoping for a City Full of Farms on Rooftops," *New York Times*, Aug. 4, 2002; R. O. Y. Wyatt, "Digging around—Growing Tomatoes Is a Cinch in Easy-to-Assemble Containers," *Atlanta Journal and Atlanta Constitution*, June 16, 1991; Mary Corcoran, "Indoor Tomato Plant Serves Salad Year Round," *San Francisco Chronicle*, Sept. 29, 1999. For information on the Aerogarden, see http://www .aerogarden.com. Image available at http://media.aerogardenimages.com/media /catalog/product/cache/1/image/398x398/9df78eab33525d08d6e5fb8d27136e95/u/l /ultra_led_mct.jpg.

58. Duane Newcomb, *The Postage Stamp Garden Book: How to Grow All the Food You Can Eat in Very Little Space* (Los Angeles: J. P. Tarcher, 1975), v–vi; Mark Stith, "Fertile Ground: Learn All About Organics," *Atlanta Journal and Atlanta Constitution*, May 5, 1991.

59. Joanna Poncavage, "Timeless Tomatoes," *Organic Gardening*, Mar. 1997; Laura Martin, "Some Have Sentimental Bond to Heirloom Plants," *Atlanta Journal and Atlanta Constitution*, Jan. 7, 1990; Mimi Fuller Foster, "Heirloom Vegetables: Treasured Varieties Are Tasty Living Link to Gardens of the Past," *Atlanta Journal and Atlanta Constitution*, Feb. 19, 1993; Dan Vierria, "Ugly Can Be Beautiful When It Comes to Tomatoes," *Sacramento Bee*, Feb. 1, 2003; Dan Vierria, "With Good Taste—Winning Tomatoes for Home Gardens," *Sacramento Bee*, Jan. 15, 2005; Dan Vierria, "Top 10 Garden Catalogs for 2006," *Sacramento Bee*, Dec. 17, 2005; Ellen Speicher, "Heirloom Tomatoes Offer Variety of Flavors," *Pittsburgh Post-Gazette*, Feb. 15, 2003. An open-pollinated plant is a plant in which fertilization occurs "naturally" by insects, wind, and other natural means. The seeds that result can be saved and can, through selection, be improved over time. A commercial hybrid variety, on the other hand, is a plant created by intentionally crossing two specific varieties, typically for the purpose of breeding in specific traits. The result is usually referred to as an F1 hybrid. The seeds from the fruits of F1 hybrid seeds cannot be saved, as they will not produce similar plants in following generations and will have significantly lower yields.

60. Collins, "Increase in Home Gardening Yields Bumper Crop of Sales"; Lane, "Baby Boomers Have Taken to Gardening." See also, "In High Favor: Tomatoes, Still Tops, Repay Early Start," *New York Times*, Mar. 20, 1955; H. Fred Dale, "Here's How to Grow Tomatoes, the Star of Most Home Gardens," *Toronto Star*, July 3, 1988.

61. George Haegel, "Vegetable Success: 'Best' Means Best Suited to Local Conditions," *New York Times*, Mar. 11, 1956. For information on the geographic diversity in tomato

production, see John Hoenig, "A Tomato for All Seasons: Innovation in American Agriculture, 1900–1945," *Business History Review* 88, no. 3 (2014): 523–44, and Alma Chesnut Moore, "Aztecs' Tomatl Is the Modern Tomato," *New York Times*, Apr. 7, 1963.

62. Walter Chandoha, "It's Almost Time to Plant the Backyard Tomato Patch," *New York Times*, May 10, 1981; Peter Tonge, "The Tomato's Firmly Rooted Popularity," *Christian Science Monitor*, Feb. 24, 1987. For an example on the debate concerning staking tomatoes, see Barbara Pleasant, "The Great Tomato Debate," *Organic Gardening*, Apr. 1992.

63. Wayne McLaurin, "Garden/Pick of the Crop: There's Nothing Better Than a Vine-Ripe Tomato," *Atlanta Journal-Constitution*, Aug. 6, 2004; Richard W. Langer, "Gardening: In and Out: Gardening to Reap a Full Vegetable Bin," *New York Times*, Apr. 7, 1977; Francis C. Coulter, "Choice Vegetables: Certain Favorites Are Better Grown at Home," *New York Times*, Mar. 19, 1950; William Evans, "Bringing Up Tomatoes," *Organic Gardening*, June–July 2004; "Inside & Out—Heirloom Seed Line Grounded in History," *Atlanta Journal and Atlanta Constitution*, Mar. 4, 1994. For a very early example describing homegrown varieties versus varieties for commercial growing and shipping, see Ruth Gannon, "The Vegetable Plot: When Properly Managed, It Can Supply Both the Freezer and the Table," *New York Times*, Mar. 13, 1949. See also, Francis Coulter, "Market or Home: Commercial Vegetable Growers Do Not Always Produce the Best Crops," *New York Times*, Apr. 15, 1956.

64. Joanna Poncavage, "Grow Great Tasting Early Tomatoes," *Organic Gardening*, Jan. 1997; Harold Faber, "An Ode to the Tomato," *New York Times*, May 2, 1971; Nadine Brozan, "What's Gone Wrong with the Tomato," *New York Times*, May 31, 1972. See also J. I. Rodale, *How to Grow Vegetables and Fruits by the Organic Method* (Emmaus, PA: Rodale Books, 1970), 5; Richard Langer, "Tomatoes: Making Memory Come Alive," *New York Times*, Apr. 2, 1978.

65. Francis C. Coulter, "Catalogues Contain the Seeds of Debate: Sales Responses Prove Amateurs Still Prefer Many Vegetables Home Grown," *New York Times*, Jan. 2, 1955; Lynette Evans, "Best and the Brightest in Tomato Season," *San Francisco Chronicle*, Mar. 1, 2008; R. R. Thomasson, "Novelty Tomatoes for Summer: Small-Fruited Kinds Yield Good Harvest from Few Plants," *New York Times*, May 7, 1961; Faber, "Ode to the Tomato"; Joan Potter, "Planning for Tomorrow's Blossoms," *New York Times*, Feb. 8, 1976; Alan Vaughn, "Certain Tomato Plant Varieties Produce Well in Home Gardens," *Times-Picayune*, Mar. 24, 1991.

CONCLUSION

1. Michael Pollan, *The Omnivore's Dilemma: A Natural History of Four Meals* (New York: Penguin, 2006); Eric Schlosser, *Fast Food Nation: The Dark Side of the American Meal* (New York: Houghton Mifflin, 2001); *Food, Inc.*, directed by Robert Kenner (Los Angeles: Magnolia Home Entertainment, 2009, DVD, 148 min.). For general

dissatisfaction with supermarket produce, see Marianne McGarry Wolf, Arianne Spittler, and James Ahern, "A Profile of Farmers' Market Consumer and the Perceived Advantages of Produce Sold at Farmers' Markets," *Journal of Food Distribution Research* 36, no. 1 (2005): 198, and Alan S. Kezis, F. Richard King, Ulrich C. Toensmeyer, Robert Jack, and Howard W. Kerr, "Consumer Acceptance and Preference for Direct Marketing in the Northeast," *Journal of Food Distribution Research* 15, no. 3 (1984): 39–41. For evidence that consumers are more dissatisfied with supermarket tomatoes than other produce, see John Booker, David B. Eastwood, and Robert H. Orr, "Consumers' Perceptions of Locally Grown Produce at Retail Outlets," *Journal of Food Distribution Research* 18, no. 1 (1987): 103–5.

2. Jeffrey Pilcher, *Planet Taco: A Global History of Mexican Food* (New York: Oxford University Press, 2012).

3. See, for example, Monsanto Inc., "Food, Inc. Movie," Monstanto.com, www .monsanto.com/food-inc/pages/default.aspx (accessed Sept. 18, 2014).

BIBLIOGRAPHY

ARCHIVAL SOURCES

DIVISION OF RARE AND MANUSCRIPT COLLECTIONS, CORNELL UNIVERSITY LIBRARY, ITHACA, NY

Macklem, Stanley, Oral History. New York State Food Processing Oral History Project, #2378. Menu Collection, #6452.

HAGLEY LIBRARY, WILMINGTON, DE

Canners' Supply Company Catalog. Bridgeton, NJ; Philadelphia, [1890s].
Dichter, Ernest Papers, Series 1, #2407A.
H. S. Mill Canning Company. Letter book, 1905–1908, #2497.

NATIONAL AGRICULTURE LIBRARY, BELTSVILLE, MD

Gilbert, Henry G., Nursery and Seed Trade Catalog Collection. Manuscript Collection #120.
    Bliss, Benjamin K. Descriptive Catalogue of a Choice Collection of Vegetable, Agricultural, and Flower Seeds . . . 1865. Springfield, MA, 1866.
    Breck, Charles H. B. Catalogue of Vegetable, Herb, Tree, Flower and Grass Seeds. Boston: Tuttle and Dennett, 1842.
    Breck, Joseph, and Co. Catalogue of Vegetable, Herb, Tree, Flower and Grass Seeds. Boston, 1840.
    Comstock, Ferre and Co. Descriptive Catalogue of Garden Seeds Cultivated and Sold at the Wethersfield Seed Garden. Wethersfield, CT, 1852.

Dreer, Henry A. Dreer's Garden Calendar, 1861. Philadelphia, 1861.

Evans, Edward J., and Co. Catalog. York, PA, 1868.

Landreth, D., and Sons. Catalog. Philadelphia, 1900.

Landreth, David, and Son. Descriptive Catalogue of the Garden Seeds Cultivated at Bloomsdale, the Seed Grounds of David Landreth & Son. Philadelphia, 1865.

Landreth, D., Seed Company. Landreth's Garden Seeds. Bristol, PA, 1915.

Leonard Seed Co. Leonard's Seeds. Chicago, 1920.

Nebraska Seed Company. Catalog. Omaha, 1905.

Prouty, David, and Co. Catalogue of Garden, Flower, Field and Grass Seeds. Boston, 1851.

Russell, John B. Catalogue of Kitchen Garden Herb, Tree, Field and Flower Seeds. Boston: New England Farmer Office, 1827.

Thorburn, G., and Son. Catalogue of Kitchen Garden, Herb, Flower, Tree and Grass Seeds. New York: Clayton and Van Norden, 1825.

Thorburn, James M. Thorburn's Catalogue of Kitchen Garden Seeds. New York: William S. Dorr, 1853.

Washburn and Co., Washburn & Co.'s Amateur Cultivator's Guide to the Flower and Kitchen Garden, 1869 Catalogue. Boston, 1869.

NATIONAL MUSEUM OF AMERICAN HISTORY, WASHINGTON DC

Burpee, W. Atlee, and Co. Catalog. Philadelphia, 1904.

——. Catalog. Philadelphia, 1905.

Sprague Canning Machinery Co. Sprague General Catalogue of Canning Machinery and Supplies. Chicago, ca. 1910.

UNIVERSITY LIBRARY, UNIVERSITY OF CALIFORNIA, DAVIS

Blackwelder Manufacturing Company Archives, #D-326. Department of Special Collections, General Library.

Dickman, A. I. Interviews with Persons Involved in the Development of the Tomato Harvester, the Compatible Processing Tomato and the New Agricultural Systems That Evolved. Davis: University of California, Davis, Oral History Office, Shields Library, 1978.

BOOKS

Alberts, Robert C. The Good Provider: H. J. Heinz and His 57 Varieties. Boston: Houghton Mifflin, 1973.

Alexander, William. The $64 Tomato. Chapel Hill, NC: Algonquin, 2006.

Allen, Arthur. *Ripe: The Search for the Perfect Tomato.* Berkeley, CA: Counterpoint Press, 2010.

American Can Company. *The Canned Food Reference Manual.* 3rd ed. New York, 1949.

American Cooking: The Melting Pot, Supplement. New York: Time-Life Books, 1972.

Anderson, J. L. *Industrializing the Corn Belt: Agriculture, Technology, and Environment, 1945–1972.* DeKalb: Northern Illinois University Press, 2008.

Appert, Nicholas. *The Art of Preserving All Kinds of Animal and Vegetable Substances.* London: Black Perry, 1812.

Apple, Rima. *Vitamania: Vitamins in American Culture.* New Brunswick, NJ: Rutgers University Press, 1996.

Barndt, Deborah. *Tangled Routes: Women, Work, and Globalization on the Tomato Trail.* New York: Rowman and Littlefield, 2002.

Bartholomew, Mel. *All New Square Foot Gardening.* Franklin, TN: Cool Springs Press, 2005.

Belasco, Warren. *Americans on the Road: From Autocamp to Motel, 1910–1945.* Baltimore: Johns Hopkins University Press, 1997.

——. *Appetite for Change: How the Counterculture Took on the Food Industry.* Ithaca, NY: Cornell University Press, 2006.

Boorstin, Daniel. *The Americans: The Democratic Experience.* New York: Random House, 1973.

"A Boston Housekeeper." *The Cook's Own Book.* Boston: Munroe and Francis, 1832.

Briggs, John W. *An Italian Passage: Immigrants to Three American Cities, 1890–1930.* New Haven, CT: Yale University Press, 1978.

Brooks, David. *Bobos in Paradise: The New Upper Class and How They Got There.* New York: Simon and Schuster, 2000.

Buist, Robert. *The Family Kitchen Gardener.* New York: J. C. Riker, 1847.

Burr, Fearing, Jr. *The Field and Garden Vegetables of America.* Boston: J. E. Tilton, 1865.

Calavita, Kitty. *Inside the State: The Bracero Program, Immigration, and the INS.* New Orleans: Quid Pro Books, 2010.

Callahan, Joan R. *50 Health Scares That Fizzled.* Santa Barbara, CA: Greenwood, 2011.

Campbell, Clyde H. *Campbell's Book: A Manual on Canning, Pickling, and Preserving.* 3rd ed. Chicago: Vance Publishing, 1950.

Campbell, Helen. *The Easiest Way in Housekeeping and Cooking: Adapted to Domestic Use or Study in Classes.* Boston: Little, Brown, 1903.

Canners Directory 1925. Washington, DC: National Canners Association, 1925.

The Canning Industry, Its History, Organization, Methods, and the Public Service Values of Its Products. Washington, DC: National Canners Association, 1952.

Canning Trade. *1916 Almanac of the Canning Industry.* Baltimore, 1916.

——. *1918 Almanac of the Canning Industry.* Baltimore, 1918.

Carson, Jane. *Colonial Virginia Cookery.* Charlottesville: University Press of Virginia, 1968.

Chadwick, Mrs. J. *Home Cookery: A Collection of Tried Receipts.* Boston: Crosby, Nichols, and Company, 1853.

Child, Lydia Marie Francis. *The Frugal Housewife.* 2nd ed. Boston: Carter and Hendee, 1830.

Cohen, Lizabeth. *A Consumers' Republic: The Politics of Mass Consumption in Postwar America.* New York: Knopf, 2003.

Collegiate Section of the U.S. Food Administration, *Food and the War: A Textbook for College Classes*. Boston: Houghton Mifflin, 1918.

Collins, Douglas. *America's Favorite Food: The Story of Campbell Soup Company*. New York: Harry N. Abrams, 1994.

Collins, James H. *The Story of Canned Foods*. New York: E. P. Dutton, 1924.

Conley, Emma. *Principles of Cooking: A Textbook in Domestic Science*. New York: American Book Company, 1914.

Cooper, Lenna Frances. *How to Cut Food Costs*. Battle Creek, MI: Good Health Publishing, 1917.

Courtwright, David. *Forces of Habit: Drugs and the Making of the Modern World*. Cambridge, MA: Harvard University Press, 2001.

Cronon, William. *Changes in the Land: Indians, Colonists, and the Ecology of New England*. New York: Hill and Wang, 2003.

——. *Nature's Metropolis: Chicago and the Great West*. New York: Norton, 1992.

Crosby, Alfred. *The Columbian Exchange*. Westport, CT: Praeger, 2003.

Cross, Gary. *All-Consuming Century: Why Commercialism Won in Modern America*. New York: Columbia University Press, 2000.

——. *The Cute and the Cool*. New York: Oxford University Press, 2004.

——. *Time and Money: The Making of Consumer Culture*. New York: Routledge, 1993.

Cross, Gary, and Robert Proctor. *Packaged Pleasures: How Engineering and Marketing Revolutionized Desire*. Chicago: University of Chicago Press, 2014.

Cruess, William V. *Home and Farm Food Preservation*. New York: Macmillan, 1918.

Cummings, Richard Osborn. *The American and His Food*. New York: Arno, 1970.

Day, Ivan. *Cooking in Europe, 1650–1850*. Westport, CT: Greenwood, 2009.

De Candolle, A. P. *Origins of Cultivated Plants*. New York: D. Appleton, 1885.

De Quattrociocchi, Niccolo. *Love and Dishes*. New York: Bobbs-Merrill, 1950.

Dichter, Ernest. *Handbook of Consumer Motivations*. New York: McGraw-Hill, 1964.

Dienstag, Eleanor Foa. *In Good Company: 125 Years at the Heinz Table*. New York: Warner Books, 1994.

Diner, Hasia R. *Hungering for America: Italian, Irish, and Jewish Foodways in the Age of Migration*. Cambridge, MA: Harvard University Press, 2001.

Doerrfeld, Dean A., David L. Ames, and Rebecca J. Siders. *The Canning Industry in Delaware, 1860 to 1940+/–: A Historic Context*. Wilmington, DE: University of Delaware, Center for Historic Architecture and Engineering, 1993.

Elias, Megan J. *Stir It Up: Home Economics in American Culture*. Philadelphia: University of Pennsylvania Press, 2008.

Estabrook, Barry. *Tomatoland: How Modern Industrial Agriculture Destroyed Our Most Alluring Fruit*. Kansas City, MO: Andrews McMeel, 2011.

Ets, Marie Hall. *Rosa: The Life of an Italian Immigrant*. Minneapolis: University of Minnesota Press, 1970.

Felt, Joseph B. *History of Ipswich, Essex, and Hamilton*. Cambridge: Charles Folsom, 1834.

Fessenden, Thomas G. *The New American Gardener*. Boston: J. B. Russell, 1828.

Fischer, David Hackett. *Albion's Seed: Four British Folkways in America*. New York: Oxford University Press, 1989.

Fitzgerald, Deborah. *Every Farm a Factory: The Industrial Ideal in American Agriculture.* New Haven, CT: Yale University Press, 2003.

Fowler, Daniel Lee. *Dining at Monticello: In Good Taste and Abundance.* Charlottesville, VA: Thomas Jefferson Foundation, 2005.

Francis, Clarence. *A History of Food and Its Preservation.* Princeton, NJ: Princeton University Press, 1937.

Freidberg, Susanne. *Fresh: A Perishable History.* Cambridge, MA: The Belknap Press of Harvard University Press, 2009.

Gabaccia, Donna R. *Italy's Many Diasporas.* Seattle: University of Washington Press, 2000.

——. *We Are What We Eat: Ethnic Food and the Making of Americans.* Cambridge, MA: Harvard University Press, 1988.

Gans, Herbert J. *The Urban Villagers: Group and Class in the Life of Italian-Americans.* New York: Free Press, 1982.

Gardner, Bruce L. *American Agriculture in the Twentieth Century: How It Flourished and What It Cost.* Cambridge, MA: Harvard University Press, 2002.

Gelber, Steven M. *Hobbies: Leisure and the Culture of Work in America.* New York: Columbia University Press, 1999.

Gentilcore, David. *Pomodoro!: A History of the Tomato in Italy.* New York: Columbia University Press, 2010.

Gentile, Maria. *The Italian Cookbook: The Art of Eating Well.* New York: Italian Book Co., 1919.

Giedion, Siegfried. *Mechanization Takes Command: A Contribution to Anonymous History.* New York: Norton, 1969.

Glasse, Hannah. *The Art of Cookery Made Plain and Easy.* Alexandria, VA, 1805.

Goldstein, Carolyn M. *Creating Consumers: Home Economists in Twentieth-Century America.* Chapel Hill: University of North Carolina Press, 2012.

Goudiss, C. Houston, and Alberta M. Goudiss. *Foods That Will Win the War and How to Cook Them.* New York: World Syndicate, 1918.

Green, Mary. *Better Meals for Less Money.* New York: Henry Holt, 1917.

Gumina, Deanna Paoli. *The Italians of San Francisco.* New York: Center for Migration Studies, 1978.

Hale, Sarah Josefa. *The Ladies' New Book of Cookery.* New York: H. Long and Brother, 1859.

Hamilton, Shane. *Trucking Country: The Road to America's Wal-Mart Economy.* Princeton, NJ: Princeton University Press, 2008.

Helstosky, Carol. *Pizza: A Global History.* London: Reaktion Books, 2008.

Herrick, Christine. *Consolidated Library of Modern Cooking and Household Recipes.* Volume 3. New York: R. J. Boomer, 1905.

Hill, Janet McKenzie. *Canning, Preserving and Jelly Making.* Boston: Little, Brown, 1915.

——. *Practical Cooking and Serving: A Complete Manual of How to Select, Prepare, and Serve Food.* New York: Doubleday, Page, 1919.

Hine, Thomas. *The Total Package: The Secret History and Hidden Meanings of Boxes, Bottles, Cans, and Other Persuasive Containers.* New York: Little, Brown, 1995.

Holt, Emily. *The Complete Housekeeper.* New York: Doubleday, Page, 1917.

Hooker, Richard J. *Food and Drink in America: A History.* New York: Bobbs-Merrill, 1981.

Hooper, Edward James. *The Practical Farmer, Gardener and Housewife.* Cincinnati: Geo. Conclin, 1840.

Horowitz, Daniel. *The Morality of Spending: Attitudes Toward the Consumer Society in America, 1875–1940.* Chicago: Elephant Paperbacks, 1992.

Horowitz, Roger. *Putting Meat on the American Table: Taste, Technology, Transformation.* Baltimore: Johns Hopkins University Press, 2005.

Howard, A. J. *Canning Technology.* Washington, DC: Sherwood Press, 1949.

Hughes, Mary B. *Everywoman's Canning Book.* 2nd ed. Boston: Whitcomb and Barrows, 1918.

Hurt, R. Douglas. *Problems of Plenty: The American Farmer in the Twentieth Century.* Chicago: Ivan R. Dee, 2002.

Jacobs, Meg. *Pocketbook Politics: Economic Citizenship in Twentieth-Century America.* Princeton, NJ: Princeton University Press, 2007.

Jameson, J. Franklin. *Johnson's Wonder-Working Providence, 1628–1651.* New York: Charles Scribner's Sons, 1910.

Jefferson, Thomas. *Notes on the State of Virginia.* Paris, 1782.

Jenkins, Virginia Scott. *The Lawn: A History of an American Obsession.* Washington, DC: Smithsonian Institution Press, 1994.

Johnson, Colleen Leahy. *Growing up and Growing Old in Italian-American Families.* New Brunswick, NJ: Rutgers University Press, 1985.

Judge, Arthur L., ed. *A History of the Canning Industry, by Its Most Prominent Men.* Baltimore: The Canning Trade, 1914.

Kalm, Peter. *The America of 1750: Peter Kalm's Travels in North America: The English Version of 1770.* Edited by Adolph B. Benson. Vol. 2. New York: Wilson-Erickson, 1937.

Kammen, Michael G. *Colonial New York: A History.* New York: Oxford University Press, 1975.

Kessner, Thomas. *The Golden Door: Italian and Jewish Immigrant Mobility in New York City, 1880–1915.* New York: Oxford University Press, 1977.

Kimball, Kristin. *The Dirty Life: On Farming, Food, and Love.* New York: Scribner, 2010.

Kitchiner, William. *The Cook's Oracle.* New York: Evert Duyckinck, 1825.

Kittredge, George Lyman. *The Old Farmer and His Almanack.* Cambridge, MA: Harvard University Press, 1904.

Kloppenburg, Jack, Jr. *First the Seed: The Political Economy of Plant Biotechnology, 1492–2000.* New York: Cambridge University Press, 1988.

Kramer, Jack. *Basket Bounty: Growing Vegetables, Fruits, and Herbs in and Around the House.* New York: Charles Scribner's Sons, 1975.

Laird, Pamela Walker. *Advertising Progress: American Business and the Rise of Consumer Marketing.* Baltimore: Johns Hopkins University Press, 1998.

Lawson, Laura J. *City Bountiful.* Berkeley: University of California Press, 2005.

Lears, T. Jackson. *Fables of Abundance: A Cultural History of Advertising in America.* New York: Basic Books, 1994.

Leslie, Eliza. *Directions for Cookery.* Philadelphia: Carey and Hart, 1840.

Levenstein, Harvey. *Revolution at the Table: The Transformation of the American Diet.* New York: Oxford University Press, 1988.

Livingston, A. W. *Livingston and the Tomato.* Columbus, OH: A. W. Livingston's Sons, 1893.

Marchand, Roland. *Advertising the American Dream: Making Way for Modernity, 1920–1940.* Berkeley: University of California Press, 1985.

Marling, Karal Ann. *As Seen on TV: The Visual Culture of Everyday Life in the 1950s.* Cambridge, MA: Harvard University Press, 1996.

Marsh, Margaret. *Suburban Lives.* New Brunswick, NJ: Rutgers University Press, 1990.

Martineau, Belinda. *First Fruit: The Creation of the Flavr Savr Tomato and the Birth of Biotech Foods.* New York: McGraw-Hill, 2001.

Marx, Karl. *Outlines of the Critique of Political Economy.* New York: Penguin, 1973.

Matteson, Emma B., and Ethel M. Newlands. *A Laboratory Manual of Foods and Cookery.* New York: Macmillan, 1917.

Matthiolus [Mattioli], Petrus Andreas. *Di Pedacio Dioscoride Anazarebo libri cinque dellas historia, et material medciciale tradotti in lingua volgare Italiana.* Venice, 1554.

May, Earl Chapin. *The Canning Clan: A Pageant of Pioneering Americans.* New York: Macmillan, 1938.

McPhee, John. *Giving Good Weight.* New York: Farrar, Straus and Giroux, 1979.

McWilliams, James E. *A Revolution in Eating: How the Quest for Food Shaped America.* New York: Columbia University Press, 2005.

Mease, James. *Archives of Useful Knowledge.* Vol. 2. Philadelphia: David Hogan, 1812.

Mintz, Sidney. *Sweetness and Power: The Place of Sugar in Modern History.* New York: Viking Penguin, 1985.

Mitchell, Alex. *The Edible Balcony: Growing Fresh Produce in Small Spaces.* New York: Rodale, 2011.

M'Mahon, Bernard. *The American Gardener's Catalog.* Philadelphia: B. Graves, 1806.

Montanari, Massimo. *Food Is Culture.* Translated by Albert Sonnenfeld. New York: Columbia University Press, 2006.

Morganelli, Adrianna. *The Biography of Tomatoes.* New York: Crabtree, 2007.

Morris, Edmund. *Ten Acres Enough.* New York: James Miller, 1864.

Morton, Nathaniel. *New England's Memorial.* Boston: Crocker and Brewster, 1826.

Neil, Marion Harris. *Canning, Preserving and Pickling.* Philadelphia: David McKay, 1914.

Nelli, Humbert S. *Italians in Chicago, 1880–1930.* New York: Oxford University Press, 1970.

Nesbitt, Florence. *Low Cost Cooking: A Manual of Cooking, Diet, Home Management and Care of Children.* Chicago: American School of Home Economics, 1915.

Newcomb, Duane. *The Postage Stamp Garden Book: How to Grow All the Food You Can Eat in Very Little Space.* Los Angeles: J. P. Tarcher, 1975.

Packard, Vance. *The Status Seekers.* New York: David McKay, 1961.

Parkin, Kathleen. *Food Is Love: Food Advertising and Gender Roles in Modern America.* Philadelphia: University of Pennsylvania Press, 2006.

Peterson, James. *Sauces: Classical and Contemporary Sauce Making.* 3rd ed. Hoboken, NJ: John Wiley and Sons, 2008.

Pilcher, Jeffrey. *Planet Taco: A Global History of Mexican Food.* New York: Oxford University Press, 2012.

Pollan, Michael. *The Omnivore's Dilemma: A Natural History of Four Meals.* New York: Penguin, 2006.

Putnam, Elizabeth H. *Mrs. Putnam's Receipt Book and Young Housekeeper's Assistant*. Boston: Ticknor, Reed, and Fields, 1850.

Raffald, Elizabeth. *The Experienced English Housekeeper*. Manchester, 1769.

Randall, Henry Stephens. *The Life of Thomas Jefferson*. Vol. 1. New York: Derby and Jackson, 1858.

Randolph, Mary. *The Virginia Housewife; or, Methodical Cook*. Mineola, NY: Dover, 1993.

Reader, John. *Potatoes: A History of the Propitious Esculent*. New Haven, CT: Yale University Press, 2008.

Rees, Jonathan. *Refrigeration Nation: A History of Ice, Appliances, and Enterprise in America*. Baltimore: Johns Hopkins University Press, 2013.

Riesman, David. *The Lonely Crowd*. New Haven, CT: Yale University Press, 1950.

Riley, John. *A History of the American Soft Drink Industry: Bottled Carbonated Beverages, 1807–1957*. Washington, DC: American Bottlers of Carbonated Beverages, 1958.

Robson, Charles, ed. *The Manufactories and Manufacturers of Pennsylvania of the Nineteenth Century*. Philadelphia: Galaxy, 1875.

Rodale, J. J. *How to Grow Vegetables and Fruits by the Organic Method*. Emmaus, PA: Rodale Books, 1970.

Rome, Adam. *Bulldozer in the Countryside: Suburban Sprawl and the Rise of American Environmentalism*. New York: Cambridge University Press, 2001.

Root, Waverly, and Richard de Rochemont. *Eating in America: A History*. New York: William Morrow, 1976.

Rosenberg, Nathan. *Technology and American Economic Growth*. New York: Harper and Row, 1972.

Rundell, Maria Eliza. *The American Domestic Cookery*. New York: Every Duyckinck, 1823.

——. *A New System of Domestic Cookery*. London: John Murray, 1808.

Sackman, Douglas Cazaux. *Orange Empire: California and the Fruits of Eden*. Berkeley: University of California Press, 2007.

Saga of a City, Lynchburg, Virginia, 1786–1936. Lynchburg, 1936.

Salmon, William. *Botanologia: The English Herbal; or, History of Plants*. London: I. Dawks for H. Rhodes and J. Taylor, 1710.

Scalon, Jennifer. *Inarticulate Longings: The Ladies' Home Journal, Gender, and the Promises of Consumer Culture*. New York: Routledge, 1995.

Schivelbusch, Wolfgang. *Tastes of Paradise*. New York: Vintage, 1992.

Schlosser, Eric. *Fast Food Nation: The Dark Side of the American Meal*. New York: Houghton Mifflin, 2001.

Serventi, Silvano, and Francoise Sabban. *Pasta: The Story of a Universal Food*. Translated by Antony Shugaar. New York: Columbia University Press, 2002.

Shephard, Sue. *Pickled, Potted, and Canned: How the Art and Science of Food Preserving Changed the World*. New York: Simon and Schuster, 2000.

Shover, John T. *First Majority—Last Minority: The Transforming of Rural Life in America*. DeKalb: Northern Illinois University Press, 1976.

Sidorick, Daniel. *Condensed Capitalism: Campbell Soup and the Pursuit of Cheap Production in the Twentieth Century*. Ithaca, NY: ILR/Cornell University Press, 2009.

Simmons, Amelia. *American Cookery; or, the Art of Dressing Viands, Fish, Poultry and Vegetables*. Albany, NY, 1796.

Smith, Andrew. *Hamburger: A Global History*. London: Reaktion, 2008.

———. *Pure Ketchup: A History of America's National Condiment*. Washington, DC: Smithsonian Institution Press, 2001.

———. *Souper Tomatoes: The Story of America's Favorite Food*. New Brunswick, NJ: Rutgers University Press, 2000.

———. *The Tomato in America: Early History, Culture, and Cookery*. Columbia: University of South Carolina Press, 1994.

Smith, E. *The Compleat Housewife*. London, 1739.

Soluri, John. *Banana Cultures: Agriculture, Consumption, and Environmental Change in Honduras and the United States*. Austin: University of Texas Press, 2006.

Stark, Tim. *Heirloom: Notes from an Accidental Tomato Farmer*. New York: Broadway Books, 2008.

Stern, Frances, and Gertrude T. Spitz. *Food for the Worker: The Food Values and Cost of a Series of Menus and Recipes for Seven Weeks*. Boston: Whitcomb and Barrows, 1917.

Stoll, Steven. *The Fruits of Natural Advantage: Making the Industrial Countryside in California*. Berkeley: University of California Press, 1998.

Strasser, Susan. *Satisfaction Guaranteed: The Making of the American Mass Market*. Washington, DC: Smithsonian Institution Press, 1989.

Sturgeon, Launcelot. *Essays, Moral, Philosophical, and Stomachical*. London: G. and W. B. Whitaker, 1823.

Thomson, Bob. *The New Victory Garden*. Boston: Little, Brown, 1987.

Trachtenberg, Alan. *The Incorporation of America: Culture and Society in the Gilded Age*. New York: Hill and Wang, 1982.

Vileisis, Ann. *Kitchen Literacy: How We Lost Knowledge of Where Food Comes from and Why We Need to Get It Back*. Washington, DC: Island Press, 2010.

Volney, C. F. *View of the Climate and Soil of the United States of America*. London: C. Mercier, 1804.

Wagner, E. *Recipes for the Preserving of Fruit, Vegetables, and Meat*. Translated by Chas. Salter. London: Scott, Greenwood and Son, 1908.

Wardall, Ruth A., and Edna Noble White. *A Study of Foods*. Boston: Ginn, 1914.

Whyte, William. *Organization Man*. Garden City, NY: Doubleday, 1956.

Williams, John Lee. *The Territory of Florida: Sketches of the Topography, Civil and Natural History*. New York: A. T. Goodrich, 1837.

———. *A View of West Florida*. Philadelphia: H. S. Tanner and the Author, 1827.

Williams, Mary E., and Katherine Rolston Fisher. *Elements of the Theory and Practice of Cookery: A Textbook of Household Science for Use in School*. New York: Macmillan, 1913.

Wilson, C. Anne. *Food and Drink in Britain: From the Stone Age to the 19th Century*. Chicago: Academy Chicago Publishers, 1991.

Woloson, Wendy. *Refined Tastes: Sugar, Confectionary, and Consumers in Nineteenth Century America*. Baltimore: Johns Hopkins University Press, 2002.

Young, Alexander. *Chronicles of the First Planters of the Colony of Massachusetts Bay, from 1623 to 1636.* Boston: Charles C. Little and James Brown, 1846.

ARTICLES

Acrelius, Israel. "A History of New Sweden." In *Memoirs of the Historical Society of Pennsylvania* 11 (1876).

Adelaja, Adesoji O., Robin G. Brumfield, and Kimberley Lininger. "Product Differentiation and State Promotion of Farm Produce: An Analysis of the Jersey Fresh Tomato." *Journal of Food Distribution Research* (1990): 73–85.

Andreatta, Susan, and William Wickliffe II. "Managing Farmer and Consumer Expectations: A Study of a North Carolina Farmers' Market." *Human Organization* 61, no. 2 (2002): 167–76.

Banerjee, Tridib. "The Future of Public Space: Beyond Reinvented Streets and Reinvented Places." *Journal of the American Planning Association* 67, no. 1 (2001): 9–24.

Brooker, John, David B. Eastwood, and Robert H. Orr. "Consumers' Perceptions of Locally Grown Produce at Retail Outlets." *Journal of Food Distribution Research* 18, no. 1 (1987): 99–107.

Brown, Allison. "Counting Farmers Markets." *Geographical Review* 91, no. 4 (2001): 655–74.

——. "Farmers' Market Research 1994–2000: An Inventory and Review." *American Journal of Alternative Agriculture* 17, no. 4 (2002): 167–76.

Brown, Cheryl. "Consumers' Preferences for Locally Produced Food: A Study in Southeast Missouri." *American Journal of Alternative Agriculture* 18, no. 4 (2003): 213–24.

Brown, Cheryl, and Stacy Miller. "The Impacts of Local Markets: A Review of Research on Farmers Markets and Community Supported Agriculture (CSA)." *Agricultural & Applied Economics Association* 90, no. 5 (2008): 1296–1302.

Darby, Kim, Marvin T. Batte, Stan Ernst, and Brian Roe. "Decomposing Local: A Conjoint Analysis of Locally Produced Foods." *American Journal of Agricultural Economics* 90 no. 2 (2008): 476–86.

Dicke, Tom. "Red Gold in the Ozarks: The Rise and Decline of Tomato Canning, 1885-1955." *Agricultural History* 79, no. 1 (2005): 1–26.

Diffenderffer, Frank Reid. "The German Immigration into Pennsylvania." In *Pennsylvania-German Society: Proceedings and Addresses* 10, no. 1. Lancaster, PA: New Era Printing Company, 1900.

Eastwood, David B., John R. Brooker, and Morgan D. Gray. "Location and Other Market Attributes Affecting Farmer's Market Patronage: The Case of Tennessee." *Journal of Food Distribution Research* 30, no. 1 (1999): 63–72.

Fowler, Cary. "The Plant Patent Act of 1930: A Sociological History of its Creation." *Journal of the Patent and Trademark Office* 82 (2000): 621–44.

Gabaccia, Donna R. "Italian-American Cookbooks: From Oral to Print Culture." *Italian-Americana* 16, no. 1 (1998): 15–23.

Gallons, James, U. C. Toensmeyer, J. Richard Bacon, and Carl L. German. "An Analysis of Consumer Characteristics Concerning Direct Marketing of Fresh Produce in Delaware: A Case Study." *Journal of Food Distribution Research* 28, no. 1 (1997): 98–106.

Grewe, Rudolf. "The Arrival of the Tomato in Spain and Italy: Early Recipes." *Journal of Gastronomy* 3 (Summer 1987): 67–83.

Hamilton, Lisa M. "The American Farmers Market." *Gastronomica: The Journal of Food and Culture* 2, no. 3 (2002): 73–77.

Hardesty, Shermain D. "The Growing Role of Local Food Markets." *Agricultural & Applied Economics Association* 90, no. 5 (2008): 1289–95.

Hoenig, John. "A Tomato for All Seasons: Innovation in American Agriculture." *Business History Review* 88, no. 3 (2014): 523–44.

Hunt, Alan R. "Consumer Interactions and Influences on Farmers' Market Vendors." *Renewable Agriculture and Food Systems* 22, no. 1 (2007): 54–66.

Jenkins, J. A. "The Origin of the Cultivated Tomato." *Economic Botany* 2, no. 4 (1948): 379–92.

Just, Richard E., and Quinn Weninger. "Economic Evaluation of the Farmers' Market Nutrition Program." *American Journal of Agricultural Economics* 79, no. 3 (1997): 902–17.

Kesiz, Alan S., F. Richard King, Ulrich C. Toensmeyer, Robert Jack, and Howard W. Kerr. "Consumer Acceptance and Preference for Direct Marketing in the Northeast." *Journal of Food Distribution Research* 15, no. 3 (1984): 38–46.

Lockeretz, William. "Consumers' Attitudes Towards Locally Grown Produce." *American Journal of Alternative Agriculture* 1, no. 2 (1986): 83–88.

Lyson, T. A., G. W. Gillespie Jr., and D. Hilchey. "Farmers' Markets and the Local Community: Bridging the Formal and Informal Economy." *American Journal of Alternative Agriculture* 10, no. 3 (1995): 108–13.

Marks, Joe. "Tomato Harvesters." *Nation's Agriculture* 40, no. 5 (1965).

Muller, C. H. "The Taxonomy and Distribution of the Genus *Lycopersicon*." *National Horticultural Magazine* 19 (1940): 157–60.

National Canners' Association. *Canned Food Pack Statistics, 1943*. Washington, DC, 1944.

——. *Canned Food Pack Statistics, 1948*. Washington, DC, 1949.

——. *Canned Food Pack Statistics: 1950, Part 1: Vegetables*. Washington, DC, June 1951.

Patterson, Paul M., Hans Olofsson, Timothy J. Richards, and Sharon Sass. "An Empirical Analysis of State Agricultural Product Promotions: A Case Study." *Agribusiness* 15, no. 2 (1999): 179–96.

Petrick, Gabriela. "'Like Ribbons of Green and Gold': Industrializing Lettuce and the Quest for Quality in the Salinas Valley, 1920–1965." *Agricultural History* 80, no. 3 (2006): 269–95.

Pyle, Jane. "Farmers' Markets in the United States: Functional Anachronisms." *Geographical Review* 61, no. 2 (1971): 167–97.

Rasmussen, Wayne D. "Advances in American Agriculture: The Mechanical Tomato Harvester as a Case Study." *Technology and Culture* 9, no. 4 (1968): 531–43.

Raspa, Richard. "Exotic Foods Among Italian-Americans in Mormon Utah: Food as Nostalgic Enactment of Identity." In *Ethnic and Regional Foodways in the United States: The Performance of Group Identity*, edited by Linda Keller Brown and Kay Mussell. Knoxville: University of Tennessee Press, 1984.

Revedin, Anna, et al. "Thirty Thousand-Year-Old Evidence of Plant Food Processing." *Proceedings of the National Academy of Sciences of the United States of America* 107, no. 44 (2010): 18815–19.

Sabine, J. "On the Love Apple or Tomato." *Royal Horticultural Society Transactions* 3 (1819): 342–54.

Schermerhorn, L. G. "Scientific Breeding Gives New Jersey the Rutgers Tomato." *New Jersey State Horticultural Society News* 15, no. 6 (1934): 1–2.

Smith, Andrew. "The Making of the Legend of Robert Gibbon Johnson." *New Jersey History* 108 (1990): 59–74.

Sommer, Robert, Margaret Wing, and Susan Aitkens. "Price Savings to Consumers at Farmers' Markets." *Journal of Consumer Affairs* 14, no. 2 (1980): 452–62.

Thilmany, Dawn, and Phil Watson. "The Increasing Role of Direct Marketing and Farmers Markets for Western U.S. Producers." *Western Economics Forum* 3, no. 1 (2004): 19–25.

Valdés, Dennis Nodín. "Machine Politics in California Agriculture, 1945–1990s." *Pacific Historical Review* 63, no. 2 (1994): 203–24.

Wolf, Marianne McGarry, Arianne Spittler, and James Ahern. "A Profile of Farmers' Market Consumers and the Perceived Advantages of Produce Sold at Farmers' Markets." *Journal of Food Distribution Research* 36, no. 1 (2006): 192–201.

Zepeda, Lydia, and Catherine Leviten-Reid. "Consumers' Views on Local Food." *Journal of Food Distribution Research* 35, no. 3 (2004): 1–6.

Zepeda, Lydia, and Jingham Li. "Who Buys Local Food?" *Journal of Food Distribution Research* 37, no. 3 (2006): 1–11.

PERIODICALS

Adams, E. E. "Packages for Hothouse Tomatoes." *Market Growers Journal*, June 29, 1912.

Adams, Emily. "Fresh from the Farm: Customers at Outdoor Markets Enjoy Chatting with Growers." *Los Angeles Times*, Oct. 4, 1992.

Adams, Virgil. "Garden Centers Doing Well, Thank You." *Atlanta Journal and Atlanta Constitution*, Jan. 21, 1990.

Adams, William D. "Get Your Veggies in a Row—Tomatoes Lead the Field of Spring Favorites." *Houston Chronicle*, Feb. 28, 1987.

Advertisement. *Genesee Farmer and Gardener's Journal* (Rochester, NY), July 20, 1833.

Advertisement. *Good Housekeeping*, July 1909, back advertising section.

Advertisement. *Good Housekeeping*, Sept. 1909, back advertising section.

Advertisement. *Good Housekeeping*, May 1919, 75.

Advertisement. *Good Housekeeping*, Apr. 1926, 240.

Advertisement. *Good Housekeeping*, May 1926, 116.

Advertisement. *New England Farmer, and Horticultural Register* (Boston), Aug. 7, 1833.

Advertisement. *New England Farmer, and Horticultural Register* (Boston), Aug. 21, 1833.

Advertisement. *Saturday Evening Post*, Feb. 27, 1909, 20–21.

"Airplane View of the Zuck Greenhouses." *Market Growers Journal*, Mar. 15, 1925.

Allen, Arthur. "Rotten Tomatoes: Scandal Strikes the Tomato-Paste Industry." *Slate*, Mar. 19, 2010. http://www.slate.com/id/2248288/.

American Farmer. "Tomato Figs." *New England Farmer, and Horticultural Register* (Boston), Sept. 1, 1841.

Applebome, Peter. "Providing Fresh Vegetables to a Community Where Fast Food Reigns." *New York Times*, Sept. 20, 2010.

Aronow, Ina. "White Plains Acts on Farmers Market." *New York Times*, May 7, 1989.

Arrington, Debbie. "As Gardening Expands, So Does Burpee Mailing List." *Sacramento Bee*, Jan. 16, 2010.

"Art. VIII.: On the Cultivation of Tomatoes; (Solanum Lycopersicum); by the Editor." *Southern Agriculturist and Register of Rural Affairs* (Charleston, SC), Feb. 1829.

Ashton, Carrie May. "Two New Year's Dinners." *Good Housekeeping*, Jan. 1900.

Atwater, W. O. "The Chemistry of Foods and Nutrition, II. How Food Nourishes the Body." *Century Illustrated Magazine*, June 1887.

——. "The Chemistry of Foods and Nutrition, V. Pecuniary Economy of Food." *Century Illustrated Magazine*, Jan. 1888.

——. "What We Should Eat." *Century Illustrated Magazine*, June 1888.

Baker, Lois. "Round the Food Stores." *Chicago Tribune*, Jan. 7, 1966.

Baird, Thos. D. "The Garden: The Tomato." *National Stockman and Farmer*, June 13, 1889.

Bedford, Christopher. "Meeting the Challenge of Local Food." *Business*, Jan. 2006.

"Beginner Tomato Preservation." *Organic Gardening*, Aug.–Oct. 2007.

"The Best Dinner Chauncey M. Depew Ever Sat Down To." *Good Housekeeping*, May 1896.

"Big Slash in Canned Vegetables." *New York Times*, June 2, 1945.

Billingsley, Sarah. "Takin' It to the Streets: From Ethnic Lunch Trucks to the Corner Hot Dog Stand, the City Is Full of Flavor." *Pittsburgh Post-Gazette*, May 7, 2004.

Blangger, Tim. "Berks Grower Finds Market for Heirloom Varieties in New York City." *Morning Call* (Allentown, PA), Sept. 12, 1996.

"Blight Hits Tomatoes." *New York Times*, Aug. 14, 1946.

"Boston Faneuil Market, Aug. 14, 1833." *New England Farmer, and Horticultural Register* (Boston), Aug. 14, 1833.

Brooke, James. "Farmers' Markets: Fresh and Folksy." *New York Times*, Aug. 28, 1985.

Brooks, Patricia. "Farmers' Markets Bring Variety to Urban Life." *New York Times*, Oct. 7, 1979.

Brown, Corie. "A Napa Just Waiting to Happen." *Los Angeles Times*, Oct. 13, 2004.

Brown, Douglas. "No Garden? No Problem—Community Plots, Other Yards Await Tilling." *Denver Post*, Apr. 11, 2008.

Brozan, Nadine. "What's Gone Wrong with the Tomato." *New York Times*, May 31, 1972.

Burros, Marian. "A Farmers' Market Worth Fighting For." *New York Times*, July 27, 1988.

Burroughs, Margaret. "Seasonable Menu—VIII." *Good Housekeeping*, Aug. 1899.

"Braceros Stream Into California." *New York Times*, Sept. 5, 1965.

Bylin, James E. "Big Tomato Harvest in California Not Likely to Cut Consumer Cost." *Wall Street Journal*, Dec. 7, 1966.

——. "Lack of Workers May Limit Tomato Crops in California; Higher Retail Prices Seen." *Wall Street Journal*, Aug. 12, 1965.

——. "Tomato Prices Expected to Fall This Year Due to Use of Harvesting Machines in West." *Wall Street Journal*, Mar. 21, 1966.

——-. "Tomato Product Prices Start to Tumble as California Fields Yield a Bumper Crop." *Wall Street Journal*, Nov. 4, 1968.

"Canning Centers Opening Rapidly." *New York Times*, Aug. 25, 1943.

"Care in Selecting Seed." *New England Farmer, and Horticultural Register* (Boston), Jan. 26, 1884.

Chandoha, Walter. "It's Almost Time to Plant the Backyard Tomato Patch." *New York Times*, May 10, 1981.

"Charges Cuba Perils Florida Tomato Crop." *Chicago Daily Tribune*, Apr. 13, 1960.

Chorlton, William. "Culture of the Tomato." *Horticulturist and Journal of Rural Art and Rural Taste*, Mar. 1, 1855.

Collins, Glenn. "Increase in Home Gardening Yields Bumper Crop of Sales: A Bumper Crop in Gardening Supplies." *New York Times*, Aug. 20, 1994.

"Convenience Foods Lift Consumption." *New York Times*, Aug. 19, 1962.

Cook, Louise. "A Plan for Jobless: Plant a Food Garden." *Philadelphia Inquirer*, Mar. 20, 1983.

"Cookery." *Tennessee Farmer* (Jonesborough), Sept. 1837.

"Cooking in a Southern Kitchen." *Good Housekeeping*, Sept. 28, 1889.

Corcoran, Mary. "Indoor Tomato Plant Serves Salad Year Round." *San Francisco Chronicle*, Sept. 29, 1999.

"Cornfield Thrives in Midtown Plot." *New York Times*, June 11, 1942.

Coulter, Francis C. "Catalogues Contain the Seeds of Debate: Sales Responses Prove Amateurs Still Prefer Many Vegetables Home Grown." *New York Times*, Jan. 2, 1955.

——. "Choice Vegetables: Certain Favorites Are Better Grown at Home." *New York Times*, Mar. 19, 1950.

——. "Market or Home: Commercial Vegetable Growers Do Not Always Produce the Best Crops." *New York Times*, Apr. 15, 1956.

——. "Raising Food for a Family of Four." *New York Times*, Mar. 21, 1943.

"Council Opens Produce Market in South Side." *Morning Call*, Aug. 30, 1990.

"Crop Damage in Jersey." *New York Times*, May 13, 1947.

Culbertson, Amy. "The Big Red One: To Savor Summer, Eat 'Real' Tomato." *Patriot News*, July 14, 2004.

"Cultivation of Tomato." *American Farmer, and Spirit of the Agricultural Journals of the Day* (Baltimore), Aug. 30, 1843.

Cultivator. "To Make Tomato Catsup." *Farmer's Register* (Richmond, VA), Dec. 1834.

"Davis Gardens, with 29 Acres Under Glass, Gives Indiana World's Biggest Range." *Market Growers Journal*, Apr. 15, 1925.

D. "Turkish Preparation of Tomato." *New York Farmer*, Oct. 1836.

D., S. M. "Canning Tomatoes (from a Reader)." *Good Housekeeping*, Sept. 28, 1889.

D'Agnese, Joseph. "From the Fields to a Parking Lot Near You." *New York Times*, July 18, 1999.

Dale, H. Fred. "Here's How to Grow Tomatoes, the Star of Most Home Gardens." *Toronto Star*, July 3, 1988.

Dan, Vierria. "Mr. Tomato—Retired NASA Worker's Rocklin Garden Is Out of This World." *Sacramento Bee*, Mar. 23, 2002.

Davies, Lawrence E. "Growers Counter Loss of Braceros." *New York Times*, Feb. 23, 1964.

Delatiner, Barbara. "Food Prices Spur Gardening in Nassau and Suffolk." *New York Times*, May 26, 1974.

Demuth, George S. "Canning Tomatoes on a Large Scale." *Market Growers Journal*, May 7, 1910.

Detloff, Edward. "Mexican Tomatoes." *Chicago Tribune*, Mar. 14, 1969.

"The Discovery of New Vitamines." *American Food Journal*, July 1922.

"Domestic Economy—VII. Recipes for Various Condiments." *Good Housekeeping*, Sept. 1896.

"Domestic Receipts." *Maine Farmer* (Augusta), Aug. 25, 1853.

Dutel-Martino, Jeanne. "Farmers Market Opens Tonight in Cranberry." *Pittsburgh Post-Gazette*, May 9, 1997.

"E. 59th St. Farmers' Market Thrives." *New York Times*, Aug. 1, 1976.

"The Earliest in the World" (May's Tomato Seed advertisement). *Market Growers Journal*, Feb. 5, 1908.

Egan, Timothy. "Growers and Shoppers Crowd Farmers' Markets." *New York Times*, Nov. 29, 2002.

"18,000,000 Gardens Urged for Victory." *New York Times*, Jan. 22, 1943.

Ellsworth, H. L. "Tomato Figs." *American Farmer, and Spirit of the Agricultural Journals of the Day* (Baltimore), July 10, 1841.

Elmer-Dewitt, P. "Fried Gene Tomatoes." *Time*, May 30, 1994.

Enright, W. J. "Supplies of Food Change Sharply." *New York Times*, Mar. 7, 1943.

Escalante, Virginia. "Compton Market Opens: Shoppers Save, Farmers Profit." *Los Angeles Times*, Sept. 24, 1981.

Etter, Gerald. "Their Approach to Food Is Fresh." *Philadelphia Inquirer*, June 20, 1982.

Evans, Lynette. "Best and the Brightest in Tomato Season." *San Francisco Chronicle*, Mar. 1, 2008.

——. "Should Gardeners Give Away the Best Produce or Keep It for Themselves." *San Francisco Chronicle*, Aug. 25, 2007.

Evans, William. "Bringing up Tomatoes." *Organic Gardening*, June–July 2004.

"An Experienced House-Keeper and a Father." "Farmers' Department." *Western Christian Advocate* (Cincinnati), Sept. 23, 1836.

F., W. "Tomatoes—Varieties and Culture." *Cultivator and Country Gentleman*, Sept. 25, 1884.

Faber, Harold. "A Good Season Is Predicted for Home Vegetable Gardens." *New York Times*, May 13, 1973.

——. "An Ode to the Tomato." *New York Times*, May 2, 1971.

——. "Sales of Seeds at Record as Home Gardening Gains Popularity." *New York Times*, Feb. 18, 1974.

Falconer, W. "Tomatoes at Christmas." *Cultivator and Country Gentleman*, Sept. 11, 1884.

"Family Receipts." *Genesee Farmer and Gardener's Journal* (Rochester), Aug. 30, 1834.

"Faneuil Hall Market." *New England Farmer, and Horticultural Register* (Boston), Sept. 9, 1835.

"Faneuil Hall Vegetable Markets." *New England Farmer, and Horticultural Register* (Boston), July 29, 1835.

"Farmers' Department." *Western Christian Advocate* (Cincinnati), Aug. 3, 1838.

"A Farmers Market in the City." *New York City*, Aug. 13, 1976.

"A Female Reader." "Domestic Economy." *Cultivator* (Albany, NY), June 1844.

——. "To Preserve Tomatoes." *Southern Planter* (Richmond, VA), Aug. 1844.

"A Few Salad Recipes." *American Food Journal*, June 1913.

"50% Loss in Tomato Crop Seen." *New York Times*, Aug. 12, 1948.

"53 'Smuggled' Mexican Farm Hands Jailed." *Chicago Daily Tribune*, Aug. 21, 1945.

"Florida Hit by Crops of Mexico." *New York Times*, May 11, 1969.

"For Housekeepers." *Saturday Evening Post*, Sept. 22, 1849.

"Forcing Tomatoes." *Meehan's Monthly: A Magazine of Horticulture, Botany and Kindred Subjects*, Jan. 1893.

Foster, Mimi Fuller. "Heirloom Vegetables: Treasured Varieties Are Tasty Living Link to Gardens of the Past." *Atlanta Journal and Atlanta Constitution*, Feb. 19, 1993.

——. "Killer Tomatoes—'Mater Mania's Taken Hold, in a Humongous-Is-Best Quest That's Just Ripe—for Competition." *Atlanta Journal and Atlanta Constitution*, June 11, 1993.

Fowler, Elizabeth M. "Home Grown: Vegetable Gardens Sprouting Anew." *New York Times*, May 21, 1972.

"From Soup Tureen to Pudding Dish." *Good Housekeeping*, Jan. 5, 1889.

"Fruits of a Victory Garden." *New York Times*, July 2, 1943.

Gallagher, Katie. "Retailers Learn to Tap Into Growing Organic Market." *Gourmet News*, Aug. 1, 2007.

Gannon, Ruth. "The Vegetable Plot: When Properly Managed, It Can Supply Both the Freezer and the Table." *New York Times*, Mar 13, 1949.

"Gardener's Club." *Market Growers Journal*, Mar. 23, 1912.

"The Gardener's Manual." *Genesee Farmer and Gardener's Journal* (Rochester, NY), Sept. 5, 1835.

"Gardening for the South." *Southern Cultivator* (Atlanta), Mar. 1850.

Garnett, James M. "Culture of the Tomato and the Indian Pea." *Farmer's Register: A Monthly Publication* (Richmond, VA), Oct. 31, 1841.

Gillingham, Karen. "Cornucopia in Gardena Parking Lot." *Los Angeles Times*, July 5, 1979.

Goff, E. S. "Mr. A. W. Livingston." *American Garden: A Monthly Illustrated Journal Devoted to Garden Art*, Mar. 1, 1887.

"Good Things for the Table." *Good Housekeeping*, May 30, 1885.

"Good Things for the Table." *Good Housekeeping*, June 27, 1885.

Goodale, D. H. R. "Company Dinners for One." *Good Housekeeping*, May 30, 1885.

Grayson, Esther C. "Especially for Salads: Out of the Victory Garden Many Good for the Big Wooden Bowl." *New York Times*, Mar. 21, 1943.

——. "Planning Those Garden Crops Eases the Burden of Canning." *New York Times*, June 14, 1942.

Green, E. C. "The Earliest Tomato." *Ohio Farmer*, Mar. 23, 1899.

Gross, Jane. "Farmers' Market Lures Office Workers at Lunchtime." *New York Times*, Aug. 3, 1985.

Grunebaum, Peter K. "Letters to the Editor of the Times: Dumping Tomatoes." *New York Times*, May 22, 1969.

H. "The Best Way of Preserving Fruits and Vegetables." *Horticulturalist and Journal of Rural Art and Rural Taste*, Sept. 1, 1851.

Haegel, George. "Vegetable Success: 'Best' Means Best Suited to Local Conditions." *New York Times*, Mar. 11, 1956.

"Half a Hundred: Recipes for Jams, Jellies, Preserves and Pickles." *Good Housekeeping*, July 20, 1889.

Hallman, Tom. "Ever Thought of 'Investing' in a Veggie Garden?—You Could Reap What You Sowed, up to Tenfold." *Atlanta Journal-Constitution*, May 5, 1986.

Hallock, N. "Experiences with Tomatoes: Results of a Large Experiment." *American Garden: A Monthly Illustrated Journal Devoted to Garden Art*, May 1890.

Hamilton, J. O., J. Cardy, and J. F. Siler. "The Country Cousin is Blossoming, Too." *Business Week*, Mar. 2, 1992.

Hardy, Dan. "Farmers' Market Flourishes: In Chester, It Offers a Cornucopia of Benefits, from Fresh Produce to Nutritional Information." *Philadelphia Inquirer*, Aug. 13, 2000.

Harris, W. H. "Earliest Crops in the Vegetable Garden." *Market Growers Journal*, Jan. 15, 1925.

"Heat Hurts Crops: Local Prices Hold." *New York Times*, Aug. 31, 1948.

Hill, Gladwin. "Mexican Trade Booms Through a New Outlet." *New York Times*, Aug. 10, 1947.

Holt, Jane. "Fresh Vegetables Plus." *New York Times*, Aug. 20, 1944.

——. "Home-Made Relishes." *New York Times*, July 11, 1943.

——. "News of Food: Output of Canning Equipment Increased to Stimulate Home Processing of Foods." *New York Times*, Feb. 10, 1944.

——. "News of Food: Recipes, with Tomatoes Basic Ingredient, Offered as Suggestions for Summer Meals." *New York Times*, Sept. 2, 1943.

——. "Vegetable Variety." *New York Times*, Aug. 19, 1945.

——. "Warm-Weather Salads." *New York Times*, July 15, 1945.

"Home Canning Outfit." *Market Growers Journal*, Jan. 15, 1908.

"Home Gardeners Show a Decline." *New York Times*, July 3, 1950.

"Hot Beds." *Cultivator* (Albany, NY), Feb. 1844.

"Hot Beds." *Genesee Farmer and Gardener's Journal* (Rochester, NY), Mar. 28, 1835.

"Hot Beds." *Southern Planter* (Richmond, VA), Feb. 1852.

"Household Affairs." *Cultivator* (Albany, NY), Oct. 1834.

"Household Affairs." *Southern Agriculturist, Horticulturist, and Register of Rural Affairs* (Charleston, SC), Sept. 1841.

"The House of Heinz." *Fortune*, Feb. 1941.

"Housewife." "Good Things for the Table." *Good Housekeeping*, Oct. 3, 1885.

"How to Keep Ag Business Profitable." *Public Opinion*, Dec. 17, 2006.

Huffstutter, P. J. "Ex-Owner of SK Foods Indicted in Tomato Scandal." *Los Angeles Times*, Feb. 19, 2010.

Hunt, Todd. "Homegrown Vegetables Will Set a Pace for the Seventies." *New York Times*, Jan. 9, 1972.

"Hurrying up the Tomatoes." *Maine Farmer* (Augusta), Aug. 26, 1852.

"In Grandpa's Shoes." *Saturday Evening Post*, June 23, 1949.

"In High Favor: Tomatoes, Still Tops, Repay Early Start." *New York Times*, Mar. 20, 1955.

"Inside and Out—Heirloom Seed Line Grounded in History." *Atlanta Journal and Atlanta Constitution*, Mar. 4, 1994.

"Is the Tomato a Medicine or an Aliment?" *Graham Journal of Health and Longevity* (New York), Oct. 13, 1838.

Jenkins, Dorothy H. "Spring and the Garden: Hope and Challenge." *New York Times*, Mar. 4, 1951.

Jerrard, G. W. P. "Early Tomato Plants." *Maine Farmer* (Augusta), Mar. 20, 1884.

"Jersey Tomato Crop Hurt." *New York Times*, Oct. 3, 1946.

Jones, Stacy V. "Walking Truck-Boat Just Puts One Pontoon Before the Other: Frozen Pizza and Dispenser of Disposable Umbrellas Also Win Patents—'Water Shield' Protects Building Next to Fire." *New York Times*, Feb. 6, 1954.

Kane, Karen. "For This Couple, Farming Is Worth the Long Days, Dirty Hands, and Low Pay." *Pittsburgh Post-Gazette*, Aug. 19, 2001.

Kelly, Erin. "A Bumper Crop of Customers." *Los Angeles Times*, July 17, 1980.

Kindall, James. "A Movement That Follows the Credo: Think Globally, Grow and Buy Locally." *New York Times*, Aug. 24, 2008.

"The Kitchen Table: Good Soup Without Milk." *Good Housekeeping*, Dec. 1896.

"The Kitchen Table: Tomato Dishes." *Good Housekeeping*, June 1895.

Klaus, Mary. "Growing Trend: Organic Produce Helps Farm Build Subscription List." *Patriot-News* (Harrisburg, PA), July 29, 2001.

Kummer, Corby. "Less Green at the Farmers' Market." *New York Times*, May 10, 2007.

"Lack of Workers Perils Coast Crop: Growers in California Find Domestic Help Unstable." *New York Times*, Mar. 14, 1965.

Landon, L. E. "Miscellaneous." *Farmer and Gardener, and Live-Stock Breeder and Manager* (Baltimore), Nov. 4, 1834.

Lane, Peggy. "Baby Boomers Have Taken to Gardening: In Record Numbers, They Are Spending Record Dollars Growing Everything from Radishes to Roses." *USA Today*, Apr. 18, 1988.

Langer, Richard W. "Gardening: In and Out: Gardening to Reap a Full Vegetable Bin." *New York Times*, Apr. 7, 1977.

——. "Tomatoes: Making Memory Come Alive." *New York Times*, Apr. 2, 1978.

Lingle, John C. "One-Over Harvest: What It Means to the Tomato Grower." *American Vegetable Grower*, Jan. 1965.

"Localvore Living." *Wayne (PA) Independent*, Sept. 9, 2011.

Logan, William Bryant. "Community Garden Experts: Trending the Green City Lots." *New York Times*, Aug. 15, 1985.

Lorenzen, Coby. "Tomato Harvester." *American Vegetable Grower*, Oct. 1956.

"Love-Apple, or Tomato Berry." *Times* (London), Sept. 22, 1820.

"Love Apple—Tomato." *Genesee Farmer and Gardener's Journal* (Rochester, NY), Apr. 7, 1832.

"Machine Is Used to Pick Tomatoes." *New York Times*, Sept. 4, 1960.

Marder, Dianna. "Sprouting in the City: Besides Good Fresh Food and Sunday Hours, Area Farmers Markets Offer a Chance to Meet the Folks Who Grow the Eats." *Philadelphia Inquirer*, Apr. 22, 2010.

Marizco, Michel. "The Tomato Trade Wars." *Fronteras*, Sept. 17, 2012. http://www.fronteras-desk.org/content/tomato-trade-wars.

Mars, Ploughman. "Keeping Tomatoes." *Maine Farmer* (Augusta), Oct. 6, 1853.

Martin, Laura. "Some Have Sentimental Bond to Heirloom Plants." *Atlanta Journal and Atlanta Constitution*, Jan. 7, 1990.

Martinson, Suzanne. "Fresh Is Best, Produce Survey Respondents Concur." *Pittsburgh Post-Gazette*, June 13, 2002.

Massey, W. F. "Timely Topics." *Market Growers Journal*, May 18, 1912.

——. "Trucking in Virginia and North Carolina—Early Tomatoes." *Southern Planter*, Feb. 1896.

McDevitt, Bette. "Fresh off the Farm." *Pittsburgh Post-Gazette*, Aug. 31, 2000.

McLaurin, Wayne. "Garden/Pick of the Crop: There's Nothing Better Than a Vine-Ripe Tomato." *Atlanta Journal-Constitution*, Aug. 6, 2004.

McMillan, Tracie. "Urban Farmers' Crops Go from Vacant Lot to Market." *New York Times*, May 7, 2008.

"Meals for the Many of Moderate Means." *Good Housekeeping*, Oct. 1, 1887.

"Method of Preserving Tomatoes." *Workingman's Advocate* (New York), Sept. 26, 1835.

"Mexican Aliens Free in Bail to Pick Tomatoes." *Chicago Daily Tribune*, Aug. 22, 1945.

"Mexican Vegetables for American Trade Increasing Yearly: Home Growers Should Get Busy." *Market Growers Journal*, Nov. 1, 1925.

Michioku, Sandra. "Farm Markets Thrive from Eureka to L.A." *Los Angeles Times*, Sept. 30, 1979.

Miller, Roxann. "Farmers Markets Equal Fresh Produce." *Public Opinion*, July 10, 2010.

"Miscellaneous." *Farmer and Gardener*, Nov. 4, 1834.

"Miscellanies." *Genesee Farmer and Gardener's Journal* (Rochester, NY), Sept. 9, 1835.

"Mississippi Tomatoes Have Wide Distribution." *Market Growers Journal*, July 15, 1925.

Mitchell, Dan. "Finally—an Indictment in the Massive Tomato Conspiracy." *Big Money*, Feb. 2, 2010. http://www.thebigmoney.com/blogs/daily-bread/2010/02/19/man-center-massive-tomato-fraud-indicted. Accessed Nov. 6, 2012.

Mitgang, Herbert. "Pizza a la Mode: In Many Variations, Italy's Famous Pie Now Rivals the Hot Dog in Popularity." *New York Times*, Feb. 12, 1956.

Moore, Alma Chesnut. "Aztecs' Tomatl Is the Modern Tomato." *New York Times*, Apr. 7, 1963.

"More Beans and Less Meat." *American Food Journal*, Jan. 1913.

Naedele, Walter F. "Seeds Fade in Favor—Just Ask Anyone Named Burpee." *Houston Chronicle*, Oct. 7, 1994.

Naughton, Jenifer. "Helping the Poor Buy Fresh Fruits and Vegetables." *New York Times*, Sept. 22, 1991.

Nickerson, Jane. "News of Food: Canned Sauces Are Here from Brussels to Enliven Left-Overs. Aid Summer Cooks." *New York Times*, June 5, 1950.

———. "News of Food: Pizza Is Newest on Packaged Mix Shelves—Dehydrated Sourdough Starter Available." *New York Times*, July 29, 1953.

———. "News of Food: Pizzas Now Offered Here Ready-to-Cook; Salad Julienne Suggested for Hot Days." *New York Times*, June 28, 1950.

———. "News of Food: Rare Taste Discovered in New Tomato Sauce—Olive Oil Paucity Seen Likely Next Year." *New York Times*, Aug. 15, 1953.

Nurin, Tara. "Farmers' Market on Wheels: Camden Gets Much-Needed Fresh Food with Help from State, Greensgrow Farms." *Philadelphia Inquirer*, July 7, 2011.

"Obituary." *American Gardening*, Nov. 26, 1898.

O'Neill, M. O. "No Substitute for Summer." *New York Times*, May 19, 1994.

O'Steen, Kitty. "2,000 Shoppers Seek Bargains at Opening of Burbank Farmers' Market." *Los Angeles Times*, Sept. 4, 1983.

Owen, June. "Food: Tomato Farmers: Family in Nassau County One of Few to Raise and Sell Crops in the Area." *New York Times*, Aug. 6, 1962.

———. "News of Food: New Macaroni Meal-in-a-Package Offered—Ready-Stewed Tomatoes Put up in Cans." *New York Times*, Apr. 23, 1952.

———. "News of Food: Spaghetti Sauces: Tomatoes First Grew in America, but Italy Put Them to Tasty Uses." *New York Times*, May 17, 1955.

P., A. M. "Pickles and Their Kindred." *Good Housekeeping*, Sept. 15, 1888.

Pableaux, Johnson. "$20 to Spend, Surrounded by Ripeness." *New York Times*, July 21, 2004.

"Palmetto." "A Spring Breakfast." *Good Housekeeping*, Apr. 2, 1887.

Parker, Eliza R. "Seasonable Work for Housekeepers." *Good Housekeeping*, Sept. 18, 1886.

———. "Some Seasonable Dishes." *Good Housekeeping*, Aug. 21, 1886.

Parloa, Maria. "Gastronomic Thoughts and Suggestions." *Good Housekeeping*, May 2, 1885.

———. "Many Meals for the Millions and a Few for the Millionaires." *Good Housekeeping*, Oct. 1892.

———. "Ten Mornings in the Kitchen." *Good Housekeeping*, July 1891.

Parsons, Mary Currier. "Canning Vegetables." *Good Housekeeping*, Aug. 21, 1886.

———. "Fall Canning, Preserving and Pickling." *Good Housekeeping*, Sept. 18, 1886.

"Part III. Miscellaneous Intelligence." *Southern Agriculturist and Register of Rural Affairs* (Charleston, SC), Oct. 1835.

Pearlstine, Norman. "Curbs on Tomatoes from Mexico Cause U.S. Prices to Rise: Mexican Farmers Are Enraged as Their Crops Rot; Florida Growers Had Urged Restraints." *Wall Street Journal*, Mar. 4, 1969.

Peirce, Neal R. "Green Revolution Plants Seeds of Hope in Cities." *Los Angeles Times*, Sept. 2, 1979.

Peto, H. B. "Mechanical Harvesting of Tomatoes." *Seed World*, Nov. 8, 1963.

"Pickles." *Good Housekeeping*, July 20, 1889.

"Pickles, Tomatoes, Etc." *Godey's Lady's Book and Magazine*, Aug. 1855.

Pleasant, Barbara. "The Great Tomato Debate." *Organic Gardening*, Apr. 1992.

Pollan, Michael. "Playing God in the Garden." *New York Times Magazine*, Oct. 25, 1998.

Poncavage, Joanna. "Food for Thought: 'Eating Local' to Help the Environment Sounds Simple. But Is It?" *Morning Call*, June 22, 2007.

——. "Grow Great Tasting Early Tomatoes." *Organic Gardening*, Jan. 1997.

——. "Timeless Tomatoes." *Organic Gardening*, Mar. 1997.

Poole, Hester M. "Vegetables." *Good Housekeeping*, July 23, 1887.

Potter, Joan. "Planning for Tomorrow's Blossoms." *New York Times*, Feb. 8, 1976.

"Preserves and Pickles." *Good Housekeeping*, Aug. 1895.

"Preserving Apples for Hogs." *New England Farmer, and Horticultural Register* (Boston), Oct. 7, 1835.

"Preserving Tomatoes." *Valley Farmer* (St. Louis), Sept. 1855.

"Raising of Early Tomatoes." *Genesee Farmer and Gardener's Journal* (Rochester, NY), Feb. 8, 1834.

Raver, Anne. "Hoping for a City Full of Farms on Rooftops." *New York Times*, Aug. 4, 2002.

"Recipes." *Southern Planter* (Richmond, VA), Sept. 1844.

"Record Heat Ruins $15,000 Tomato Crop." *New York Times*, Aug. 30, 1948.

"Record Tomato Crop Forces Prices Down; Some Packers Impose Ceilings on Deliveries." *Wall Street Journal*, Oct. 15, 1962.

Reichstein, Frank. "Plant Tomatoes Now." *Better Homes and Gardens*, Apr. 1946.

"Rockland Farmer Fleeing Bumper Crop of Red Tape." *New York Times*, Oct. 3, 1956.

Robbins, L. H. "15,000,000 Victory Gardens." *New York Times*, Aug. 23, 1942.

Rose, William T. "No Mexican Tomatoes?" *Chicago Tribune*, Mar. 27, 1969.

Rowe, Emma Louise Hauck. "Soups and Soup Stocks." *Good Housekeeping*, Jan. 1899.

Rozhon, Tracie. "Urban Farmers Develop Their Own Market." *New York Times*, Sept. 6, 1981.

Rubin, Pat. "A Garden Plan That's Strictly on the Square." *Sacramento Bee*, Apr. 5, 2008.

Ruth, Pamela. "The Perfect Tomato Plan." *Organic Gardening*, Apr. 2007.

Ryerson, Lucy. "Pickles and Sauces." *Good Housekeeping*, June 1893.

Salgado, Robert J. "Lots Once Strewn with Rubble Are Becoming Urban Farms." *New York Times*, Aug. 9, 1987.

"Sanitation in Mechanical Harvesting and Bulk Handling of Canning Tomatoes." *Food Technology* 18 (1964).

Sankel, K. "What the Tasters Say." *San Francisco Chronicle*, May, 19, 1994.

Saul, Louise. "Home Gardening Making Strides." *New York Times*, Apr. 29, 1984.

Schmidt, Jimmy. "Heirloom Tomatoes: A Luscious Legacy to Bring to the Table." *Philadelphia Inquirer*, Sept. 3, 1997.

Scovil, Elizabeth Robinson. "Tomatoes." *Good Housekeeping*, Sept. 15, 1888.

Seabrook, J. "Tremors in the Hothouse." *New Yorker*, July 19, 1993.

"Secrets of Success with Early Tomatoes: A Summary of the Experience of Thirty-Six Growers." *Market Growers Journal*, Mar. 9, 1912.

"$75-Million 'Town' to Rise on 640 Acres Near Miami." *New York Times*, Dec. 31, 1967.

Severson, Kim. "Greenmarket at 30, Searching for Itself." *New York Times*, July 19, 2006.

"Shoppers Look to Supermarkets for Produce Purchases." *Supermarket News*, May 23, 2012.

Shrader, J. H. "Economies in Tomato Manufacturing." *American Food Journal*, Aug. 1918.

——. "The Manufacture of Tomato Paste." *American Food Journal*, Sept. 1919.

Shriver, J. Alexis. "Canned-Tomato Industry in Italy." *American Food Journal*, Aug. 1915.

Sitth, Mark. "Three Experts Share Their Secrets for Growing Terrific Tomatoes—Enjoy a Late Harvest of Luscious Home-Growns." *Atlanta Journal and Atlanta Constitution*, July 28, 1991.

"Some Seasonable Dishes." *Good Housekeeping*, July 24, 1886.

Speicher, Ellen. "Heirloom Tomatoes Offer Variety of Flavors." *Pittsburgh Post-Gazette*, Feb. 15, 2003.

Starns, John A., Jr. "Lots of Tomatoes." *St. Petersburg Times*, Jan. 20, 2001.

Stith, Mark. "Fertile Ground: Learn All About Organics." *Atlanta Journal and Atlanta Constitution*, May 5, 1991.

Stolberg, Sheryl. "Growers Eager to Sell Their Bounty Find City Folks Wanting to Stock Up at San Pedro's Farmer's Market." *Los Angeles Times*, Sept. 24, 1989.

Stout Ries, S. K and B. A. "Status of Tomato Harvester." *Canner/Packer*, Mar. 1963.

"Strictly Fresh." *Good Housekeeping*, May 1896.

Strom, Stephanie. "United States and Mexico Reach Tomato Deal, Averting a Trade War." *New York Times*, Feb. 3, 2013.

Sugarman, C. "Tasting . . . 1,2,3, Tasting . . ." *Washington Post*, June 8, 1994.

Sullivan, Ronald. "Jersey Migrant Camp Squalor Called Worst in U.S. by Witness." *New York Times*, Sept. 22, 1966.

——. "Migrant Workers Add New Charges: Jersey Negroes Complain of Loan Rates up to 50%." *New York Times*, Aug. 27, 1967.

"This Week's Topic." *Market Growers Journal*, Mar. 9, 1912.

"This Week's Topic." *Market Growers Journal*, Mar. 16, 1912.

Thomasson, R. R. "Novelty Tomatoes for Summer: Small-Fruited Kinds Yield Good Harvest from Few Plants." *New York Times*, May 7, 1961.

Thorpe, John. "Fruits and Vegetables Under Glass." *American Garden: A Monthly Illustrated Journal Devoted to Garden Art*, Sept. 1, 1889.

"To Cook Tomatoes." *New England Farmer, and Horticultural Register* (Boston), July 30, 1845.

"To Make Tomato Ketchup." *New England Farmer, and Horticultural Register* (Boston), Sept. 11, 1829.

"The Tomato." *Farmers Cabinet and American Herd Book, Devoted to Agriculture, Horticulture, and Rural and Domestic Affairs* (Philadelphia), Sept. 15, 1843.

"Tomato." *New England Farmer, and Horticultural Register* (Boston), Oct. 14, 1835.

"Tomato Blight in Pennsylvania." *New York Times*, Aug. 26, 1948.

"Tomato Catsup." *Ohio Cultivator* (Columbus), Sept. 1, 1850.

"Tomato Crop Blight Descends on Jersey." *New York Times*, Aug. 23, 1946.

"Tomato Growing in Tennessee." *Market Growers Journal*, Apr. 1, 1925.

"Tomato Harvest Sets Record." *New York Times*, Oct. 12, 1947.

"Tomato, or Love Apple." *American Magazine of Useful and Entertaining Knowledge* (Boston), Sept. 1835.

"Tomato Paste Being Added to Cotton Board Dealings." *Wall Street Journal*, Oct. 15, 1970.

"Tomato Pickers Needed." *Philadelphia Tribune*, Sept. 1, 1970.

"Tomato Picking Becomes a Vast Production." *Chicago Daily Tribune*, Aug. 23, 1957.

"Tomato Sauce." *New England Farmer, and Horticultural Register* (Boston), Dec. 19, 1828.

"Tomato Sauce and Butter." *Maine Farmer* (Augusta), Sept. 5, 1850.

"Tomatoes." *Christian Watchman and Reflector* (Boston), Aug. 12, 1852.

"Tomatoes." *Workingman's Advocate*, Sept. 1, 1832.

"Tomatoes and Trade." *Wall Street Journal*, Mar. 14, 1969.

"Tomatoes Jam Canneries." *New York Times*, Aug. 25, 1947.

"Tomatoes Under Glass." *Meehan's Monthly: A Magazine of Horticulture, Botany and Kindred Subjects*, Feb. 1892.

Tonge, Peter. "Grow Your Own Food and Bank the Savings." *Christian Science Monitor*, Jan. 8, 1982.

——. "The Tomato's Firmly Rooted Popularity, and the Vegetable Owes It All, Some Say, to Colonel Johnson's Heroic Act." *Christian Science Monitor*, Feb. 24, 1987.

——. "TV Series Whets the Appetite for Simple Backyard Garden." *Christian Science Monitor*, May 14, 1982.

Trussell, C. P. "Braceros' Entry Sought in Senate." *New York Times*, July 29, 1963.

Tunks, Jim. "Bounty from Our Rooftop." *San Francisco Chronicle*, Sept. 27, 2009.

Tuttle, Angelina M. "The Uncertain Tomato." *Good Housekeeping*, Aug. 1893.

"25 to 40% Cut Seen in Canned Food." *New York Times*, June 8, 1945.

U., C. A. "A Farmer's Report on Tomato Growing." *Market Growers Journal*, Feb. 5, 1908.

Untitled article. *Atkinson's Saturday Evening Post* (Philadelphia), Aug. 8, 1835.

Untitled article. *Baltimore Monument*, Oct. 15, 1836.

Untitled article. *Cincinnati Mirror, and Western Gazette of Literature, Science, and the Arts*, Sept. 6, 1834.

Untitled article. *The Cultivator* (Albany, NY), Mar. 1835.

Untitled article. *Farmer and Gardener's Journal* (Rochester, NY), Aug. 17, 1833.

Untitled article. *Good Housekeeping*, Mar. 1891.

Untitled article. *New England Farmer, and Horticultural Register* (Boston), Nov. 13, 1829.

Untitled article. *New England Farmer, and Horticultural Register* (Boston), Oct. 14, 1835.

Untitled article. *New England Farmer, and Horticultural Register* (Boston), July 19, 1837.

Untitled article. *New England Farmer, and Horticultural Register* (Boston), Sept. 6, 1837.

Untitled article. *Valley Farmer* (St. Louis), Sept., 1855.

Untitled recipe. *Cincinnati Mirror, and Western Gazette of Literature, Science, and the Arts*, Aug. 8, 1835.

"Upstate Growers Vie for Pickers." *New York Times*, Aug. 21, 1966.

"U.S. Admits 6,000 Braceros." *New York Times*, Aug. 2, 1966.

Valle, Victor, M. "Fast-Growing Farmers' Market Sales in the Green." *Los Angeles Times*, July 15, 1982.

"Varieties of Tomatoes." *Michigan Farmer*, Feb. 15, 1890.

Vaughn, Alan. "Certain Tomato Plant Varieties Produce Well in Home Gardens." *Times-Picayune* (New Orleans), Mar. 24, 1991.

"Vegetable Exports of the United States." *Market Growers Journal*, Apr. 1, 1925.

"Vegetable Imports Jump $3,000,000 Over Totals of First Half of 1924." *Market Growers Journal*, Oct. 15, 1925.

"Victory Gardens Held Vital to U.S." *New York Times*, Mar. 3, 1944.

Vierria, Dan. "Top 10 Garden Catalogs for 2006." *Sacramento Bee*, Dec. 17, 2005.

—— "Ugly Can Be Beautiful When It Comes to Tomatoes." *Sacramento Bee*, Feb. 1, 2003.

——. "With Good Taste—Winning Tomatoes for Home Gardens." *Sacramento Bee*, Jan. 15, 2005.

"Virtues of the Tomato." *Christian Register and Boston Observer*, Aug. 22, 1835.

"Virtues of the Tomato." *New England Farmer, and Horticultural Register* (Boston), Sept. 2, 1835.

Waid, C. W. "Growing Tomatoes Under Glass." *Market Growers Journal*, Jan. 1, 1908.

——. "Packages for Greenhouse Tomatoes." *Market Growers Journal*, May 18, 1912.

Warden, Philip. "Senator Asks U.S. for Ban on Cuban Tomato." *Chicago Daily Tribune*, Nov. 23, 1960.

Watts, R. L. "Victory Garden Thoughts." *Pennsylvania Farmer*, Feb. 13, 1943.

Werman, Marco, and Jason Margolis. "NAFTA 20 Years After: Florida's Tomato Growers Struggling." *World*, Dec. 17, 2012. http://www.pri.org/stories/2012-12-17/nafta-20-years -after-floridas-tomato-growers-struggling.

"What Are Vitamines?—Best Described by What They Do." *American Food Journal*, Jan. 1921.

Wilcox, E. V. "Are Vegetable Growers Meeting Consumers Half Way?" *Market Growers Journal*, Oct. 15, 1925.

Wilkins, Jennifer. "Think Globally, Eat Locally." *New York Times*, Dec. 18, 2004.

"Winter-Grown Vegetables." *Meehan's Monthly: A Magazine of Horticulture, Botany and Kindred Subjects*, Mar. 1896.

"Work for March." *Western Farmer and Gardener* (Cincinnati), Mar. 1844.

Wyatt, R. O. Y. "Digging Around—Growing Tomatoes Is a Cinch in Easy-to-Assemble Containers." *Atlanta Journal and Atlanta Constitution*, Sept. 29, 1999.

"A Yankee Housewife." "Good Things for the Table." *Good Housekeeping*, Aug. 22, 1885.

Young, Karen Newell. "Appetite for Unusual Feeds Gourmet Markets." *Los Angeles Times*, Nov. 4, 1988.

Zeldes, Leah. "Eat This! Chow Chow and Piccalili Pickle the Southern Harvest." *Dining Chicago*, Aug. 18, 2010. http://www.diningchicago.com/blog/2010/08/18/eat-this-southern -pickles-and-relishes/.

GOVERNMENT DOCUMENTS

App, Frank, and Allen G. Waller. "Costs, Profits and Practices of the Can-House Tomato Industry in New Jersey." New Jersey Agricultural Experiment Station Bulletin 353. Apr. 1921.

Arthur, Charles M. "Marketing Tomatoes in New Jersey." New Jersey State Agricultural Collection Extension Bulletin 1, no. 6. 1915.

Atwater, W. O. "Foods: Nutritive Value and Cost." USDA Farmers' Bulletin 23. 1894.

Beattie, James. "Greenhouse Tomatoes." USDA Farmers' Bulletin 1431. Dec. 1924.

———. "Tomatoes for Canning and Manufacture." USDA Farmers' Bulletin 1233. Oct. 1921.

Boswell, Victor R., and Robert E. Wester. "Growing Vegetables in Town and City." USDA Home and Garden Bulletin 7. 1951.

Bureau of Labor Statistics. "Labor Force Statistics from the Current Population Survey." https://data.bls.gov/timeseries/LNU04000000?years_option=all_years&periods_option=specific_periods&periods=Annual+Data. Accessed Mar. 10, 2017.

Essary, S. H. "Notes on Tomato Diseases with Results of Selection for Resistance." Tennessee Agricultural Experiment Station Bulletin 95. Jan. 1912.

Gaylord, F. C., and K. I. Fawcett. "A Study of Grade, Quality and Price of Canned Tomatoes at Retail in Indiana." Purdue University Agricultural Experiment Station Bulletin 438. 1939.

———. "A Study of Grade, Quality and Price of Canned Tomatoes Sold at Retail in Indiana." Purdue University Agricultural Experiment Station Bulletin 495. 1944.

Hiatt, William R., et al. PG Gene and Its Use in Plants. U.S. Patent 4,801,540, filed Jan. 2, 1987, and issued Jan. 31, 1989.

Hunt, Caroline L., and Helen W. Atwater. "How to Select Foods." USDA Farmers' Bulletin 808. 1917.

James, Henry A. "Tomatoes for Marketing and Canning." University of Maryland Agricultural Experiment Station Bulletin 248. Feb. 1922.

Lorenzen, Coby, Frederick L. Hill, and Istvan Szluka. Tomato Harvester. U.S. Patent 3,199,604a, filed Sept. 28, 1960, and issued Aug. 10, 1965.

Low, Sarah A., and Stephen Vogel. "Direct and Intermediated Marketing of Local Foods in the United States." ERR-128. USDA Economic Research Service. Nov. 2011.

McCue, C.A. "Tomatoes for the Canning Factory." Delaware College Agricultural Experiment Station Bulletin 101. 1912.

Muller, C. H. "A Revision of the Genus *Lycopersicon*." USDA Misc. Publication 382. 1940.

Payne, Tim. "U.S. Farmers Markets—2000: A Study of Emerging Trends." USDA Agricultural Marketing Service. 2002.

Sando, Charles E. "The Process of Ripening in the Tomato, Considered Especially from the Commercial Standpoint." USDA Bulletin 859. Sept. 1920.

Shewmaker, Christine K., et al. Anti-Sense Regulation of Gene Expression in Plant Cells. U.S. Patent 5,107,065, filed Aug. 30, 1988, and issued Apr. 21, 1992.

Stuckey, H. P., and J. C. Temple. "Tomatoes: Two Parts." Georgia Experiment Station Bulletin 96. 1911.

U.S. Census Bureau. *1935 Census of Agriculture*. U.S. Department of Commerce: Government Printing Office, 1937.

U.S. Census Bureau. *Fifteenth Census of the United States: 1930; Agriculture*. Washington, DC: Government Printing Office, 1932.

———. *Fourteenth Census of the United States*. Vol. 5, Chap. 12. Washington, DC: Government Printing Office, 1922.

——. *1940 Census of Agriculture.* Washington, DC: Government Printing Office, 1942.

——. *1945 Census of Agriculture.* Washington, DC: Government Printing Office, 1946.

——. *1954 Census of Agriculture.* Washington, DC: Government Printing Office, 1956.

——. *1969 Census of Agriculture.* Washington, DC: Government Printing Office, 1973.

——. *1978 Census of Agriculture.* Washington, DC: Government Printing Office, 1981.

——. *1987 Census of Agriculture.* Washington, DC: Government Printing Office, 1989.

——. *Statistics of the Population of the United States at the Tenth Census.* Washington, DC: Government Printing Office, 1883.

——. *Twelfth Census of the United States.* Vol. 1. Washington, DC: Government Printing Office, 1901.

——. *Twelfth Census of the United States.* Vol. 2. Washington, DC: Government Printing Office, 1902.

U.S. Department of Agriculture. *2002 Census of Agriculture.* Washington, DC: Government Printing Office, 2004.

——. *Yearbook of Agriculture: Gardening for Food and Fun.* Washington, DC: Government Printing Office, 1977.

U.S. Department of Agriculture, Agricultural Marketing Service. "Farmers' Market Program Fact Sheet." http://www.ams.usda.gov/AMSv1.0/getfile?dDocName=STELPRDC 5080175&acct=frmrdirmkt. Accessed Oct. 20, 2014.

U.S. Department of Agriculture, Bureau of Agricultural Economics. "Car-Lot Shipments and Unloads of Important Fruits and Vegetables for the Calendar Years 1924–1926." Statistical Bulletin 23. Apr. 1928.

——. "Car-Lot Shipments and Unloads of Important Fruits and Vegetables for the Calendar Years 1927 and 1928." Statistical Bulletin 30. May 1930.

——. "Car-Lot Shipments and Unloads of Important Fruits and Vegetables for the Calendar Years 1929 and 1930." Statistical Bulletin 35. Oct. 1931.

——. "Commercial Truck Crops: Revised Estimates of Acreage, Production and Value, 1928–1941, Under New Seasonal Groupings." Statistical Bulletin. Oct. 1943.

——. *Consumption of Food in the United States, 1909–1952.* Agricultural Handbook 62. 1953.

——. "Shipments and Unloads of Certain Fruits and Vegetables, 1918–1923." Statistical Bulletin 7. Apr. 1925.

——. *Supplement for 1961 to Consumption of Food in the United States 1909–52.* Supplement to Agricultural Handbook 62. 1962.

——. "Vegetables for Commercial Processing: Acreage, Production, Value; Revised Estimates, 1918–50." Statistical Bulletin 132. June 1953.

U.S. Department of Agriculture, Economic Research Service. "Tomatoes—Per Capita Availability." *Food Availability (Per Capita) Data System.* https://www.ers.usda.gov/data -products/food-availability-per-capita-data-system/.

——. "Food Consumption, Prices, and Expenditures, 1970–1997." Statistical Bulletin SB-965. April 1999. https://www.ers.usda.gov/publications/pub-details/?pubid=47115.

U.S. Food Administration. *Food Guide for War Service at Home.* New York: Charles Scribner's Sons, 1918.

Wester, Robert. "Growing Vegetables in the Home Garden." USDA Home and Garden Bulletin 202. 1972.

MISCELLANEOUS SOURCES

Berrenson, E. "A Comparison of Purchasing Behaviors and Consumer Profiles at San Luis Obispo's Thursday Night Farmer's Market: A Case Study." Senior Project, California State University, San Luis Obispo, 2003.

Gallup Poll (AIPO). June 1981. Retrieved Feb. 19, 2014, from iPoll Databank, Roper Center for Public Opinion Research, University of Connecticut. http://www.ropercenter.uconn .edu/data_access/ipoll/ipoll.html.

GrowNYC. "Frequently Asked Questions." http://www.grownyc.org/greenmarket/faq#q_ available. Accessed 5/7/2014.

Food, Inc. Directed by Robert Kenner. Los Angeles: Magnolia Home Entertainment, 2009. DVD, 148 min.

Lisle, Benjamin. "Thinking for Myself, Building for Myself: The 1970s Post-Industrial Homestead in Maine." Paper presented at "A Hands-On Approach: The Do-It-Yourself Culture and Economy in the 20th Century," German Historical Institute, Washington, DC, Apr. 24, 2014.

Monsanto Inc. "Food, Inc. Movie." Monsanto.com. www.monsanto.com/food-inc/pages /default.asps. Accessed Sept. 18, 2014.

Moran, Rachel Louise. "Body Politic: Government and Physique in Twentieth Century America." PhD. diss., Pennsylvania State University, 2013.

Scarry, C. Margaret. "Plant Remains from Fort Matanzas." Unpublished paper, Feb. 1991.

INDEX

Lorenzen, Coby, 122, 125–26, 128–30
Los Angeles, 104
Los Angeles Times (newspaper), 164
Louisiana, 91
Lundy, Ronni, 169–70
Lycopersicon esculentum, 16
Lyson, T. A., 151

Macklem, Stanley, 60–61
Macy's, 145
magazines. See periodicals; specific
    magazines
Maine, 173–74
Marchand, Roland, 56
Market Growers Journal (magazine), 61–62,
    70, 71
marketing, 9–10, 43, 55, 56–57, 146
Marks, Joe, 125–26
Marx, Karl, 198n3
Maryland, 44, 52, 62–63, 67, 116
Maryland Agricultural Experiment
    Station, 63
Massey, W. F., 39, 75
Massey Ferguson, 130
Mattioli, Petrus Andreas, 17
McCarthy, Richard, 167
McCollum, E. V., 86
McCormick, Cyrus, 11, 194
McCue, C. A., 66
McDonald's, 148
McLaurin, Wayne, 186
McMurry, Sally, 209n30
McPhee, John, 173
Mease, James, 27
meat, 20, 24, 26, 85
meatpacking industry, 7, 42
mechanical harvesters, 10–12, 118, 121–25,
    123, 128–34, 131, 143
Merrell and Soule, 49–50
Mertineau, Belinda, 141
Mexico: migrant farm workers from,
    117–22, 125; tomato cultivation in, 1, 10,
    16, 17–18, 72, 73, 75, 134–39

Michigan, 67
Michigan State University, 133
migrant labor, 11, 117–22, 125, 194
Miller, Stacy, 158
minerals, 86
Miracle-Gro, 178–79
Mississippi, 11, 73–74, 75, 113
Missouri, 63
Mitchell, Alex, 182
M'Mahon, Bernard, 21
Monsanto, 139, 142
Montanari, Massimo, 20
Moore and Bristol, 50
Morris, Edmund, 33
mushrooms, 26, 28

National Canners Association, 59–60, 64
National Gardening Association, 161–62
National Stockman and Farmer (journal), 34
Nation's Agriculture (magazine), 125–26
Nebraska Seed Company, 71
Neubert, Charles, 119
New England Farmer (journal), 32–33
New Jersey: farmers' markets in, 165,
    166–67, 170; labor shortages and
    migrant workers in, 119, 120; tomato
    production in, 11, 44, 62–63, 72, 75–76,
    116–17
New Jersey Experiment Station, 63
New York City: community gardens in,
    180; farmers' markets in, 157, 165,
    167–68, 170, 171, 173; fresh tomato in, 74,
    75–76; tomato production in, 117; war
    and home gardening in, 104–105, 155,
    158, 180
New York Cotton Exchange (NYCE), 146
New Yorker (magazine), 173
New York State: farmers' markets in, 157,
    165; home and community canning in,
    105; labor shortages and migrant
    workers in, 119–20; pasta industry in,
    99; tomato production in, 11, 116–17; war
    and home gardening in, 154–55, 175–76

ARTS AND TRADITIONS OF THE TABLE:
PERSPECTIVES ON CULINARY HISTORY

Albert Sonnenfeld, Series Editor

Building a Meal: From Molecular Gastronomy to Culinary Constructivism, Hervé This,
translated by M. B. DeBevoise

Eating History: Thirty Turning Points in the Making of American Cuisine,
Andrew F. Smith

The Science of the Oven, Hervé This, translated by Jody Gladding

Pomodoro! A History of the Tomato in Italy, David Gentilcore

Cheese, Pears, and History in a Proverb, Massimo Montanari,
translated by Beth Archer Brombert

Food and Faith in Christian Culture, edited by Ken Albala and Trudy Eden

The Kitchen as Laboratory: Reflections on the Science of Food and Cooking,
edited by César Vega, Job Ubbink, and Erik van der Linden

Creamy and Crunchy: An Informal History of Peanut Butter,
the All-American Food, Jon Krampner

Let the Meatballs Rest: And Other Stories About Food and Culture,
Massimo Montanari, translated by Beth Archer Brombert

The Secret Financial Life of Food: From Commodities Markets to Supermarkets,
Kara Newman

Drinking History: Fifteen Turning Points in the Making of American Beverages,
Andrew F. Smith

Italian Identity in the Kitchen, or Food and the Nation, Massimo Montanari,
translated by Beth Archer Brombert

Fashioning Appetite: Restaurants and the Making of Modern Identity,
Joanne Finkelstein

The Land of the Five Flavors: A Cultural History of Chinese Cuisine,
Thomas O. Höllmann, translated by Karen Margolis

The Insect Cookbook: Food for a Sustainable Planet, Arnold van Huis, Henk van Gurp,
and Marcel Dicke, translated by Françoise Takken-Kaminker
and Diane Blumenfeld-Schaap

Religion, Food, and Eating in North America, edited by Benjamin E. Zeller, Marie W. Dallam,
Reid L. Neilson, and Nora L. Rubel

Umami: Unlocking the Secrets of the Fifth Taste, Ole G. Mouritsen and Klavs Styrbæk,
translated by Mariela Johansen and designed by Jonas Drotner Mouritsen